Developing Skills in
ALGEBRA ONE

Harold Taylor ■ Loretta Taylor

Book B

DALE SEYMOUR PUBLICATIONS

Cover Design: Michael Rogondino
Technical Illustrations: Pat Rogondino

Order Number DS01442
ISBN 0-86651-222-5

**DALE
SEYMOUR
PUBLICATIONS**
P.O. BOX 10888
PALO ALTO, CA 94303

13 14 15 16 17 18 19 20 -ML- 99 98 97

CONTENTS

(over)

Rational Expressions

INTRODUCTION

In order to master algebra, most students need a great deal of practice—practice allowing them to discover mathematical patterns, to make generalizations, and to consolidate their mathematical learning—practice that helps them see and understand the workings of algebra. Algebra textbooks, by their very nature, cannot provide the quantity of problems necessary for a beginning algebra course. In order to cover the complete range of problems related to a topic, most textbook exercise sets move very quickly from simple to complex problems, giving only a few of those in-between bread-and-butter problems that students need. As a result, algebra teachers are continually looking for problems to supplement their texts.

About the Series

Developing Skills in Algebra One was created primarily to help teachers in their search for extra algebra problems. The series was not designed to be a classroom text, rather it is a back-up resource containing problems for class examples, chalkboard work, quizzes, test preparation, and extra practice. *Developing Skills in Algebra One* is a four-book series of reproducible worksheets that provides extensive practice in all the work covered in the traditional first high school course in algebra.

> *Book A* starts at the beginning of the school year with exercises in simplifying numerical expressions, and continues through to simple equations in one variable.

> *Book B* includes operations with polynomials, factoring polynomials, solving polynomial equations, and working with rational expressions.

> *Book C* covers ratio, proportion, graphing linear equations, solving systems of linear equations, plus inequalities and absolute value equations.

> *Book D* completes the algebra one course with roots and radicals, quadratic equations, and analysis of quadratic functions.

By design, the books in the *Developing Skills in Algebra One* series are appropriate for use in any algebra one course, whether it is taught in ninth grade, tenth grade, seventh or eighth grade, or in a two-year algebra program. The books also provide review work for second-year algebra students, practice for students studying high school algebra at the college level, and exercises for adults reviewing algebra on their own.

Pick-and-Choose Pages

Book B is the second book in *Developing Skills in Algebra* series. It contains 122 worksheets with more than 3000 problems that you can duplicate and use with your students. There is no required order for presenting the exercises in this book but, for maximum convenience, the worksheets are arranged sequentially, concept by concept. You may choose to select worksheets from the book as back-up for your algebra lessons. You might assign a worksheet to a single student who needs practice in a specific skill. Or, you may decide to keep certain pages as your own personal resource of problems on a particular topic. The contents in the front of this book and the labels at the top of each worksheet page will help you identify the exercises that best meet your needs.

Paired Worksheets and Exercises

As you glance through this book, you will discover that the worksheets come in pairs; there are at least two parallel worksheets for every concept so that students can learn on one set of problems and practice on the next. Several pairs of worksheets are included for particularly troublesome topics. Each pair of worksheets practices only one or two specific skills (noted at the top left of the pages), carefully sequenced and organized. Most worksheet exercises are also paired, by odds and evens, to allow for two-day assignments or for practice and testing. And, clear simple worksheet instructions along with handwritten samples of the exercises allow students to get right to work with a minimum of fuss.

Checking Work

In order to provide a quantity of problems—enough problems on a page to make it worth copying—and in order to give you complete coverage of algebra topics, we have limited the amount of workspace allowed for some exercises. We suggest that you have students show all their work on separate sheets of paper, but transfer their answers to the worksheets. You (or your students) will have a quick way to check answers as well as access to the work you must see to diagnose students' errors of understanding.

You will find answers to every problem in this book. The answers are located after the worksheet pages.

About Practice

Practice is an important part of learning, but it's not the only part. Practice makes sense only after instruction and demonstrated understanding. To help students master algebra, we must aim for a regular and consistent blend of practice with meaningful instruction, taking pains to individualize practice as much as possible. *Developing Skills in Algebra One* is one tool you can use to achieve that goal, but it is just a tool. The hard work and dedication are up to you and your students.

Developing Skills in

ALGEBRA ONE

Using Exponents

Rewrite using exponents.

1. $aaaaa$ a^5 **2.** bbb _____

3. $xxyyy$ _____   **4.** $mmmmn$ _____

5. $3aaaccc$ _____   **6.** $6xxxyy$ _____

7. $(x - y)(x - y)$ _____   **8.** $(r + t)(r + t)(r + t)$ _____

9. $5(mn)(mn)(mn)$ _____   **10.** $11(abc)(abc)$ _____

11. $5(4 + x)(4 + x)$ _____   **12.** $13(x - 8)(x - 8)(x - 8)$ _____

Rewrite without using exponents.

13. x^5 $x\ x\ x\ x\ x$ **14.** y^7 _____

15. $x^3 y^2$ _____   **16.** $m^4 n^3$ _____

17. $(m + n)^3$ _____   **18.** $(a + b)^5$ _____

19. $3(rt)^4$ _____   **20.** $9(bcd)^3$ _____

Evaluate.

21. 10^2 _____   **22.** 2^3 _____

23. 5^3 _____   **24.** 7^2 _____

Evaluate for the given value of the variable.

25. a^3; 3   27   **26.** $4x^2$; 5 _____

27. $(3x)^3$; 2 _____   **28.** $(5r)^3$; 2 _____

29. $(x + 1)^4$; 3 _____   **30.** $(y - 2)^5$; 4 _____

Using Exponents

Rewrite using exponents.

1. xxxxx $\qquad x^5$

2. cc _____

3. aaaab _____

4. yyxxx _____

5. 4mmmnn _____

6. 9ppqqqq _____

7. $(2a - 3)(2a - 3)$ _____

8. $(x + 2)(x + 2)(x + 2)$ _____

9. $3(ac)(ac)(ac)(ac)$ _____

10. $8(rst)(rst)(rst)$ _____

11. $3(a + 2b)(a + 2b)$ _____

12. $7(3x - 5)(3x - 5)$ _____

Rewrite without using exponents.

13. $4y^3$ $\qquad 4yyy$

14. p^2q^4 _____

15. r^2s^3t _____

16. $5x^3y$ _____

17. $(5a - 3b)^2$ _____

18. $(2x + 7y)^3$ _____

19. $7(vw)^3$ _____

20. $3(mnp)^2$ _____

Evaluate.

21. 4^3 _____

22. 3^4 _____

23. 6^2 _____

24. 8^2 _____

Evaluate for the given value of the variable.

25. b^6; 2 $\qquad 64$

26. $3y^3$; 4 _____

27. $(2x)^4$; 5 _____

28. $(3s)^2$; 6 _____

29. $(3x + 2)^2$; 3 _____

30. $(5a + 1)^3$; 2 _____

Developing Skills in Algebra   Book B

Classifying Polynomials

State the degree and the numerical coefficient of each term.

1. $4x^2$ *two*   *4*   **2.** $17y$ ____ ____

3. $3y$ ____ ____   **4.** $-8z^4$ ____ ____

5. 7 ____ ____   **6.** $15xz^3$ ____ ____

7. $-5xy^2z$ ____ ____   **8.** $-21y^2z^2$ ____ ____

9. $-8x^3y^2z$ ____ ____   **10.** 28 ____ ____

Write the highest degree term of each polynomial.

11. $3x^3y - 4xz + 2xy^2 + 7$ *$3x^3y$*   **12.** $2x^2yz - 5x^3y^2 + 10xz - 5$ _____

13. $2xyz + 3x^3y^2z - 5xy^2z$ _____   **14.** $-3xy + 3yz + 2xyz + 6$ _____

15. $10xy^2z - 3x^2yz + 2x^2y^2z^2$ _____   **16.** $4x^3y - 2x^2y^2 + 3xy^3z - 4$ _____

State the degree of each polynomial.

17. $7y + 4y^3 - 2y^2 + 3$ *three*   **18.** $-5x^3 + 3x^4 - 8x + 1$ _____

19. $2x^2 + 3xy + 5y^2$ _____   **20.** $9x^3 - 2xy + 7xyz^2 - 9$ _____

21. $4x^3yz - 3xyz + 7xy^2z$ _____   **22.** $13xy^2z + 2x^2y^2z - 8xyz$ _____

Write each polynomial in descending powers of the variable.

23. $14x + 2 - 3x^2 + 5x^3$ *$5x^3 - 3x^2 + 14x + 2$*

24. $8z^2 - 2z + 7 - 9z^3$ _____

25. $2y - 7y^5 + 3y^2 + 2$ _____

26. $x^3 - 2x^2 + 7x^5 + 4$ _____

Classifying Polynomials

State the degree and the numerical coefficient of each term.

1. $5a^3$ *three*   *5*   **2.** $13z^4$ _____ _____

3. 10 _____ _____   **4.** $13a^4b^3$ _____ _____

5. $9x^2y^2z^2$ _____ _____   **6.** $5 - 2mn^5$ _____ _____

7. $13rs^4t$ _____ _____   **8.** 25 _____ _____

9. $18v^3w$ _____ _____   **10.** $8m^3n^3p$ _____ _____

Write the highest degree term of each polynomial.

11. $2ab^4 - 3a^2b^2 + ab + 5$ *$2ab^4$*   **12.** $7mn^4 + 2m^3n^3 - 4m^5 + 6n$ _____

13. $x^3y^2z^2 + 2y^4z + 7x^2y^3$ _____   **14.** $14abc^4 + 2a^2b^2 - 3c^5$ _____

15. $5a^2b^2 + 2a^3b^2c^3 + 7$ _____   **16.** $9x^2y + 3xy^4 + 5x^3y^2z$ _____

State the degree of each polynomial.

17. $2a + 3a^4 - 5a^3 + 7$ *four*   **18.** $7ac^4 + 5a^3c^2 + 2a^2c$ _____

19. $3r^5 + 2rs + 7s + 2$ _____   **20.** $4mn + 3m^3n^2 - 3m^2n + 1$ _____

21. $3z^3 + 2xyz - 5x^2y + 7$ _____   **22.** $5p^2q^2 + 7p^3q - 8pq^3 + 2$ _____

Write each polynomial in descending powers of the variable.

23. $23 - 4y^4 + 7y^2 + 4y$ *$-4y^4 + 7y^2 + 4y + 23$*

24. $8x^3 - 3x + 2x^2 - 5$ _____

25. $7z^2 + 2 - 6z^4 + z$ _____

26. $16y + 2y^5 - 1 + 10y^2$ _____

Addition of Polynomials

Name _____

Date _____ Period _____

Circle like terms.

1. (x^2y) $5xy$, $10xy^2$, $(3x^2y)$ $(-2x^2y)$

2. xyz, $46xy$, $12zx$, $-6xy$, $8yz$

3. 132, $4x^2y$, $16zp$, $4x^3h$, $-12hx^3$

4. $3x^3p$, $12pxy$, $3x^3z$, $-4px^3$, $13px^3$

5. $7ha$, $8ah$, $9hz^2$, $5p^3x^4$, $11ah^2$

6. $2xy$, ut^2x, $2xt^2u$, $14xz$, $-7xut^2$

7. mnr, m^2nr, mn^2r, mnr^2, mn^2r

8. $4pqs$, $2p^2qs$, $-11pq^2s$, $13pq^2s$

9. $13x$, 17, $126zu$, $31p$, -72, $14xy$

10. πr^2, $2\pi r$, $3\pi r^3$, $5\pi r^2$, $8\pi r^3$

Find the indicated sums.

11. $(2a - 6) + (3a + 8)$ $5a + 2$

12. $(3x + 2) + (5x - 1)$

13. $(9m + 7n) + (-4m + 3n)$

14. $(4r + 2u) + (-7r - 87)$

15. $(2x + 4y - 1) + (-x - 7 - 6y)$

16. $(3c + 7d - 5) + (6d + 4 - 2c)$

17. $(3p + 2r) + (12r - 2p + 7)$

18. $(7x - 3y + 9) + (4y - 8)$

19. $(2k + 3kn) + (-6kn + 4k)$

20. $(7ax + 13by + 5) + (-3ax + 4)$

21. $(7u^2 - 10r) + (-3u^2 + 8 - 2r)$

22. $(2a^3 + 7a^2b + b^3) + (a^3 + 7b^3)$

23. $(x^2 + 3x + 2) + (3x^2 + 4x - 9)$

24. $(2a^2 + 4a - 1) + (a - 6a^2 + 2)$

25. $(abc + 3a^2b + 2) + (4abc - 5)$

26. $(x^2y^2z^2 + 3x^3y) + (7x^3y + 2)$

27. $(2mn + 3a + 7d) + (-5mn + 7a)$

28. $(6r^2t + 5rt^2) + (9rt^2 - 9r^2t)$

29. $(17a + 9b + c) + (-7b + 10c)$

30. $(x + 15y - 9z) + (7x - 8y + z)$

31. $(5ab + 2ac - 6bc) + (-4ac + 2bc)$

32. $(7a^2x - 9b^2x) + (2a^2x - b^2x)$

Addition of Polynomials

Name _____

Date _____ Period _____

Circle like terms.

1. $\widehat{ab^3}$, $3a^2b$, $9ab$, $2a^3b$, $\widehat{-2ab^3}$

2. rst, 25, $7r^2s^2t^2$, 13, $-14r^3st$

3. x^3y, $7x^3y$, $13xy$, $3x^3y$, 45

4. $5r^3s$, $10rst$, $2sr^3$, $-3rst$, 5

5. $5mn$, $9m^5n^2$, $2mn$, -7, $14mn$

6. $7ac$, cy, -2, $3cy$, $12cd$, $-5cy$

7. $8h^3p$, ph, $3hp$, $11ph$, $9h^2p$

8. $7pqr$, $-12p^3r$, $9q^3p^2r^2$, $13p^2r^2q^3$

9. $4xz^3$, $4x^2z$, $16x^2z$, $-12x^3z$

10. a^3h, $4a^2h$, $4ha$, $-7a^3h$, h^3a

Find the indicated sums.

11. $(3x + 5) + (5x - 9)$ $8x - 4$

12. $(4a - 3) + (-7a + 3)$

13. $(7b + 3c) + (-8b + 5c)$

14. $(6d + 7x) + (-7x + 9d)$

15. $(3a + 6b + 2) + (2a - 5b + 1)$

16. $(9x - 3y + 1) + (3x + 2y - 5)$

17. $(7n - 5r) + (6r - 5 + 3n)$

18. $(8a + 2b - 5) + (3b + 4a - 2)$

19. $(9ax + 5by) + (6yb - 7ax)$

20. $(9x + 10y - 9) + (y - x + 2)$

21. $(8a^3 - 9b^3) + (-2a^3 + 1 - 3b^3)$

22. $(3x + 2y + z) + (-x + 5z - 3y)$

23. $(r^2 + 2r - 1) + (3r^2 - 7r + 2)$

24. $(7x^2 + 3x + 4) + (x^2 - 3x + 1)$

25. $(mn^3 + 2m^2n + mn) + (3mn + m^2n)$

26. $(a^2x + b^2y^2 + 2) + (5 - 3a^2x)$

27. $(5rc + 5r - 2c) + (7r - 5c + 1)$

28. $(m^3n^2 + 3) + (7m^3n^2 - 5)$

29. $(4b^2 + 3b + 2) + (9b^2 - 7b)$

30. $(7x^3y^2 + 3x^4) + (5x^3y^2 - 2x)$

31. $(8rst - 5rs + 2) + (-12 + 8rs)$

32. $(15m^2n^3 - 3x^2y) + (12m^2n^3 - 2)$

Addition of Polynomials

Name _____

Date _____ Period _____

Find the sums of the following polynomials.

1. $2a + 3b$
   $\underline{a - 4b}$
   $3a - b$

2. $14x - 7y$
   $\underline{6x + 5y}$

3. $15z - 6$
   $\underline{-3z + 8}$

4. $2s - 3p + 6$
   $\underline{s + 10p - 3}$

5. $8q - 3h$
   $\underline{-3q + 5h + 1}$

6. $7b - 3a$
   $\underline{3b + 8a + c}$

7. $12m - 5n - 3$
   $\underline{-3m + 7n}$

8. $2x^2 - 3x$
   $\underline{-4x^2 + 5x}$

9. $11y^2 + 6y$
   $\underline{-3y^2 - 8y}$

10. $8z^2 + 7$
    $\underline{5z^2 - 2z - 3}$

11. $u^2 + 2u$
    $\underline{-3u^2 + 6}$

12. $h^3 + 2h^2 + h$
    $\underline{-4h^3 - 5h^2 + 3h}$

13. $2x^2 - 13$
    $\underline{ + x + 5}$

14. $x - 6$
    $\underline{x^2 - 8}$

15. $x^2 + 2x - 3$
    $\underline{x^2 - 6}$

16. $x^3 - 2x^2 + x - 3$
    $\underline{ - x^2 + 8}$

17. $(x^2 - 3x - 11)$ and $(x^2 - 4x + 7)$

18. $(x^3 - 6x^2 - 7)$ and $(-3x^3 + 2x^2 - 9)$

19. $(x^3 - 2x + 5)$ and $(x^2 - 6)$

Addition of Polynomials

Name _____

Date _____ Period _____

Find the sums of the following polynomials.

1. $\quad 5a - 7b$
$\quad \underline{-6a - 9b}$
$\quad -a - 16b$

2. $\quad -17x + 2y$
$\quad \underline{3x - 9y}$

3. $\quad 11z - 13$
$\quad \underline{-14z + \;\; 6}$

4. $\quad 8s - 11p - 7$
$\quad \underline{-3s + 15p + 2}$

5. $\quad 14q - 8h$
$\quad \underline{-9q + 3h - 4}$

6. $\quad 12b - 14a$
$\quad \underline{8b - \;\; 5a + 4c}$

7. $\quad 19m + 3n - 15$
$\quad \underline{-8m - 9n + 16}$

8. $\quad -8x^2 + 15x$
$\quad \underline{3x^2 - 11x}$

9. $\quad 13y^2 + 7y + 19$
$\quad \underline{-4y^2 \qquad - 12}$

10. $\quad 12z^2 + 3z - 5$
$\quad \underline{-11z^2 \qquad + 9}$

11. $\quad 14u^2 + 5u + 8$
$\quad \underline{-7u^2 - 9u}$

12. $\quad -18h^3 + 3h^2 + 4h + 2$
$\quad \underline{5h^3 - 2h^2 \qquad - 7}$

13. $\quad 5x^2 + 9x - 9$
$\quad \underline{6x^2 + 3x - 2}$

14. $\quad 3x^2 + 7x + 2$
$\quad \underline{4x^2 - 6x + 3}$

15. $\quad 7x^2 - 15x + 13$
$\quad \underline{-9x^2 - 13x + 11}$

16. $\quad 2x^3 + 7x^2 + 4x - 9$
$\quad \underline{8x^3 - 3x^2 + 2x - 3}$

17. $(x^3 - 5x + 15)$ and $(x^3 - 7x^2 + 3x - 17)$

18. $(-8x^3 + 3x^2 - 4)$ and $(12x^4 - 7x^3 - 15)$

19. $(7x^2 - 4x + 12)$ and $(3x^2 - 8)$

Subtraction of Polynomials

Name _____

Date _____ Period _____

Find the indicated differences.

1. $(2a - 3b) - (3a + 5b)$ $-a - 8b$

2. $(x - c) - (2x - 4c)$

3. $(12z - 6) - (-3z + 7)$

4. $(6p - 4q) - (-9p + 6q - 1)$

5. $(7x + 4y) - (3x + 8y + c)$

6. $(u^2 + 2u) - (2u^2 + 1)$

7. $(6z^2 + 3) - (5z^2 - 2z - 6)$

8. $(h^2 - 15) - (h + 5)$

9. $(x^2 - 6x - 11) - (x^2 - 4x + 7)$

10. $(x^2 - 6x - 7) - (-3x^2 + 2x)$

11. $(x^2 + 2x - 3) - (x^2 - 3)$

12. $(x - 6) - (2x^2 - 5)$

13. $(6x^3 - 3x^2 - x) - (x^3 - 6x + 2)$

14. $(-x^3 + 6x + 5) - (6x^3 + 2x)$

15. $(4a - 7b - 2) - (3a + 9b - 5)$

16. $(7x - 9y + 3) - (5x - 8y + 6)$

17. $(9r + 7n) - (3r - 2 + 11n)$

18. $(9c + 3d - 3) - (7d - 3c + 8)$

19. $(7mn - 6rs) - (8rs + 3mn)$

20. $(6x - 11y - 3) - (4y + x - 7)$

21. $(7s - 3t) - (13t + 13 - 14s)$

22. $(7x - 5y + z) - (2x + 8z - y)$

23. $(x^2 + 4x - 9) - (5x^2 - 3x + 7)$

24. $(9z^2 + 2z - 9) - (z^2 - 7z + 2)$

25. $(pq + 4rs - 9mn) - (6mn + 3rs)$

26. $(6b^2 + 4b + 1) - (8 - b^2 + 2b)$

27. $(13m^2 + 6m - 7) - (m^2 - 3m + 2)$

28. $(c^2d^2 + 5) - (8c^2d^2 - 8)$

29. $(12x^2 + 3x - 9) - (12x + 13)$

30. $(8x^3y^2 - 5x^2) - (-3x^3y^2 + 7x)$

31. $(9nm^2 + 3nm + 5) - (-14 - 6nm)$

32. $(32a^2 + 5a - 3) - (14a^2 + 13)$

9

Developing Skills in Algebra   Book B

Subtraction of Polynomials

Name _____

Date _____ Period _____

Find the indicated differences.

1. $(7x - 9y) - (13x - 9y)$ $-6x$

2. $(13a - 5b) - (9b - 3a)$

3. $(15a - 9) - (10a + 3)$

4. $(7r - 8s) - (15s - 2r + 8)$

5. $(5n^2 - 2n) - (6n^2 - 5 + 3n)$

6. $(3x^2 + 5x) - (7x - 2x^2)$

7. $(3r^2 + 4) - (7r^2 - 5r - 9)$

8. $(y^2 - 7y) - (8y + 3 - 9y^2)$

9. $(7x + 2) - (9x^2 + 3x - 7)$

10. $(8b^2 + 3b + 1) - (15b^2 + 3b)$

11. $(r^2 - 5r - 8) - (r^2 - 2)$

12. $(x^2 - 6x) - (2x^2 - 5 + 3x)$

13. $(4y^2 - 7y + 2) - (y^2 - 3y + 1)$

14. $(3x^2 + 2x - 9) - (7x^2 - 13)$

15. $(6m - 3n + 5) - (7n + 8m - 2)$

16. $(8z^2 + 3z + 2) - (7z + 15)$

17. $(2a - 9b) - (6b - 3a - 7)$

18. $(3x - 9y - 13) - (4x - 2 + 9y)$

19. $(9cd - 6pq) - (5pq + 2cd)$

20. $(7x^2 + 2x + 3) - (15x^2 + 13)$

21. $(5z^2 - 7z) - (13z + 15 - 9z^2)$

22. $(9a - 3b + 7) - (8a - 7b + 6)$

23. $(14rst - 8xy) - (15xy + 10rst)$

24. $(3m^2 - 5m + 7) - (m^2 + 3m - 5)$

25. $(st - 3pq + 10) - (15 - 7pq)$

26. $(5r + 3s - 2) - (6 + 7s + 2r)$

27. $(29ab + 3cd) - (18cd + 12ab)$

28. $(11mn^2 + 3m^2n) - (6m^2n - 2mn^2)$

29. $(3x^2 - 5x^3 + 3) - (7x^3 + 17)$

30. $(9rt + 3zy) - (12rt + 2zy + 4)$

31. $(8cq - 2q + 7) - (-10 + 2q)$

32. $(17b^2 + 3b - 7) - (22b^2 - 21)$

Subtraction of Polynomials

Name _____

Date _____ Period _____

Find the differences of the following polynomials.

1. $3x - 2y$
    $-4x + 3y$

    $7x - 5y$

2. $22a + 3b$
    $15a - 7b$

3. $13c - 15d$
    $22c - 9d$

4. $7r - 12t + 3$
    $-4r - 11t + 9$

5. $-18x + 3$
    $-7x - 9$

6. $15r + 10s$
    $-4r + 17s - 2t$

7. $21c - 7d + 25$
    $-11c - 2d + 11$

8. $-3x - 13y$
    $8x + 25y$

9. $-22m^2 + 3m - 17$
    $-8m^2 + 22$

10. $13r^2 - 5r + 16$
    $-15r^2 + 2r + 7$

11. $-18c^2 - 9c + 12$
    $-9c^2 - 8c - 15$

12. $13x^3 - 5x^2 + 15x + 2$
    $-11x^3 - 3x^2 + 9$

13. $8z^2 + 7z - 15$
    $-6z^2 + 4z - 15$

14. $9a^2 + 3a + 24$
    $-2a^2 - 5a + 13$

15. $11b^2 - 13b - 21$
    $-8b^2 + 13b + 16$

16. $13x^3 + 2x^2 - 9x - 15$
    $15x^3 + 2x^2 - 7x - 23$

17. $(x^2 - 8x + 22)$ and $(x^2 - 5x + 15)$

18. $(-7x^2 + 8x - 6)$ and $(13x^2 + 3x - 22)$

19. $(9x^2 - 2x + 13)$ and $(5x^2 - 7x - 2)$

Developing Skills in Algebra   Book B

Subtraction of Polynomials

Name _____

Date _____ Period _____

Find the differences of the following polynomials.

1. $\quad 7x + 9y$
$\quad \underline{-8x - 2y}$

$\quad 15x + 11y$

2. $15r + 3s$
$\quad \underline{22r + 5s}$

3. $28a - 22b$
$\quad \underline{14a - 22b}$

4. $\quad 6x - 11y + 7$
$\quad \underline{-9x - 14y + 3}$

5. $23m + 22$
$\quad \underline{-6m + 15}$

6. $\quad 16z + 22w$
$\quad \underline{-11z + 13w - 9}$

7. $\quad 28x - 5y + 13z$
$\quad \underline{-13x - 3y + 14z}$

8. $-9a + 22b - 4c$
$\quad \underline{-9a + 21b + 2c}$

9. $-19r^2 + 2r - 15$
$\quad \underline{-2r^2 - 5r}$

10. $\quad 16s^2 - 3s + 27$
$\quad \underline{-11s^2 - 7s + 13}$

11. $-16z^2 - 8z + 17$
$\quad \underline{-11z^2 - 8z + 13}$

12. $\quad 21y^3 - 2y^2 + 11y + 4$
$\quad \underline{-13y^3 - 7y^2 - 8y}$

13. $\quad 4a^2 + 9a - 27$
$\quad \underline{-8a^2 + 3a - 13}$

14. $17x^2 + 3x - 22$
$\quad \underline{-6x^2 + 3x + 19}$

15. $\quad 22r^2 - 15r - 28$
$\quad \underline{-17r^2 + 11r + 14}$

16. $15m^3 + 2m^2 - 3m - 18$
$\quad \underline{13m^3 - 4m^2 - 2m + 13}$

17. $(z^2 - 2z + 14)$ and $(2z^2 - 8z + 22)$

18. $(15y^2 - 7y - 13)$ and $(15y^2 + 12y - 18)$

19. $(23x^2 - 7x - 19)$ and $(6x^2 - 7x + 24)$

Addition and Subtraction of Polynomials

Name _____

Date _____ Period _____

Simplify.

1. $a + (3a - 2b) - (4a - 3b)$ b

2. $4x - (6x - 2y) + (2x - 7y)$

3. $7a + [4a - 6b - (8a + 2b)]$

4. $3x + [2x + 3y - (4x - 7y)]$

5. $(2a - 5) + (3a - 1) - (4a + 2)$

6. $(3y - 2) - (6y + 4) + (8y + 2)$

7. $(3x + 2) - (4x - 7) + (3x + 1)$

8. $(7m + 3) + (6m + 1) - (4m + 7)$

9. $(x^2 - 3x) + (5x + 2) - (x^2 + 3)$

10. $(7a^2 - 5) - (4a - 3) + (2a + 1)$

11. $(2x^2 - 3x + 2) + (5x^2 - 3x + 7) - (13x^2 + 6x - 5)$

12. $(4a^2 + 2a^3 - 6) - (7a^3 - 8a^2 + 3a - 1) + (7a^2 - 9a + 3)$

13. $(21x^2 - 5xy + 13y^2) - (15y^2 - 7xy + 13x^2) + (12x^2 - 9xy + 13y^2)$

14. $(13a^2 + 12ab - 15b^2) + (11b^2 - 16ab + 13a^2) - (7a^2 + 12ab - 16b^2)$

15. $(14m^2n - 18m^2n^2 + 16n) - (12mn - 17m^2n^2 + 3n) + (11m - 13m^2n^2 + 2m^2)$

16. $(21c^2 + 14c^2d - 8) + (11cd^2 - 14) + (2c^2d - 15cd^2 - 19d^2)$

17. $(16r^2 + 2r - 7) + (9r - 15r^2 - 1) - (22 + 3r^2 - 9r)$

18. $(16k^2 + 4km - 2m^2) + (3m^2 + 7km - 11k^2) - (22km + 8k^2 - 3m^2)$

19. $(14x + 3y - 7z) - (11y - 4x + 7z) - (11z + 3x - 10y)$

20. $(8x^3 + 3x^2 - 5x + 4) - (2x^3 - 3x + 2 - 7x^2) + (14x^2 - 9)$

21. $(5mn + 2pq - 8rs) - (7pq - 11rs + 13mn) - (4rs + 2pq + 7mn)$

22. $(8xy + 7xz - 11yz) - (15yx + 2xz - 7yz) - (13yz + 11xz - 15xy)$

    13   Developing Skills in Algebra   Book B

Addition and Subtraction of Polynomials

Simplify.

1. $x + (7x - 4y) - (2x - 9y)$ $6x + 5y$

2. $3c - (7d - 4c) + (7c - 9d)$

3. $3v - [7w - 8v - (7v - 4w)]$

4. $9a - [3b + 2a - (5a - 8b)]$

5. $(2x - 9) + (6x - 7) - (3x + 1)$

6. $(5c - 9) - (7c + 3) + (1 - 8c)$

7. $(7x - 5) + (3x - 2) + (8x + 9)$

8. $(9r + 7) - (3 - 7r) + (2r - 9)$

9. $(a^2 - 7a) + (3a + 7) - (a^2 + 3)$

10. $(9x^2 - 2) - (7x + 5) + (3x - 2)$

11. $(11a^2 - 7a + 1) + (2a^2 - 9a + 13) - (17a^2 + 2a - 11)$

12. $(6x^3 + 7x^2 - 4) - (3x^3 - 2x^2 - 5x + 3) + (8x^3 - 7x + 1)$

13. $(15c^2 - 8cd + 19d^2) - (14d^2 - 2cd + 11c^2) + (7c^2 - 12cd + 14d^2)$

14. $(12m^2 - 11mn + 17n^2) + (13n^2 + 2mn + 15m^2) - (2m^2 - 15mn + 7n^2)$

15. $(13a^3 + 9a^2 - 2a) + (7a^2 - 2a + 3) - (7a^3 - 2a^2 - 5a + 2)$

16. $(14m^3 - 8m^2 + 3m^4) + (11m^4 + m^2 - 2m + 4) - (16m^3 - 5m^2 + 2)$

17. $(19x^2 + 7x - 2) + (4x + 11x^2 - 7) - (15 + 5x^2 - 9x)$

18. $(22r^2 - 2rs - 3s^2) + (4s^2 + 9rs - 14r^2) - (27rs - 7r^2 - 2s^2)$

19. $(2a - 4b + 8c) - (16b - 2c + 4a) + (15c + 3a - 12b)$

20. $(9x^3 - 5x^2 - 2x + 3) - (7x^3 - 5x + 4 - 9x^2) + (22x^3 - 13)$

21. $(6ac + 5bc - 7ab) - (9bc - 15ab + 11ac) - (3ab - 7ac + 9bc)$

22. $(14mn + 8mp - 13np) - (11np + 5mp - 8mn) - (15mp - 13np - 17mn)$

Products of Monomials

Name _____

Date _____ Period _____

Simplify.

1. $a^3 \cdot a^2$ a^5 2. $b^4 \cdot b$ _____

3. $3a^2 \cdot a^3$ _____   4. $7b^2 \cdot b^5$ _____

5. $6a^3 \cdot 5a^4$ _____   6. $2b^3 \cdot 3b^4$ _____

7. $4a^3(-6a)^3$ _____   8. $7b^4(-3b)^2$ _____

9. $(-7a)^2(-5a)^2$ _____   10. $(-2b)^3(-6b)^2$ _____

11. $(3x^2y^3)(2x^3y)$ _____   12. $(7m^4n^2)(3m^4n)$ _____

13. $(7x^3y^3)(-5x^2y)$ _____   14. $(-4m^3n)(3m^2n)$ _____

15. $a^2(a^3)(a^3)$ _____   16. $b^3(b^2)(b^2)$ _____

17. $a^4(-a^5)(a^2)$ _____   18. $b^5(-b)^2(-b)^3$ _____

19. $13x^2y^2(-2x^3)(-4y)$ _____   20. $-7m^3n^4(4m^5)(6n)$ _____

21. $7ab^3(-2a^2b)(3ab)$ _____   22. $-5a^4(6a^2b^2)(4b)$ _____

23. $8a^5(9b)(-6a^2b^2)$ _____   24. $2m^4(-3m^3n^2)(-8m)$ _____

25. $10^2(10^3)$ _____   26. $2^5(2^2)$ _____

27. $5^3(5^2)(5^4)$ _____   28. $3^3(3^2)(3^2)$ _____

29. $a^2(a^r)$ _____   30. $b^3(b^m)$ _____

31. $r(r^2)(r^x)$ _____   32. $x^3(x)(x^n)$ _____

33. $2y^x(-3y^2)(4y)$ _____   34. $-2r^c(3r)(-5r^2)$ _____

15

Products of Monomials

Name _____

Date _____ Period _____

Simplify.

1. $x^5 \cdot x$ x^6

2. $y^3 \cdot y^2$ _____

3. $5x^3 \cdot x^4$ _____

4. $4y^2 \cdot y^5$ _____

5. $2x^3 \cdot 7x^3$ _____

6. $9y^2 \cdot 5y^2$ _____

7. $3x^5(-7x)^2$ _____

8. $5y^4(-2y)^5$ _____

9. $(-4x)^2(-7x)^2$ _____

10. $(-3y)^3(-7y)^2$ _____

11. $(7a^3b^2)(3a^3b)$ _____

12. $(6r^4s^2)(2r^2s)$ _____

13. $(6a^3b^3)(-4a^4b)$ _____

14. $(-9r^3s)(5r^5s)$ _____

15. $c^3(c^2)(c^4)$ _____

16. $z^3(z^2)(z^5)$ _____

17. $m(-m^2)(-m^3)$ _____

18. $t^4(-t^2)(t^3)$ _____

19. $17a^3b^2(-2a^4)(-3b)$ _____

20. $-2s^3t^2(5s^4)(7t)$ _____

21. $4xy(-3x^3y)(2xy^4)$ _____

22. $3m^3(2m^2n^2)(-3n)$ _____

23. $3r^4(2s)(-5r^2s^2)$ _____

24. $5c^3(2c^3d^2)(-11d)$ _____

25. $12^2(12^2)$ _____

26. $3^4(3^2)$ _____

27. $7^3(7^3)(7^2)$ _____

28. $2^4(2^5)(2^2)$ _____

29. $c^3(c^r)$ _____

30. $d^4(d^s)$ _____

31. $a(a^3)(a^x)$ _____

32. $r^y(r)(r^3)$ _____

33. $5x^a(-2x^3)(-3x)$ _____

34. $12d^r(-2d)(-7d^2)$ _____

Powers of Monomials

Simplify.

1. $(a^2)^3$ a^6 2. $(x^4)^2$ _____

3. $(x^3)^2$ _____   4. $(b^2)^5$ _____

5. $(u^7)^{10}$ _____   6. $(z^8)^5$ _____

7. $(2x^2)^3$ _____   8. $(3y^3)^4$ _____

9. $(-3x^2)^2$ _____   10. $(-5y^3)^3$ _____

11. $(\frac{1}{2}x^4)^2$ _____   12. $(\frac{1}{3}y^3)^2$ _____

13. $(0.2x^3)^3$ _____   14. $(0.3y^2)^4$ _____

15. $2(3a^2)^3$ _____   16. $4(-2x^3)^3$ _____

17. $\frac{1}{2}(4x^3)^2$ _____   18. $\frac{1}{3}(3t^2)^3$ _____

19. $0.1(10x^2)^3$ _____   20. $0.01(10y^2)^3$ _____

21. $(-x^2)^3$ _____   22. $(-2y^3)^2$ _____

23. $(-3x^3)^2$ _____   24. $(-5y^2)^3$ _____

25. $(a^m)^n$ _____   26. $(b^x)^y$ _____

27. $(3b^s)^3$ _____   28. $(5x^p)^2$ _____

29. $(x^m)^2(2x^n)^2$ _____ 30. $(a^r)^3(a^s)^2$ _____

31. $(x^2)^b(x^{3b})^2$ _____ 32. $(y^3)^c(y^{2c})^4$ _____

33. $(2x^m)^3(x^2)^m$ _____ 34. $(3y^r)^2(y^3)^r$ _____

     17   Developing Skills in Algebra   Book B

Name _____

Date _____ Period _____

Simplify.

1. $(c^3)^4$ c^{12} **2.** $(t^2)^5$ _____

3. $(c^4)^2$ _____   **4.** $(t^3)^2$ _____

5. $(m^5)^5$ _____   **6.** $(y^6)^4$ _____

7. $(3a^2)^4$ _____   **8.** $(2b^3)^5$ _____

9. $(-5a^3)^2$ _____   **10.** $(-2b^4)^4$ _____

11. $(\frac{1}{4}c^3)^3$ _____   **12.** $(\frac{1}{5}m^3)^2$ _____

13. $(0.4x^3)^2$ _____   **14.** $(0.1y^5)^3$ _____

15. $5(2x^3)^4$ _____   **16.** $7(-3y^2)^3$ _____

17. $\frac{1}{3}(6x^2)^3$ _____   **18.** $\frac{1}{2}(6t^2)^3$ _____

19. $0.2(10a^2)^3$ _____   **20.** $0.03(19b^3)^2$ _____

21. $(-a^3)^4$ _____   **22.** $(-3b^4)^3$ _____

23. $(-2a^6)^5$ _____   **24.** $(-4b^3)^2$ _____

25. $(x^p)^q$ _____   **26.** $(y^r)^s$ _____

27. $(2m^x)^4$ _____   **28.** $(9n^y)^2$ _____

29. $(a^r)^3(2a^s)^2$ _____   **30.** $(c^p)^2(c^q)^3$ _____

31. $(t^3)^c(t^{2c})^3$ _____   **32.** $(n^4)^x(n^{3x})^2$ _____

33. $(3a^y)^2(a^3)^y$ _____   **34.** $(5b^t)^3(b^4)^t$ _____

Name _____

Date _____ Period _____

Simplify.

1. $(2a^3)(3a^4) + (2a^4)(3a)^3$ $60a^7$

2. $(5b^2)(6b^3) + (3b)^3(4b^2)$

3. $(-2c)^2(3c)^3 + (4c^3)(3c)^2$

4. $(4d)^3(2d^3) + (-3d)^2(2d)^4$

5. $(8a)^2(4a)^3 + (2a^3)(4a^2)$

6. $(6x)^4(3x)^2 + (7x^3)(2x)^3$

7. $(4ab)^2(2a^2b^2) + 2(ab)^3(4ab)$

8. $(9xy)^2(3x^3y^3) + 3(xy)^4(2xy)$

9. $(2x^2)(3x)^2(2x^3) + (3x)^3(3x^4)$

10. $(5y^2)(2y)^3(3y^3) + (4y)^2(2y^6)$

11. $(2a)^5(3ab)^3 + (3a^5)(2ab)^3$

12. $(7x)^2(2xy)^3 + (4x^2)(6xy)^3$

13. $(3n)^2(-4m)^3 + (2m)^3(-7n)^2$

14. $(5r)^2(-2s)^5 + (3s)^5(-4r)^2$

15. $(2a^4)(3ab)^2 - (2b)^2(3a^2)^3$

16. $(7c^3)(2ac)^2 - (3c)^3(2ac)^2$

17. $(xy^2z)(x^2yz) - (2xy)^2(xyz^2)$

18. $(r^2st)(rs^2t) - (4rs)^3(t^2)$

19. $(2x^2ab)^2(2a^2b^2) - (abx)^3(3abx)$

20. $(7tu)(2t^2uv) - (3tu)^2(4tv)$

21. $(ab^3c^2)(2ab)^3 - (ab)^2(3ab^2c)^2$

22. $(c^3d^3t)(3t)^2 - (2cdt)^2(4cdt)$

23. $(-2nm)(3nm)^3 - (-8mn)^2(mn)^2$

24. $(5x^2y^2)(-xy)^3 - (4xy)^3(xy)^2$

25. $(2up^2)(4up)^3 - (3u^4p)(9p^4)$

26. $(7rs)^3(3rs^2) - (7s)(-2rs)^4$

27. $(-3ab)^2(3ab^3) - (5b)^2(-10ab)^3$

28. $(4c)^2(-2cd^3) - (8d)^2(-3c^3d)$

29. $(3x^2zu)(-2zu^3) - (-6x^2)(zu^2)^2$

30. $(-5a^2bc)(-2bc^2) - (-a^2c)(bc)^2$

31. $(-2x^3)(-3a^3x) - (6ax)^3(x)$

32. $(12mr^2)(-2m^2r) - (7mr)(2mr)^2$

33. $(11a^2)(+3ab)^3 - (2a^4)(4ab^3)$

34. $(7uv)(-5uv^2)^2 - (-5uv)^2(7uv^3)$

        Developing Skills in Algebra   Book B

Name _____

Date _____ Period _____

Simplify.

1. $(3b^2)(4b^3) + (5b^2)(2b)^3$ $52b^5$

2. $(3x^4)(2x^2) + (3x)^3(8x^3)$

3. $(3m)^4(-8m)^2 + (5m^5)(3m)$

4. $(3r)^2(7r)^3 + (-2r)^3(5r)^2$

5. $(3d)^4(2d)^3 + (9d^5)(7d^2)$

6. $(8r)^3(2r)^2 + (5r^4)(-3r)$

7. $(3xy)^2(4x^3y^3) + 6(xy)^4(5xy)$

8. $(7mn)^2(2m^2n^2) + 4(mn)^3(3mn)$

9. $(7a^5)(2a)^2(5a^2) + (3a^3)(9a^3)^2$

10. $(7b^2)(3b)^3(8b^2) + (2b)^4(4b^3)$

11. $(6x)^2(4xy)^5 + (9x^2)(2xy)^5$

12. $(6a)^2(5a^3b^2) + (7a^2b^2)(2a)^3$

13. $(5s)^2(-2t)^4 + (3t)^4(-2s)^2$

14. $(3c)^2(-5d)^2 + (4c)^2(-2d)^2$

15. $(7x^2)(4xy)^3 - (3x^2y)^2(5xy)$

16. $(8m^3)(3mr)^2 - (2m)^3(5mr)^2$

17. $(pq^3r)(p^2qr) - (5pq)^2(pq^2r^2)$

18. $(a^3bc)(a^2b^2c) - (3ab)^3(ac)^2$

19. $(5x^3yz^2)(3xy)^2 - (xy)^3(2xz)^2$

20. $(5mr)(3m^2rt^5) - (2mt)^3(2rt)^2$

21. $(fg^2h)(3fg)^2 - (fg)^3(2gh)$

22. $(p^2qr)(2qr)^4 - (3pqr)^2(2qr)^3$

23. $(-3xy)^2(4xy)^3 - (-6xy)^2(xy)^3$

24. $(7ab)(-ab)^3 - (3ab)^3(ab)$

25. $(3gt^2)(2gt)^3 - (5g^3t^5)(8g)$

26. $(8ms)^2(2ms^5) - (5s)(-3ms^2)^3$

27. $(-2x)^4(4xy^3) - (3x)^4(-12xy^3)$

28. $(7u)^2(-3uv)^3 - (2uv)^3(-4u^2)$

29. $(5s^3tu)(-4tu^3) - (-7t^2u)(su)^3$

30. $(-3d^3ef)(-2de)^3 - (-d^2f)(de)^4$

31. $(-9ab^2)(-2a^2b) - (7ab)(ab)^2$

32. $(-3rs^2)(-4r^2s) - (8rs)(5rs)^2$

33. $(13gh^2)(-5g^3h) - (3g)(7gh)^3$

34. $(9xy^3)(-7x^2y) - (12xy)^2(3xy^2)$

Developing Skills in Algebra   Book B

Multiplication of a Polynomial and a Monomial

Name _____

Date _____ Period _____

Multiply.

1. $3(x + 5)$ $3x + 15$

2. $5(2x + 3)$

3. $x(x - 3)$

4. $y(y - 5)$

5. $3x(x + 7)$

6. $5y(y - 9)$

7. $2c(c - 3d)$

8. $4m(m + 7n)$

9. $-3a(2a + 3b)$

10. $-7x(5x - 4y)$

11. $-7c(3c - 4d)$

12. $-4t(7t + 3u)$

13. $2x(x^2 - 3x + 5)$

14. $4y(y^2 + 7y - 2)$

15. $-4c(c^2 + 6c - 2)$

16. $-9x(x^2 - 7x + 15)$

17. $9st(5s + 3t - 9)$

18. $11pq(5p - 7q + 4)$

19. $-8mn(14m - 8n + 3)$

20. $-7uv(12u + 6v - 11)$

21. $xy(xy - u)$

22. $pq(5pq + v)$

23. $x^2y(x^3 - y)$

24. $ab^2(3a + 2b)$

25. $x^3z(z^2 - 5)$

26. $r^2s(s^3 - 7)$

27. $3x^3(y^2 + 2x)$

28. $4z^2(2y + 7z)$

29. $x^2y^2(x^2y - 2y)$

30. $m^2n^2(m^3n + 3n)$

31. $xa^4(x^2a - 8c)$

32. $mr^3(mr + 9t)$

33. $4x^2y(2x^3y + 15z)$

34. $-7c^3d(3c^2d - 14e)$

Multiplication of a Polynomial and a Monomial

Name _____

Date _____ Period _____

Multiply.

1. $8(y + 4)$ $8y + 32$

2. $9(3a - 5)$

3. $c(c - 7)$

4. $z(z + 15)$

5. $2y(y + 8)$

6. $3p(p - 11)$

7. $7a(a - 4b)$

8. $3d(d + 2g)$

9. $-5z(3y + 4z)$

10. $-4m(2m - 3n)$

11. $-3t(4t + 7u)$

12. $-3r(2s - 4r)$

13. $7z(z^2 - 5z + 9)$

14. $8a(a^2 + 3a - 5)$

15. $-4t(t^2 + 7t - 5)$

16. $-3a(a^2 - 6a + 17)$

17. $7ab(2a + 4b - 6)$

18. $13rs(12r + 6s - 7)$

19. $-7mr(12m - 7r + 5)$

20. $-9st(12s + 3t - 15)$

21. $pq(pq - v)$

22. $ab(7ab + c)$

23. $a^3b(a^2 - b)$

24. $xy^3(4x + 3y)$

25. $r^2s(s^3 - 9)$

26. $v^2w(w^3 - 14)$

27. $7x^2(x^3 - 7y)$

28. $9b^2(7b + 8c)$

29. $c^3d^2(c^2d - 2d)$

30. $v^3w^2(v^2w + 9v)$

31. $pq^2(p^3q - 9r)$

32. $st^3(st + 7u)$

33. $-5x^3y(3x^2y^2 + 15z)$

34. $8rs(3r^2s + 12t)$

    22   Developing Skills in Algebra   Book B

Multiplication of a Polynomial and a Monomial

Name _____

Date _____ Period _____

Multiply.

1. $4x^2(2x^2 - 3x + 1)$ $8x^4 - 12x^3 + 4x^2$

2. $9y^2(7y^2 + 5y - 3)$

3. $7x^2y(3x^2 + 2xy - 5y^2)$

4. $3a^3b(2a^2 - 4ab + 7b^2)$

5. $x^2y^2(y^3 + y + 2)$

6. $a^2b^2(2b^2 - 5b + 1)$

7. $-x^3(ax^2 + 5a + 3)$

8. $-y^4(by - 6b - 9)$

9. $a^2b^2(a^2 + 2a + 1)$

10. $c^2d^2(d^2 + 3d - 7)$

11. $-\frac{1}{3}a(3a^2 - 6a + 9)$

12. $-\frac{1}{2}c(6c^2 + 8c - 4)$

13. $0.2x(10x^2 + 30x - 20)$

14. $0.3y(50y^2 - 70y + 10)$

15. $x^2y^2z^3(3x^2y + 4yz + 7)$

16. $p^2q^3r^2(4p^2q + 2qr - 9)$

17. $a^2b(3a^3b^2 - 9a^2b^3c + 3b^2c^3)$

18. $r^3s^2(7r^3s + 6r^2s^2t - 2st)$

19. $3m^2n^3p^2(14m^2n^3p - 9mp^3)$

20. $2r^2u^2v^3(12r^2u^3v^2 + 19rv^4)$

21. $-6wxy^5(3wx + 2wy - 7xy)$

22. $-9rs^3t^2(5rs + 2st - 8rt)$

23. $13a^2b^3c^3(2a^2b^3 + 3a^3c^2)$

24. $9m^3n^2r^2(3mn^2 - 2nr^2 + 3m^3r^2)$

25. $11zy^3x(14x^3 - 12zy + 7)$

26. $-15p^2q^3(8p^2q^3 - 7q^3r^2 + 2)$

27. $23a^4d^2(5a^2d^2 - 7dc + 4)$

28. $16u^3v^2(6u^2v^3 + 9vt - 8)$

29. $9x^3z(3x^2 + 4z^2 + 2y^2z^3)$

30. $14a^3t(2a^3 - 3t + 3tu)$

31. $9d^2c(14d^2 - 12c + 3b)$

32. $-7p^3q^2(4p^3 + 2q - 9r)$

33. $-8m^2n(12m^3n + 5mt - 7nt^3)$

34. $6r^2s^2(9r^2s^2 - 6r^3t + 5su)$

   23   Developing Skills in Algebra   Book B

Multiplication of a Polynomial and a Monomial   Name _____

Date _____ Period _____

Multiply.

1. $5a^2(3a^2 - 7a + 4)$ $15a^4 - 35a^3 + 20a^2$ **2.** $7c^3(8c^2 + 2c - 9)$

3. $3m^3n(5m^2 - 4mn - 8n^2)$ **4.** $6x^2y(3x^2 - 5xy + 9y^2)$

5. $p^2q^2(q^2 + q - 5)$ **6.** $m^3n^2(5n^2 - 7n + 2)$

7. $-z^3(az^3 - 9a + 5)$ **8.** $-b^3(ab - 7b + 13)$

9. $r^2a^2(r^2 + 5r - 7)$ **10.** $x^3y^2(y^2 - 9y + 14)$

11. $-\dfrac{2}{3}x(6x^2 - 9x + 3)$ **12.** $-\dfrac{3}{4}z(8z^2 + 16z - 12)$

13. $0.3x(20x^2 + 50x - 10)$ **14.** $0.5y(20y^2 - 16y + 24)$

15. $a^2b^2c^3(4a^2b + 9bc + 3)$ **16.** $t^3u^2v^2(2u^3v - 3vt - 11)$

17. $r^2t(7r^2t^2 - 3r^2t^3q + 5t^3q)$ **18.** $z^3w^2(4z^2w + 9y^3z^2w - 5yz)$

19. $9v^2u^3w^2(13v^2u^3w - 8uw)$ **20.** $7a^3b^2t^3(11a^2b^2t + 11at^3)$

21. $-7cde^4(5ce + 4de - 8cd)$ **22.** $-2ab^2c^3(7bc - 3ac - 9ab)$

23. $11m^2n^3r^3(3m^2n^3 - 7n^3r^2)$ **24.** $5r^3s^2t^2(2rs^3 - 3st^2 - 5r^2t^3)$

25. $19cd^3e(11c^2 - 12de + 5)$ **26.** $-23r^3t^2(6r^3t^2 + 3r^3q^2 - 7)$

27. $15m^2t^3(3m^2t^3 - 4mn - 7)$ **28.** $13x^4z^2(4x^3z^2 + 6xy - 9)$

29. $3a^4c(5a^2 + 2c^3 - 7a^2c^2)$ **30.** $6b^3q(3b^2 - 5q - 8bq)$

31. $4r^3t^2(15r^3 - 11t + 5c^3)$ **32.** $-9z^2y^2(3y^3 - 2z^2 - 5d)$

33. $-2b^3r(11b^2r^2 + 3ab - 6rt)$ **34.** $7t^4q(7t^2q^2 - 8t^3x - 4st)$

24   Developing Skills in Algebra   Book B

Name _____

Date _____ Period _____

Multiply.

1. $(x + 3)(x + 1)$ $x^2 + 4x + 3$

2. $(x + 6)(x + 5)$

3. $(x + 3)(2x + 1)$

4. $(2x + 7)(2x + 3)$

5. $(x + 5)(3x + 2)$

6. $(4x + 3)(3x + 2)$

7. $(3x + 2)(4x + 1)$

8. $(x + 8)(4x + 7)$

9. $(x + 4)(5x + 1)$

10. $(2x + 3)(5x + 3)$

11. $(x + 8)(5x + 8)$

12. $(x + 5)(6x + 5)$

13. $(2x + 1)(x + 2)$

14. $(x + 6)(2x + 5)$

15. $(x + 8)(3x + 1)$

16. $(3x + 2)(4x + 3)$

17. $(2x + 9)(5x + 1)$

18. $(3x + 2)(5x + 3)$

19. $(2x + 7)(5x + 8)$

20. $(2x + 7)(7x + 2)$

21. $(x + 4)(7x + 6)$

22. $(x + 4)(7x + 3)$

23. $(3x + 7)(x + 3)$

24. $(4x + 1)(x + 7)$

25. $(4x + 5)(2x + 3)$

26. $(2x + 3)(2x + 9)$

27. $(2x + 3)(x + 6)$

28. $(x + 8)(3x + 4)$

29. $(x + 5)(3x + 7)$

30. $(x + 5)(4x + 3)$

31. $(x + 6)(3x + 7)$

32. $(x + 3)(5x + 8)$

33. $(x + 3)(x + 4)$

34. $(2x + 5)(x + 3)$

Products of Binomials

Name _____

Date _____ Period _____

Multiply.

1. $(x + 4)(x + 7)$ $x^2 + 11x + 28$

2. $(x + 7)(2x + 1)$

3. $(3x + 5)(3x + 1)$

4. $(3x + 5)(x + 6)$

5. $(x + 4)(4x + 5)$

6. $(x + 1)(4x + 9)$

7. $(2x + 9)(5x + 8)$

8. $(2x + 3)(4x + 7)$

9. $(5x + 1)(4x + 1)$

10. $(4x + 7)(x + 8)$

11. $(x + 4)(2x + 7)$

12. $(2x + 5)(4x + 3)$

13. $(3x + 7)(5x + 4)$

14. $(2x + 1)(7x + 3)$

15. $(x + 7)(7x + 6)$

16. $(x + 5)(5x + 6)$

17. $(x + 6)(6x + 7)$

18. $(x + 6)(4x + 9)$

19. $(x + 1)(2x + 7)$

20. $(2x + 7)(x + 6)$

21. $(x + 8)(x + 3)$

22. $(4x + 5)(x + 5)$

23. $(4x + 7)(3x + 1)$

24. $(2x + 1)(3x + 7)$

25. $(5x + 9)(x + 3)$

26. $(5x + 1)(2x + 5)$

27. $(2x + 3)(3x + 1)$

28. $(7x + 1)(3x + 7)$

29. $(4x + 3)(5x + 8)$

30. $(5x + 4)(7x + 1)$

31. $(3x + 2)(7x + 5)$

32. $(4x + 5)(7x + 8)$

33. $(5x + 3)(x + 9)$

34. $(5x + 4)(x + 1)$

Products of Binomials

Name _____

Date _____ Period _____

Multiply.

1. $(x - 1)(x - 5)$ $x^2 - 6x + 5$

2. $(x - 5)(2x - 3)$

3. $(2x - 3)(x - 2)$

4. $(x - 1)(3x - 4)$

5. $(x - 7)(3x - 5)$

6. $(2x - 7)(4x - 5)$

7. $(4x - 1)(5x - 2)$

8. $(x - 3)(6x - 7)$

9. $(3x - 2)(5x - 6)$

10. $(x - 1)(7x - 1)$

11. $(2x - 7)(4x - 1)$

12. $(3x - 1)(2x - 9)$

13. $(x - 3)(x - 7)$

14. $(4x - 5)(4x - 9)$

15. $(2x - 3)(5x - 7)$

16. $(2x - 3)(7x - 4)$

17. $(x - 7)(7x - 2)$

18. $(3x - 5)(3x - 2)$

19. $(2x - 5)(x - 9)$

20. $(x - 4)(x - 2)$

21. $(5x - 3)(x - 4)$

22. $(x - 9)(2x - 3)$

23. $(x - 3)(3x - 1)$

24. $(4x - 1)(x - 7)$

25. $(5x - 1)(6x - 1)$

26. $(3x - 1)(7x - 2)$

27. $(x - 1)(7x - 8)$

28. $(5x - 4)(3x - 4)$

29. $(5x - 3)(5x - 1)$

30. $(x - 4)(5x - 4)$

31. $(x - 8)(6x - 5)$

32. $(2x - 9)(x - 5)$

33. $(3x - 4)(2x - 7)$

34. $(6x - 7)(4x - 3)$

Multiply.

1. $(x - 8)(x - 5)$ $x^2 - 13x + 40$

2. $(x - 3)(3x - 4)$

3. $(3x - 4)(5x - 7)$

4. $(x - 6)(2x - 9)$

5. $(x - 1)(4x - 3)$

6. $(3x - 7)(4x - 5)$

7. $(3x - 5)(x - 5)$

8. $(x - 3)(7x - 3)$

9. $(5x - 8)(5x - 3)$

10. $(4x - 7)(4x - 3)$

11. $(3x - 5)(2x - 1)$

12. $(x - 1)(3x - 1)$

13. $(2x - 9)(x - 8)$

14. $(5x - 3)(7x - 5)$

15. $(2x - 1)(7x - 8)$

16. $(2x - 3)(6x - 5)$

17. $(x - 7)(4x - 3)$

18. $(x - 4)(x - 9)$

19. $(4x - 1)(2x - 7)$

20. $(5x - 6)(3x - 2)$

21. $(2x - 1)(4x - 9)$

22. $(x - 4)(7x - 1)$

23. $(2x - 5)(3x - 5)$

24. $(3x - 4)(7x - 4)$

25. $(x - 3)(4x - 1)$

26. $(x - 1)(7x - 4)$

27. $(x - 4)(7x - 9)$

28. $(4x - 7)(x - 9)$

29. $(6x - 5)(x - 5)$

30. $(2x - 9)(x - 3)$

31. $(x - 3)(x - 8)$

32. $(4x - 1)(3x - 4)$

33. $(5x - 6)(4x - 7)$

34. $(x - 7)(5x - 8)$

Developing Skills in Algebra   Book B

Name _____

Date _____ Period _____

Multiply.

1. $(x - 8)(2x + 5)$ $2x^2 - 11x - 40$ **2.** $(2x + 9)(x - 6)$

3. $(x + 8)(5x - 1)$ **4.** $(2x - 5)(5x + 1)$

5. $(4x + 3)(3x - 7)$ **6.** $(5x + 3)(2x - 7)$

7. $(3x - 7)(x + 8)$ **8.** $(6x - 1)(2x + 5)$

9. $(3x - 5)(4x + 7)$ **10.** $(x + 9)(5x - 7)$

11. $(3x + 1)(5x - 2)$ **12.** $(x - 6)(x + 2)$

13. $(4x - 1)(2x + 1)$ **14.** $(x - 9)(7x + 1)$

15. $(2x + 9)(5x - 3)$ **16.** $(3x + 7)(7x - 5)$

17. $(5x + 7)(7x - 4)$ **18.** $(4x - 3)(5x + 7)$

19. $(x + 9)(3x - 2)$ **20.** $(2x - 9)(2x + 1)$

21. $(x - 9)(x + 1)$ **22.** $(x - 1)(x + 9)$

23. $(4x - 5)(3x + 5)$ **24.** $(x + 3)(5x - 2)$

25. $(5x + 3)(5x - 7)$ **26.** $(2x + 5)(7x - 6)$

27. $(x - 9)(4x + 3)$ **28.** $(3x - 4)(2x + 9)$

29. $(x - 6)(7x + 9)$ **30.** $(3x - 2)(x + 3)$

31. $(6x + 1)(x - 1)$ **32.** $(5x + 6)(4x - 3)$

33. $(x - 7)(5x + 4)$ **34.** $(5x - 1)(7x + 2)$

Products of Binomials

Multiply.

1. $(x - 6)(3x + 4)$ $3x^2 - 14x - 24$ 2. $(x - 3)(4x + 9)$

3. $(2x - 3)(7x + 1)$ 4. $(5x - 3)(x + 3)$

5. $(2x - 3)(3x + 2)$ 6. $(x - 8)(5x + 3)$

7. $(5x - 7)(x + 7)$ 8. $(7x + 2)(3x - 2)$

9. $(3x + 4)(7x - 2)$ 10. $(2x + 7)(3x - 7)$

11. $(5x + 8)(3x - 2)$ 12. $(3x + 2)(x - 9)$

13. $(x + 5)(4x - 9)$ 14. $(x - 1)(7x + 3)$

15. $(3x - 7)(2x + 9)$ 16. $(5x + 4)(6x - 1)$

17. $(2x - 1)(2x + 5)$ 18. $(3x + 4)(x - 1)$

19. $(5x - 4)(2x + 9)$ 20. $(4x - 5)(x + 7)$

21. $(7x - 1)(x + 4)$ 22. $(6x - 1)(4x + 7)$

23. $(x + 4)(7x - 8)$ 24. $(3x + 1)(6x - 5)$

25. $(x + 6)(4x - 5)$ 26. $(4x - 7)(x + 4)$

27. $(x - 4)(x + 5)$ 28. $(6x - 5)(3x + 5)$

29. $(3x + 5)(5x - 8)$ 30. $(x - 2)(3x + 1)$

31. $(3x + 5)(5x - 1)$ 32. $(x - 7)(5x + 8)$

33. $(4x - 7)(7x + 6)$ 34. $(2x + 3)(5x - 8)$

30   Developing Skills in Algebra   Book B

Products of Binomials

Multiply.

1. $(3x + 7)(3x + 1)$ $9x^2 + 24x + 7$ 2. $(x - 3)(5x + 1)$

3. $(5x - 9)(5x - 7)$ 4. $(x + 5)(x + 1)$

5. $(x + 9)(3x - 4)$ 6. $(4x - 1)(x + 4)$

7. $(x - 8)(7x + 3)$ 8. $(6x - 1)(5x - 2)$

9. $(x + 7)(4x - 5)$ 10. $(x - 1)(3x + 7)$

11. $(2x + 9)(2x + 3)$ 12. $(3x + 5)(x + 2)$

13. $(5x - 7)(x - 9)$ 14. $(7x + 1)(x - 1)$

15. $(2x - 1)(5x + 8)$ 16. $(5x + 4)(4x - 3)$

17. $(3x + 4)(x - 6)$ 18. $(7x - 4)(6x + 5)$

19. $(5x - 1)(2x + 9)$ 20. $(4x - 5)(6x - 7)$

21. $(x - 6)(5x - 7)$ 22. $(6x + 5)(2x - 5)$

23. $(2x + 5)(x - 2)$ 24. $(x + 4)(7x + 4)$

25. $(5x + 8)(7x + 2)$ 26. $(3x - 1)(4x + 1)$

27. $(5x - 3)(4x + 9)$ 28. $(2x - 7)(6x - 7)$

29. $(7x - 3)(x - 8)$ 30. $(3x + 2)(5x - 4)$

31. $(x + 5)(3x - 7)$ 32. $(4x + 7)(x + 1)$

33. $(6x + 7)(3x + 5)$ 34. $(2x - 3)(7x - 6)$

31   Developing Skills in Algebra   Book B

Products of Binomials

Multiply.

1. $(4x - 3)(2x - 3)$ $\quad 8x^2 - 18x + 9$

2. $(x + 9)(5x - 1)$

3. $(x + 4)(5x - 8)$

4. $(3x - 1)(x + 5)$

5. $(x + 1)(5x + 2)$

6. $(7x - 1)(x + 7)$

7. $(3x - 5)(4x + 7)$

8. $(2x + 5)(x + 8)$

9. $(5x + 8)(6x - 1)$

10. $(4x - 1)(5x - 4)$

11. $(5x + 6)(x - 3)$

12. $(2x + 3)(6x + 7)$

13. $(x + 6)(2x + 3)$

14. $(5x + 9)(2x - 7)$

15. $(2x - 7)(3x + 1)$

16. $(7x - 2)(4x + 7)$

17. $(3x + 7)(5x + 6)$

18. $(x - 8)(2x - 1)$

19. $(4x - 7)(4x - 9)$

20. $(6x + 1)(x - 5)$

21. $(7x + 6)(x - 7)$

22. $(4x - 5)(4x - 1)$

23. $(x - 3)(4x + 5)$

24. $(5x + 3)(x + 7)$

25. $(7x - 4)(3x - 4)$

26. $(5x - 7)(4x + 1)$

27. $(3x + 4)(5x + 6)$

28. $(2x - 1)(x - 8)$

29. $(5x - 1)(7x + 5)$

30. $(6x + 5)(5x - 3)$

31. $(x + 9)(x - 7)$

32. $(x + 5)(7x + 2)$

33. $(5x - 4)(3x - 2)$

34. $(x - 2)(5x + 8)$

Developing Skills in Algebra   Book B

Products of Binomials

Name _____

Date _____ Period _____

Multiply.

1. $(9x - 1)(9x + 1)$ $81x^2 - 1$

2. $(3x + 1)(3x - 1)$

3. $(x - 5y)(x + 5y)$

4. $(6 - c)(6 + c)$

5. $(7a - 1)(7a + 1)$

6. $(2x + 1)(2x - 1)$

7. $(4rs + 3)(4rs - 3)$

8. $(8r^2 - s^2)(8r^2 + s^2)$

9. $(7 - 8d)(7 + 8d)$

10. $(4a - 9b)(4a + 9b)$

11. $(x - y)(x + y)$

12. $(9r - 2s)(9r + 2s)$

13. $(5p - 4)(5p + 4)$

14. $(3x + 4y)(3x - 4y)$

15. $(7 - 5ab)(7 + 5ab)$

16. $(4a^3 - 3)(4a^3 + 3)$

17. $(2r - 5)(2r + 5)$

18. $(6a - 3b)(6a + 3b)$

19. $(3a + b)(3a - b)$

20. $(r - 3s)(r + 3s)$

21. $(5x + 8y)(5x - 8y)$

22. $(2b^2 - 9)(2b^2 + 9)$

23. $(9a - 5b)(9a + 5b)$

24. $(1 - 4v)(1 + 4v)$

25. $(5c^2 - 2d^2)(5c^2 + 2d^2)$

26. $(8a - 7b)(8a + 7b)$

27. $(v - 4)(v + 4)$

28. $(3 - 5u)(3 + 5u)$

29. $(4rs - 1)(4rs + 1)$

30. $(5x + 1)(5x - 1)$

31. $(9x - 7y)(9x + 7y)$

32. $(5x + 7y)(5x - 7y)$

33. $(6 - c^3)(6 + c^3)$

34. $(1 - 9x)(1 + 9x)$

Products of Binomials

Multiply.

1. $(4q^2 + 7)(4q^2 - 7)$ $16q^4 - 49$

2. $(5x - 3)(5x + 3)$

3. $(a - 2b)(a + 2b)$

4. $(7 - 6r)(7 + 6r)$

5. $(5x + 7y)(5x - 7y)$

6. $(4a + 5b)(4a - 5b)$

7. $(6 - 5a)(6 + 5a)$

8. $(c^2d^2 + 5)(c^2d^2 - 5)$

9. $(2r - 3s)(2r + 3s)$

10. $(3x - 2y)(3x + 2y)$

11. $(7c + 2)(7c - 2)$

12. $(5 - 2a)(5 + 2a)$

13. $(8a - 3b)(8a + 3b)$

14. $(3x - 7y)(3x + 7y)$

15. $(4xy + 7)(4xy - 7)$

16. $(7c - 3)(7c + 3)$

17. $(5r - 9)(5r + 9)$

18. $(a + 6b)(a - 6b)$

19. $(1 - d^2)(1 + d^2)$

20. $(2x^2 - 7)(2x^2 + 7)$

21. $(2 - 7t)(2 + 7t)$

22. $(8 - xy)(8 + xy)$

23. $(7x - 4y)(7x + 4y)$

24. $(2 + 9t)(2 - 9t)$

25. $(a - 3b)(a + 3b)$

26. $(6r + 7s)(6r - 7s)$

27. $(ab - 7)(ab + 7)$

28. $(9a + 4b)(9a - 4b)$

29. $(x^3 - 5)(x^3 + 5)$

30. $(9 - 8c)(9 + 8c)$

31. $(8x - 9y)(8x + 9y)$

32. $(r - 8s)(r + 8s)$

33. $(2y^2 - 3)(2y^2 + 3)$

34. $(3 - 2a)(3 + 2a)$

Powers of Binomials

Name _____

Date _____ Period _____

Multiply.

1. $(5 + x)^2$ $25 + 10x + x^2$

2. $(2y + 1)^2$

3. $(3ab - 4)^2$

4. $(7x - 2)^2$

5. $(c + 1)^2$

6. $(8a - b)^2$

7. $(4x - 3y)^2$

8. $(x + 9y)^2$

9. $(3 + 2d)^2$

10. $(9x + 2y)^2$

11. $(5r - 8)^2$

12. $(p - 2)^2$

13. $(4a + 5b)^2$

14. $(5ab - 2)^2$

15. $(7x - 3y)^2$

16. $(6 - 5xy)^2$

17. $(q - 3)^2$

18. $(9s + 1)^2$

19. $(8 - 5t)^2$

20. $(ab + 8)^2$

21. $(9a + 4b)^2$

22. $(3 - 5m)^2$

23. $(5v + 3)^2$

24. $(5z + 9)^2$

25. $(7c - 4d)^2$

26. $(6x + y)^2$

27. $(x + 1)^3$

28. $(2c - 1)^3$

29. $(2a - 3b)^3$

30. $(r + 4)^3$

31. $(1 - c)^4$

32. $(2d + 1)^4$

33. $(3x + 2y)^4$

34. $(1 - 4r)^4$

Powers of Binomials

Name _____

Date _____ Period _____

Multiply.

1. $(3a - b)^2$ $9a^2 - 6ab + b^2$

2. $(5cd + 4)^2$

3. $(x - 4)^2$

4. $(4x + 9y)^2$

5. $(7 + 5a)^2$

6. $(7x - 9y)^2$

7. $(4b + 7)^2$

8. $(7 - 8x)^2$

9. $(5a - 7b)^2$

10. $(m + 5)^2$

11. $(7 + r)^2$

12. $(9x - 5)^2$

13. $(3 + 7xy)^2$

14. $(2a - 5b)^2$

15. $(7s + 6t)^2$

16. $(2m + 9)^2$

17. $(8a - 9b)^2$

18. $(4t + 1)^2$

19. $(v + 6)^2$

20. $(5x - 6y)^2$

21. $(8xy + 3)^2$

22. $(9a + 7b)^2$

23. $(2 + 3z)^2$

24. $(2y - 7)^2$

25. $(8 - 7x)^2$

26. $(6a + 7)^2$

27. $(3a - b)^3$

28. $(r + 2)^3$

29. $(3 + p)^3$

30. $(1 - 10x)^3$

31. $(3a + 1)^4$

32. $(x - 2)^4$

33. $(x - 3y)^4$

34. $(r + 10)^4$

36

Products of Polynomials

Name _____

Date _____ Period _____

Multiply.

1. $(2a + 1)(a^2 + 3a - 4)$ $\quad 2a^3 + 7a^2 - 5a - 4$

2. $(3 + 2x)(9 - x + x^2)$

3. $(c - 1)(4c^2 - c - 1)$

4. $(8r - 2s)(4r^2 - 7rs + s^2)$

5. $(4m + 3n)(2m^2 - 5mn + 2n^2)$

6. $(c + 7)(7c^2 - c - 2)$

7. $(s - 6)(3s^2 - 6s - 7)$

8. $(3m - 8n)(4m^2 + 5mn + 3n^2)$

9. $(3 + 2c)(7 + c + c^2)$

10. $(6a + 5)(a^2 + a - 1)$

11. $(s - 8)(s^2 - s + 2)$

12. $(4r + 9)(3r^2 - r + 2)$

13. $(3x + y)(8x^2 + xy - 2y^2)$

14. $(8s + 7t)(6s^2 - 7st + t^2)$

15. $(9s - 5)(5s^2 + 2s + 2)$

16. $(3u - v)(7u^2 + 2uv - 2v^2)$

17. $(9r - 5s)(6r^2 - rs + 3s^2)$

18. $(7c + 6)(3c^2 - 8c - 2)$

19. $(5p + 4q)(3p^2 + pq + 5q^2)$

20. $(6 - r)(5 + r - 3r^2)$

21. $(7c + 9)(7c^2 + c - 3)$

22. $(x + 1)(3x^2 + 4x - 6)$

23. $(8r - 5)(4r^2 - 6r - 1)$

24. $(5s + 8)(4s^2 + 9s + 2)$

25. $(7u + 3t)(u^2 - 8ut - 3t^2)$

26. $(3cd - 7d)(6c^2d^2 + cd - 5)$

27. $(5 - 9a)(8 - a - a^2)$

28. $(9r + 5)(3r^2 + 3r + 1)$

29. $(r - 5)(5r^2 - r + 6)$

30. $(3x + 4y)(x^2 + 7xy - 2y^2)$

31. $(2c + 1)(9c^2 + c - 2)$

32. $(5a + 2)(6a^2 + 6a + 1)$

33. $(4u + 5t)(6u^2 - 6ut + t^2)$

34. $(6 - 5c)(7 + 3c + c^2)$

Developing Skills in Algebra   Book B

Products of Polynomials

Multiply.

1. $(4s - 1)(5s^2 + s + 1)$ $20s^3 - s^2 + 3s - 1$

2. $(6u + t)(2u^2 + 6ut - t^2)$

3. $(r + 3)(2r^2 - 4r + 1)$

4. $(x - 2)(7x^2 + 2x + 1)$

5. $(2c - 7d)(3c^2 + 7cd + 5d^2)$

6. $(3x + 4y)(x^2 - xy + 5y^2)$

7. $(2 - 5u)(8 + u + 3u^2)$

8. $(5v + 2w)(4v^2 - vw - 3w^2)$

9. $(6r + 5)(5r^2 - 5r + 6)$

10. $(8 - 3s)(3 + s + 2s^2)$

11. $(x + 8)(6x^2 + 2x - 1)$

12. $(r + 4s)(8r^2 + rs + 5s^2)$

13. $(3u - 2)(5u^2 + 2u + 1)$

14. $(3w + 7)(w^2 + 2w - 3)$

15. $(2c - 7d)(3c^2 - 4cd - 2d^2)$

16. $(4 + 5a)(3a^2 + 7a - 1)$

17. $(3r + 4)(6r^2 - 7r - 1)$

18. $(5u + 3t)(2u^2 + 3ut + 4t^2)$

19. $(x + 9)(2x^2 + 2x + 7)$

20. $(5r - 1)(4r^2 + 8r + 1)$

21. $(6s - 7)(7s^2 - s + 4)$

22. $(9s - 4t)(4s^2 + 4st + t^2)$

23. $(7a + 1)(6a^2 + 8a + 1)$

24. $(3x + y)(3x^2 + 2xy - 5y^2)$

25. $(7c + 3d)(7c^2 - 3cd + 2d^2)$

26. $(8s - 9)(s^2 - 6s - 3)$

27. $(5x - 3)(4x^2 + 3x + 3)$

28. $(3r - 7s)(5r^2 - rs + 8s^2)$

29. $(9r - 7)(8r^2 - r + 4)$

30. $(s + 6)(s^2 + 2s + 7)$

31. $(5c - 8d)(7c^2 + 4cd + d^2)$

32. $(7x - 8)(7x^2 + x - 2)$

33. $(2 + 3s)(9 - s - 4s^2)$

34. $(9m - 8n)(3m^2 - mn - 7n^2)$

38 Developing Skills in Algebra   Book B

Products of Polynomials

Multiply.

1. $(5x - 1)(3x^2 + 9x + 1)$ $15x^3 + 42x^2 - 4x - 1$ **2.** $(4 - 3r)(3 - 2r + 3r^2)$

3. $(2c + 5d)(3c^2 - 8cd + d^2)$ **4.** $(2a + 1)(3a^2 + a + 6)$

5. $(a - 3)(6a^2 + 3a - 1)$ **6.** $(4x + y)(2x^2 - 3xy + 5y^2)$

7. $(7 + r)(7 + r - 3r^2)$ **8.** $(c + 2)(4c^2 + 7c - 3)$

9. $(a + 5)(7a^2 - 5a + 1)$ **10.** $(3x + 5y)(2x^2 - 9xy + 6y^2)$

11. $(3c - 8)(3c^2 + 5c + 1)$ **12.** $(8a - 7)(4a^2 + 5a + 1)$

13. $(4r - 7)(r^2 - 4r + 3)$ **14.** $(2s - 3t)(7s^2 + 3st + t^2)$

15. $(7x - 4)(9x^2 + 2x + 1)$ **16.** $(1 - 9c)(2 - 8c - 3c^2)$

17. $(7s - 2)(5s^2 + 6s - 1)$ **18.** $(6m + 5n)(4m^2 - 4mn - 7n^2)$

19. $(2s + 9)(s^2 + 9s + 2)$ **20.** $(6a - 7b)(5a^2 - 2ab - 2b^2)$

21. $(5c + 4)(6c^2 - c + 4)$ **22.** $(5r + 6s)(6r^2 + 4rs - s^2)$

23. $(9r + 1)(7r^2 + 2r + 2)$ **24.** $(4x + 7)(2x^2 - 7x + 1)$

25. $(5x - 9y)(7x^2 + xy + 5y^2)$ **26.** $(8 + 3c)(5 + 7c - c^2)$

27. $(9a - 7b)(4a^2 - 2ab + 5b^2)$ **28.** $(9a + 4)(5a^2 + 2a - 5)$

29. $(5c + 7)(8c^2 + c + 7)$ **30.** $(6r - 1)(7r^2 + r + 4)$

31. $(2x + 5y)(9x^2 - 3xy - y^2)$ **32.** $(1 + 7x)(4 + 3x - 7x^2)$

33. $(3r - 5)(6r^2 + 2r + 1)$ **34.** $(4c + 7d)(c^2 - cd + 6d^2)$

Products of Polynomials

Multiply.

1. $(9c + 1)(c^2 + c + 5)$ $9c^3 + 10c^2 + 46c + 5$ **2.** $(c - d)(c^2 - cd + 5d^2)$

3. $(x + 4y)(4x^2 - 2xy - y^2)$ **4.** $(1 + 6r)(7 + 2r + r^2)$

5. $(4r - 5s)(5r^2 - 2rs + 5s^2)$ **6.** $(2s + 9)(8s^2 - 3s + 1)$

7. $(7 - 6c)(1 + 5c + 6c^2)$ **8.** $(x - 3)(7x^2 + 5x + 1)$

9. $(x + 7y)(9x^2 + 2xy - 3y^2)$ **10.** $(4c - d)(3c^2 + 5cd - 5d^2)$

11. $(2a + 3b)(3a^2 - 2ab - b^2)$ **12.** $(7 + 2r)(6 - 5r + 3r^2)$

13. $(8r - s)(r^2 + 9rs - 4s^2)$ **14.** $(5c + 7)(9c^2 + 2c - 2)$

15. $(9c - 2d)(8c^2 - 2cd - 3d^2)$ **16.** $(x - 4)(7x^2 - x - 6)$

17. $(7x + 5y)(7x^2 + xy + 5y^2)$ **18.** $(4r + 9)(4r^2 + 2r - 4)$

19. $(7m - 4n)(6m^2 - mn + 3n^2)$ **20.** $(9a + 2b)(8a^2 - ab + 4b^2)$

21. $(3 + 5s)(3 + 3s - 7s^2)$ **22.** $(c - 9)(5c^2 - 3c + 3)$

23. $(5c - 6d)(6c^2 + 5cd + d^2)$ **24.** $(2r + 7)(6r^2 - 3r + 1)$

25. $(x + 2)(7x^2 - 4x - 3)$ **26.** $(7x - 5y)(5x^2 - 8xy - 2y^2)$

27. $(2a + 9)(8a^2 - 2a + 1)$ **28.** $(3s + 2)(5s^2 - 2s + 3)$

29. $(9r - 8s)(5r^2 - 4rs + s^2)$ **30.** $(1 - 8a)(8 + 4a - a^2)$

31. $(4 - 3c)(7 + c + 2c^2)$ **32.** $(8c + d)(5c^2 - 9cd + d^2)$

33. $(7s + 1)(9s^2 - s + 5)$ **34.** $(9r + 4t)(4r^2 + 3rt - t^2)$

Products of Binomials

Multiply.

1. $(x + 5)(x - 2)(x + 3)$ $x^3 + 6x^2 - x - 30$

2. $(x + 1)(x + 6)(x - 8)$

3. $(x - 1)(5x - 1)(5x - 7)$

4. $(3x + 5)(x - 2)(5x - 3)$

5. $(2 + 7x)(1 + x)(2 + 3x)$

6. $(x + 2)(3x - 7)(x + 7)$

7. $(4x - y)(5x + 6y)(4x + 6y)$

8. $(x - 6y)(5x + 2y)(x - 4y)$

9. $(x - 9)(7x + 1)(x + 3)$

10. $(6x - 5)(x + 1)(3x - 2)$

11. $(5x - y)(2x + y)(5x - 2y)$

12. $(7x - 3)(6x - 5)(4x + 7)$

13. $(7x + 2)(2x - 5)(7x + 2)$

14. $(2x - 9y)(2x - 3y)(2x - 5y)$

15. $(8x + 5)(x + 5)(x + 2)$

16. $(9x - 4)(7x + 2)(6x - 7)$

17. $(3x + 4y)(6x + y)(x + 7y)$

18. $(5x - 2)(3x - 7)(9x + 1)$

19. $(6 - x)(2 + 9x)(2 - 5x)$

20. $(8x + 7y)(9x + y)(5x - 8y)$

21. $(9x + 2)(8x + 1)(3x - 7)$

22. $(4 - 5x)(5 - 7x)(7 - 5x)$

23. $(4x + 9)(3x + 5)(3x + 1)$

24. $(7x + 8)(9x - 7)(x + 3)$

25. $(x + 1)(8x + 9)(8x - 7)$

26. $(x + 6)(7x - 6)(7x + 9)$

27. $(5x + 7y)(7x - 5y)(x - 6y)$

28. $(5 - 8x)(7 - x)(3 - x)$

29. $(x + 5y)(9x + 5y)(4x + y)$

30. $(2x + 1)(8x + 3)(4x - 3)$

31. $(7x + 6)(x - 6)(7x + 8)$

32. $(x - 2)(2x - 1)(3x - 8)$

33. $(x + 9)(3x + 1)(6x + 5)$

34. $(6x + y)(2x - 7y)(5x - y)$

41

Products of Binomials

Multiply.

1. $(x - 7)(x - 8)(3x + 4)$
   $3x^3 - 41x^2 + 108x + 224$

2. $(3x + 1)(x + 5)(x + 1)$

3. $(x + 3)(2x - 5)(x + 1)$

4. $(5x - 4)(9x + 4)(5x - 3)$

5. $(2x - 3y)(8x - 5y)(4x - 5y)$

6. $(x - 4)(x - 4)(5x - 6)$

7. $(5 + 3x)(1 - 7x)(1 - 9x)$

8. $(2x + 5y)(5x - 4y)(2x + 3y)$

9. $(7x + 4)(9x + 2)(7x + 1)$

10. $(1 + 8x)(6 - 7x)(2 + x)$

11. $(5x - 9y)(3x + 8y)(x - 5y)$

12. $(7 + x)(1 + 4x)(2 - x)$

13. $(8x - 1)(x + 3)(5x + 4)$

14. $(x + 8)(x + 9)(4x + 3)$

15. $(3x + 2y)(9x + 8y)(7x - 4y)$

16. $(9x - y)(7x - 9y)(8x + 3y)$

17. $(x - 3)(5x - 3)(2x - 7)$

18. $(3x + 8)(2x + 7)(x - 6)$

19. $(6 - 7x)(7 + 8x)(8 - x)$

20. $(5x + 6y)(7x - 4y)(6x - y)$

21. $(7x - 3)(x + 8)(4x - 9)$

22. $(8 - 3x)(3 - 4x)(3 - 5x)$

23. $(8x + 9y)(9x + 3y)(x - 8y)$

24. $(7 - 5x)(1 - 4x)(5 + x)$

25. $(4x - 3)(3x - 2)(5x - 9)$

26. $(4x + 7)(5x - 9)(7x - 3)$

27. $(9 - 5x)(5 - 8x)(1 - 4x)$

28. $(9 + 7x)(2 - 3x)(2 - 9x)$

29. $(x + 7)(6x + 7)(2x + 1)$

30. $(x - 4)(8x - 7)(7x + 6)$

31. $(2x + 3)(x + 3)(8x - 5)$

32. $(2x - 5y)(3x + 5y)(x - 5y)$

33. $(7 - 2x)(1 + 9x)(3 - 5x)$

34. $(6x - 5y)(4x - 3y)(6x - y)$

42   Developing Skills in Algebra   Book B

Name _____

Date _____ Period _____

Solve.

1. $(x - 1)(x - 1) + (x + 3)(x - 4) - (2x + 3)(x + 2) = 3$ $x = -2$

2. $(x + 3)(x - 1) + (2x + 5)(x + 3) - (x + 1)(3x + 4) = -2x$

3. $(x - 2)(x + 2) + (x + 4)(x - 1) - (2x + 7)(x + 3) = -9$

4. $(x - 5)(x + 1) + (2x - 5)(x + 2) - (x + 7)(3x - 4) = 2$

5. $(2x - 1)(x - 8) - (x + 2)(x - 6) - (x + 4)(x - 3) = -10$

6. $(2x - 1)(x - 4) + (x - 5)(x - 5) - (x - 4)(3x - 4) = -11$

7. $(2x - 9)(x - 2) + (x - 7)(x - 3) - (x - 8)(3x - 1) = 1$

8. $(2x + 1)(2x + 1) - (x - 6)(x + 2) - (x + 4)(3x - 5) = 0$

9. $(2x + 3)(2x - 1) + (2x - 3)(x + 5) - (3x + 2)(2x + 1) = 0$

10. $(x + 10)(x - 5) + (x - 6)(3x - 4) - (2x + 7)(2x - 9) = -2$

11. $(2x - 3)(2x + 5) + (x - 1)(x + 5) - (5x + 2)(x + 1) = 0$

12. $(2x - 1)(x + 7) + (x - 3)(x + 3) - (3x - 1)(x - 4) = 6$

13. $(2x + 7)(x - 5) - (x - 5)(x + 3) - (x + 2)(x + 4) = 0$

14. $(2x + 5)(2x + 5) - (x + 1)(x - 6) - (x + 6)(3x - 5) = 1$

15. $(x - 4)(2x + 3) + (x + 3)(2x - 7) - (4x - 1)(x - 7) = 6$

16. $(x + 8)(x + 1) + (x + 7)(x - 7) - (2x + 9)(x - 4) = 0$

17. $(2x + 5)(x - 7) + (x - 8)(x + 5) - (3x - 1)(x - 2) = -2$

Polynomial Equations

_____

Solve.

1. $(x - 1)(x + 2) + (x - 3)(x + 6) - (2x + 3)(x + 7) = 11$ $x = 4$

2. $(2x + 7)(x - 7) + (2x - 3)(2x + 7) - (2x - 1)(3x + 1) = -1$

3. $(x + 6)(x - 5) + (3x + 1)(x + 5) - (4x + 1)(x - 2) = 1$

4. $(2x + 9)(x - 7) + (x + 1)(x - 4) - (3x + 1)(x - 7) = 0$

5. $(2x - 5)(x - 9) + (3x + 1)(2x + 1) - (4x + 3)(2x - 1) = 9$

6. $(3x - 2)(x + 2) - (x + 6)(x - 3) - (2x + 1)(x + 2) = 0$

7. $(x + 9)(x - 6) + (x + 7)(x + 8) - (x - 3)(2x + 3) = -1$

8. $(2x + 1)(x + 2) + (2x + 5)(x + 5) - (4x - 3)(x + 1) = -8$

9. $(x - 9)(x + 1) + (x + 2)(x + 3) - (2x + 7)(x - 2) = -1$

10. $(x - 8)(2x + 3) + (x + 6)(2x - 5) - (4x + 1)(x - 5) = 3$

11. $(2x + 5)(2x - 3) - (x - 6)(x + 6) - (3x + 2)(x + 3) = 1$

12. $(x - 9)(x + 3) + (x - 7)(x + 4) - (2x + 3)(x - 4) = 1$

13. $(3x + 2)(x - 5) + (x + 6)(x + 4) - (2x + 1)(2x + 5) = -1$

14. $(3x + 4)(x - 2) - (x + 6)(x + 2) - (x + 1)(2x + 3) = 2$

15. $(x + 6)(x + 1) + (x + 8)(x + 4) - (x + 2)(2x + 9) = 2$

16. $(3x + 1)(x + 6) + (x + 2)(x + 1) - (4x - 1)(x + 2) = 0$

17. $(x + 5)(x + 8) + (x + 3)(x + 9) - (2x - 7)(x + 9) = 4$

Polynomial Word Problems

Name _____

Date _____ Period _____

Show a complete solution for each problem.

1. Jenny is 5 years older than her brother. Four years ago the product of their ages was the same as 37 more than Jenny's present age subtracted from the square of the brother's present age. Find each of their present ages.

j = Jenny's age
$j - 5$ = brother's age

$(j - 4)[(j-5) - 4] = (j-5)^2 - (37 + j)$ Jenny is 24.
$j^2 - 13j + 36 = j^2 - 11j - 12$ Her brother
$-2j = -48$ is 19.
$j = 24$

2. Darrell has $2 less than five times as much money as Bob. Mary has as much money as Darrell and Bob together. If all three of them together have $80, how much money does Mary have?

3. One circle has a radius twice that of a smaller circle. The sum of the circumferences of the two circles is 180π. Find the radius of the larger circle.

4. The side of one square is five times that of another square. The difference in the areas of the two squares is 96. Find the sum of the areas of the two squares.

5. Wally and Anna each sold tickets to the school play. Anna sold 3.5 times as many tickets as Wally did. The total number of tickets they sold was 72. Find the number of tickets each person sold.

6. The second side of a triangle is four more than the first side, and the third side is five more than the second. If the product of the first and third sides is added to the product of the second and third sides, the result is 124 more than twice the square of the first side. Find the perimeter of the triangle.

7. A concrete walk 5 m wide is built around a grass court. The length of the court is 12 m more than its width. The area of the walk is 560 m². Find the dimensions of the grass court.

8. Cleve is three more than six times as old as his son Rob. If seven times Rob's present age is subtracted from the product of their present ages, the result is 418 less than the product of their ages five years from now. Find each of their present ages.

Polynomial Word Problems

Name _____

Date _____ Period _____

_____

Show a complete solution for each problem.

1. Harold has one-half as much money invested as Loretta does. One-half the product of the two investments is equal to $500 more than the amount of Loretta's investment subtracted from the square of Harold's investment. Find how much Loretta has invested.

   $l = $ Loretta's money
   $\frac{1}{2} l = $ Harold's money

   $\frac{1}{2}(l)(\frac{1}{2}l) = 500 + [(\frac{1}{2}l)^2 - l]$

   $\frac{1}{4}l^2 = \frac{1}{4}l^2 - l + 500$

   $l = 500$

   Loretta has $500 invested.
   Harold has $250 invested.

2. John won a stock car race with an average rate of 1.25 times that of Susan's average rate. If Susan's rate is subtracted from John's rate, the difference is 22.5 km/h. What was Susan's average rate for the race?

3. Two cylinders, each one open on the ends, have the same height, *h,* but one of them has a radius four times that of the other one. The difference in the surface areas of the two cylinders is $240\pi h$. Find the radius of the smaller cylinder.

4. The first of two rectangles has length 10 cm more than its width. The width of the second rectangle is 1 cm more than the width of the first, and the length is 5 cm less than that of the first. The sum of the areas of the two rectangles is 85 cm^2 more than twice the square of the width of the first rectangle. Find the dimensions of the first rectangle.

5. Art has $21 more in his savings account than Charlotte did before Art made a deposit of $20 and Charlotte made a deposit of $5. If the product of the original amounts in savings is subtracted from the product of their savings after the deposits, the result is $2705. What did each have in savings after the deposits?

6. The second side of a triangle is 3 cm less than twice as long as the first side. The third side of the triangle is 7 cm more than three times as long as the first side. The altitude to the third side of the triangle is 1 cm more than twice the first side. Twice the area of the triangle is 88 cm^2 more than the product of the second and third sides. What is the area of the triangle?

7. A second airplane has a seating capacity of 112 more than that of the first airplane, while a third one seats 190 more than the first one. When the products of these seating capacities are multiplied together by pairs in all possible ways and added together, the result is 117,920 more than three times the square of the capacity of the first plane. Find the seating capacity of the first plane.

8. The base of a parallelogram is 25 cm more than the altitude. The area is 1200 cm^2 less than the square of the base. Find the altitude and base of the parallelogram.

Name _____

Date _____ Period _____

Show a complete solution for each problem.

1. Tom is 2 years older than his brother. The product of their ages 6 years from now will be 120 more than the product of their present ages. Find each of their ages.

t = Tom's age

t − 2 = brother's age

$(t + 6)[(t − 2) + 6] = 120 + (t)(t − 2)$

$t^2 + 10t + 24 = t^2 − 2t + 120$

$12t = 96$

$t = 8$

Tom is 8 years old and his brother is 6 years old.

2. In the Silver Streak Race, Jack ran 2 km/h slower than Carole did. If 5 is subtracted from Carole's rate and then that number is multiplied by Jack's rate, the result is 62 km/h less than Carole's rate multiplied by 4 more than Jack's rate. How fast did Jack run the race?

3. The length of one rectangle is 7 m more than the width. The width of a smaller rectangle is 4 m less than and the length is 3 m more than the width of the larger rectangle. The difference in the areas of the two rectangles is 108 m². Find the length of the smaller rectangle.

4. Jane has $5 more than three times as much money as Lonnie has. Bob has $1 less than four times as much money as Lonnie has. All three of them together have $92. Find how much money Lonnie has.

5. A rectangular swimming pool with uniform depth is 12 ft wider than twice the depth and 10 ft longer than five times the depth. The volume of the pool is 5640 ft³ less than the sum of ten times the cube of the depth and eight times the product of the length and width. Find the length of the pool.

6. The longer base of a trapezoid is 14 cm more than the height, and the shorter base is 6 cm less than the longer base. The area of the trapezoid is 167 cm² less than the product of the bases. Find the height of the trapezoid.

7. The width of a rectangular gravel pit is 1 m less than 4 times its depth, and the length is 3 m more than 16 times the depth. The volume is 45 m³ less than the difference between 64 times the cube of the depth and 4 times the square of the depth. Find the length of the gravel pit.

8. If the radius of a circle were increased by 15 cm, the area would be 300 cm² more than one-half the product of the original radius and the circumference of the enlarged circle. Find the radius of the circle.

Developing Skills in Algebra   Book B

Polynomial Word Problems

Name _____

Date _____ Period _____

Show a complete solution for each problem.

1. Bill has three times as much money invested as Pat does. One-third the product of the two investments equals $630 more than the amount of Bill's investment subtracted from the square of Pat's investment. Find the amount of Bill's investment.

p = Pat's money
$3p$ = Bill's money

$\frac{1}{3}(p)(3p) = 630 + p^2 - 3p$
$p^2 = p^2 - 3p + 630$
$3p = 630$
$p = 210$

Bill invested $630. (Pat invested $210.)

2. James is 5 years older than Jennifer. Three years ago the product of their ages was 36 less than the product of their present ages. Find Jennifer's present age.

3. One circle has radius 7 more than the radius of another circle. The difference in the areas of the two circles is 77π. Find the radius of the larger circle.

4. A ditch has a cross-section that is a trapezoid whose bottom is 5 ft wider than the depth. The top is 3 in. wider than the bottom. The area of the cross-section is 66 in.^{2} more than the product of the bottom and the depth. How deep is the ditch?

5. A rectangular hay barn on the Adam's ranch is 14 ft wider than it is high and 16 ft longer than it is wide. If each dimension were increased by 2 ft, the volume would be increased by 3280 ft^3 plus six times the square of the height. Find the length of the barn.

6. A concrete walk 9 ft wide is built around a garden. The length of the garden is 9 ft more than its width. The area of the walk is 1458 ft^2. Find the length of the garden.

7. Each of two cylinders has the same height, 6 in. The radius of the smaller cylinder is 7 in. less than the radius of the larger one. The difference in their volumes is 1554π in^3. Find the radius of the larger cylinder.

8. The second side of a triangle is 8 cm more than the first side. The third side of the triangle is 5 cm more than twice the first side, and the altitude to the third side is 1 cm more than the first side. Twice the area of the triangle is 31 cm^2 less than twice the product of the first two sides. Find the area of the triangle.

Name _____

Date _____ Period _____

Simplify.

1. $\dfrac{a^3}{a^2}$ a

2. $\dfrac{b^4}{b}$

3. $\dfrac{ab^7}{ab^2}$

4. $\dfrac{c^3d^4}{c^2d}$

5. $\dfrac{12x^4y^7}{2x^2y^2}$

6. $\dfrac{-10m^5n^3}{5mn}$

7. $\dfrac{2a^{10}b^5}{8a^5b^2}$

8. $\dfrac{-13x^{15}y^{11}}{39x^7y^{10}}$

9. $\dfrac{-8x^2y^4}{16x^2y^7}$

10. $\dfrac{6x^3y^7}{24x^5y^9}$

11. $\dfrac{-15x^5y}{45xy^3}$

12. $\dfrac{30a^4b^2}{60a^2b^7}$

13. $\dfrac{(2a^3)^2}{4a^2}$

14. $\dfrac{-(3x^2)^3}{9x^4}$

15. $\dfrac{27a^4}{(3a^2)^4}$

16. $\dfrac{25x^4y^7}{(10x^2y)^2}$

17. $\dfrac{26(a^3b^6)^2}{39(a^3b^4)^3}$

18. $\dfrac{15(r^2t^5)^3}{45(r^3t^2)^4}$

19. $\dfrac{a^4}{a^r}$

20. $\dfrac{x^5}{x^t}$

21. $\dfrac{8x^m}{(2x)^2}$

22. $\dfrac{(2m^2)^4}{8m^r}$

23. $\dfrac{(a^2b^3)^r}{(a^4b)^r}$

24. $\dfrac{10^5}{10^2}$

25. $\dfrac{2^9}{2^3}$

26. $\dfrac{3^7}{3^2}$

27. $\dfrac{7^{10}}{7^5}$

28. $\dfrac{11^6}{11^3}$

29. $\dfrac{(2a^3b^4)^3}{(2ab^2)^5}$

30. $\dfrac{(3x^5y^3)^5}{(6x^{10}y^7)^2}$

31. $\dfrac{(2x^ry^t)^2}{3x^5y^7}$

32. $\dfrac{(2a^mb^t)^3}{5a^6b^2}$

33. $\dfrac{7a^sb^v}{11a^rb^t}$

34. $\dfrac{(2x^4y^5)^r}{(2x^3y^2)^r}$

35. $\dfrac{(3a^7b^2)^m}{(3a^2b^5)^m}$

36. $\dfrac{(10c^3d^7)^p}{(10c^6d^3)^p}$

Developing Skills in Algebra   Book B

Using Exponents

Name _____

Date _____ Period _____

Simplify.

1. $\dfrac{x^9}{x^6}$ x^3

2. $\dfrac{b^7}{b^2}$

3. $\dfrac{mn^8}{mn^4}$

4. $\dfrac{m^5 n^2}{m^2 n}$

5. $\dfrac{25 a^9 b^3}{5 a^4 b}$

6. $\dfrac{24 a^8 b^2}{10 a^5 b}$

7. $\dfrac{4 a^{15} b^4}{20 a^7 b^3}$

8. $\dfrac{-15 x^{10} y^{15}}{60 x^3 y^7}$

9. $\dfrac{12 x^3 y^2}{48 x^5 y^8}$

10. $\dfrac{5 x^7 y^2}{40 x^{10} y^7}$

11. $\dfrac{-13 x^6 y^2}{39 x^3 y^7}$

12. $\dfrac{12\, m^5 n^3}{36 m^2 n^{10}}$

13. $\dfrac{(3 a^4)^2}{3 a^5}$

14. $\dfrac{(2 x^2)^5}{4 x^7}$

15. $\dfrac{18 x^5}{(6 x^4)^2}$

16. $\dfrac{27 a^7 b^8}{(9 a^2 b^3)^2}$

17. $\dfrac{25 (r^5 s^2)^3}{75 (r^3 s^2)^5}$

18. $\dfrac{20 (a^5 b^3)^5}{60 (a^3 b^2)^3}$

19. $\dfrac{x^7}{x^m}$

20. $\dfrac{a^{10}}{a^n}$

21. $\dfrac{3 x^r}{(3 x)^2}$

22. $\dfrac{(2 m^4)^3}{16 m^x}$

23. $\dfrac{(x^3 y^4)^t}{(x^2 y^3)^t}$

24. $\dfrac{5^{10}}{5^3}$

25. $\dfrac{7^{11}}{7^6}$

26. $\dfrac{13^5}{13^2}$

27. $\dfrac{3^9}{3^7}$

28. $\dfrac{12^7}{12^5}$

29. $\dfrac{(3 x^4 y^5)^2}{(3 x y^3)^2}$

30. $\dfrac{(2 x^7 y^4)^3}{(6 x^9 y^7)^2}$

31. $\dfrac{(3 a^m b^n)^3}{54 a^3 b^2}$

32. $\dfrac{(5 a^r b^s)^3}{250 a^7 b^6}$

33. $\dfrac{12 x^m y^n}{24 x^s y^t}$

34. $\dfrac{(5 a^5 b^2)^x}{(5 a^2 b^3)^x}$

35. $\dfrac{(7 m^7 n^2)^r}{(7 m^3 n^4)^r}$

36. $\dfrac{(9 p^3 q^3)^s}{(9 p^2 q^2)^s}$

Division of Polynomials

Name _____

Date _____ Period _____

Simplify.

1. $\dfrac{10r + 10s}{10}$ $r + s$

2. $\dfrac{15c + 15d}{15}$

3. $\dfrac{3x + 9x^2}{3x}$

4. $\dfrac{25x^2 + 5x}{5x}$

5. $\dfrac{12a^3b - 8ab^4}{4ab}$

6. $\dfrac{18r^4s^3 + 27r^2s^5}{9r^2s^2}$

7. $\dfrac{16a^5b^3 + 20a^3b^8}{4a^3b^3}$

8. $\dfrac{14a^9b^5 + 28a^7b^3}{7a^3b^2}$

9. $\dfrac{27a^7b^5c - 36a^5b^3}{9a^4b^3}$

10. $\dfrac{30c^5d^{10} - 48c^8d^5e}{6c^3d^4}$

11. $\dfrac{28r^{10}s^6t^2 - 42r^7s^5}{-7r^5s^4}$

12. $\dfrac{48x^9y^4 - 32x^5y^9z}{-8x^3y^3}$

13. $\dfrac{44a^{11}b^{15} - 66a^7b^{12}}{11a^4b^7}$

14. $\dfrac{85a^7b^{11} - 34a^8b^7}{17a^5b^5}$

15. $\dfrac{4x + 12x^2 - 16x^3}{4x}$

16. $\dfrac{25a^4 - 15a^3 + 5a}{5a}$

17. $\dfrac{9cd - 18c^2d^2 + 27c^3d^3}{9cd}$

18. $\dfrac{84a^4b^4 - 42a^2b^2 + 14ab}{14ab}$

19. $\dfrac{5a^2b^2 + 15a^3b^3 - 20a^4b^4}{-5a^2b^2}$

20. $\dfrac{48x^6y^6 - 24x^3y^3 + 4xy}{-4xy}$

21. $\dfrac{10m^3n^5 + 20m^5n^2 - 30m^7n}{10mn}$

22. $\dfrac{65a^7b^4 - 52a^5b^3 + 13a^3b^2}{13ab}$

23. $\dfrac{28s^9t^5 - 14s^7t^8 - 7s^5t^{10}}{7s^2t^3}$

24. $\dfrac{11a^3b^8 - 33a^5b^5 - 66a^9b^3}{11a^2b^2}$

Developing Skills in Algebra   Book B

Division of Polynomials

Simplify.

1. $\dfrac{2a + 2b}{2}$ $a + b$

2. $\dfrac{6x + 6y}{3}$

3. $\dfrac{4c + 4c^2}{4c}$

4. $\dfrac{9r + 18r^2}{9r}$

5. $\dfrac{8m^2n - 6mn^2}{2mn}$

6. $\dfrac{15x^3y^2 - 10x^4y^3}{5xy}$

7. $\dfrac{12a^3b^4 + 8a^2b^5}{4a^2b^2}$

8. $\dfrac{28a^3b^2 + 35a^4b^5}{7a^3b^2}$

9. $\dfrac{18c^4d^5e - 27c^5d^3}{-9c^3d^2}$

10. $\dfrac{20x^7y^3 - 30x^3y^2z}{10x^2y}$

11. $\dfrac{24a^3b^7 - 36a^{10}b^5c^2}{6a^3b^3}$

12. $\dfrac{16p^6q^5r^4 - 28p^7q^2}{4p^2q^2}$

13. $\dfrac{35m^6n^2 + 50m^8n^4}{-5m^6n^2}$

14. $\dfrac{39a^9b^4 + 52a^7b^9}{-13a^5b^3}$

15. $\dfrac{3a + 7a^3 + 12a^5}{a}$

16. $\dfrac{9x^7 + 5x^4 + 8x}{x}$

17. $\dfrac{15x^3y^2 - 9x^2y + 3xy}{3xy}$

18. $\dfrac{21a^5b^3 - 14a^3b^2 + 7ab}{7ab}$

19. $\dfrac{5xy + 15x^3y^4 - 25x^5y^7}{-5xy}$

20. $\dfrac{3mn + 18m^4n^2 + 27m^9n^5}{-3mn}$

21. $\dfrac{4m^5n - 16m^3n^4 + 20m^7n^5}{4mn}$

22. $\dfrac{7c^7d^6 - 21c^3d^3 + 28c^2d^5}{7c^2d^2}$

23. $\dfrac{18x^9y^4 + 27x^5y^6 + 45x^2y^8}{9x^2y^4}$

24. $\dfrac{33a^{10}b^2 + 55a^6b^6 + 99a^2b^{10}}{11a^2b^2}$

Divide.

1. $(x^2 + 9x + 14) \div (x + 2)$ $x + 7$

2. $(x^2 + 8x + 15) \div (x + 3)$

3. $(x^2 - 3x - 28) \div (x - 7)$

4. $(x^2 - 4x - 45) \div (x - 9)$

5. $(2x^2 + 11x + 12) \div (x + 4)$

6. $(3x^2 + 20x + 12) \div (x + 6)$

7. $(4x^2 - 22x + 10) \div (x - 5)$

8. $(5x^2 - 38x + 21) \div (x - 7)$

9. $(4x^2 + 4x - 35) \div (2x - 5)$

10. $(6x^2 - 25x + 14) \div (2x - 7)$

11. $(6x^2 - 25x + 24) \div (2x - 3)$

12. $(15x^2 - 26x + 8) \div (3x - 4)$

13. $(10x^2 - 21x - 10) \div (5x + 2)$

14. $(21x^2 + 2x - 3) \div (3x - 1)$

15. $(x^3 - 4x^2 - 7x + 10) \div (x + 2)$

16. $(x^3 + 6x^2 + 11x + 6) \div (x + 3)$

17. $(x^3 + x^2 - 18x + 8) \div (x + 4)$

18. $(x^3 - 3x^2 - 13x + 15) \div (x - 5)$

19. $(2x^3 - 17x^2 + 27x + 18) \div (2x + 1)$

20. $(2x^3 - 9x^2 + 29x - 30) \div (2x - 3)$

21. $(3x^3 - 5x^2 - 88x + 60) \div (3x - 2)$

22. $(4x^3 + 3x^2 - 49x + 12) \div (4x - 1)$

23. $(x^3 - 13x - 12) \div (x - 4)$

24. $(x^3 - 21x + 20) \div (x - 1)$

25. $(x^3 - 27x - 54) \div (x + 3)$

26. $(x^3 - 39x - 70) \div (x + 2)$

27. $(x^3 - 1) \div (x - 1)$

28. $(27x^3 - 1) \div (3x - 1)$

29. $(x^4 - 256) \div (x + 4)$

30. $(16x^4 - 1) \div (2x + 1)$

31. $(x^5 - 32) \div (x - 2)$

32. $(243x^5 + 1) \div (3x + 1)$

Developing Skills in Algebra   Book B

Name _____

Date _____ Period _____

Divide.

1. $(x^2 - 2x - 15) \div (x + 3)$ $x - 5$

2. $(x^2 - 2x - 8) \div (x - 4)$

3. $(x^2 + 5x - 14) \div (x - 2)$

4. $(x^2 + 8x - 9) \div (x - 1)$

5. $(2x^2 - x - 6) \div (x - 2)$

6. $(3x^2 + 11x + 6) \div (x + 3)$

7. $(4x^2 + 19x - 5) \div (x + 5)$

8. $(5x^2 - 3x - 2) \div (x - 1)$

9. $(6x^2 + x - 15) \div (2x - 3)$

10. $(8x^2 - 18x - 5) \div (2x - 5)$

11. $(6x^2 - 5x - 6) \div (3x + 2)$

12. $(6x^2 + 11x - 10) \div (2x + 5)$

13. $(2x^2 - 9x - 5) \div (2x + 1)$

14. $(14x^2 + x - 3) \div (7x - 3)$

15. $(x^3 - 8x^2 + x + 42) \div (x - 7)$

16. $(x^3 + 3x^2 - 34x - 80) \div (x + 4)$

17. $(x^3 - 6x^2 + 11x - 12) \div (x - 4)$

18. $(x^3 + 7x^2 + 2x - 40) \div (x - 2)$

19. $(2x^3 - x^2 - 13x - 6) \div (2x + 1)$

20. $(3x^3 - x^2 - 34x - 40) \div (3x + 5)$

21. $(10x^3 + 31x^2 - 9) \div (5x + 3)$

22. $(2x^3 + x^2 - 9) \div (2x - 3)$

23. $(15x^3 - 19x^2 + 4) \div (5x + 2)$

24. $(12x^3 + 7x^2 - 9) \div (4x - 3)$

25. $(x^3 - 2x^2 - 10x - 25) \div (x - 5)$

26. $(x^3 - 4x^2 - 19x + 6) \div (x + 3)$

27. $(x^3 - 9x - 28) \div (x - 4)$

28. $(x^3 - 59x + 70) \div (x - 7)$

29. $(x^3 - 216) \div (x - 6)$

30. $(64x^3 - 1) \div (4x - 1)$

31. $(81x^4 - 1) \div (3x - 1)$

32. $(x^4 - 256) \div (x - 4)$

Quotients of Polynomials

Name _____

Date _____ Period _____

Divide.

1. $(x^2 + 2x + 2) \div (x - 1)$ $x + 3 + \dfrac{5}{x-1}$ **2.** $(x^2 - 4x - 80) \div (x - 11)$

3. $(x^2 - 10x + 22) \div (x - 3)$ **4.** $(x^2 - 3x - 100) \div (x - 12)$

5. $(x^2 + 9x + 27) \div (x + 5)$ **6.** $(x^2 - 10x - 90) \div (x + 5)$

7. $(x^2 - 7x - 23) \div (x - 9)$ **8.** $(x^2 + 28x + 150) \div (x + 8)$

9. $(x^2 - 11x + 27) \div (x - 5)$ **10.** $(x^2 + 6x - 75) \div (x + 13)$

11. $(x^2 + 3x - 120) \div (x + 12)$ **12.** $(x^2 + 2x + 5) \div (x + 5)$

13. $(x^2 + 10x + 30) \div (x + 4)$ **14.** $(x^2 + 17x + 60) \div (x + 10)$

15. $(x^2 - 2x - 70) \div (x + 7)$ **16.** $(x^2 - 12x - 75) \div (x - 17)$

17. $(2x^2 - x - 9) \div (x - 1)$ **18.** $(2x^2 - 3x - 65) \div (x - 7)$

19. $(2x^2 + 11x + 20) \div (x + 3)$ **20.** $(2x^2 - 17x + 40) \div (2x - 9)$

21. $(3x^2 - 5x + 8) \div (x - 2)$ **22.** $(4x^2 - 16x - 20) \div (2x + 1)$

23. $(4x^2 + 12x + 9) \div (2x + 1)$ **24.** $(6x^2 - 5x + 10) \div (2x + 3)$

25. $(6x^2 - x - 15) \div (2x - 3)$ **26.** $(5x^2 + 43x + 42) \div (x + 7)$

27. $(15x^2 - 4x - 28) \div (3x - 5)$ **28.** $(4x^2 - 37x + 23) \div (x - 8)$

29. $(4x^2 + 19x - 50) \div (x + 7)$ **30.** $(9x^2 + 18x + 18) \div (3x + 5)$

31. $(2x^2 + 9x - 100) \div (2x - 11)$ **32.** $(18x^2 - 25x - 10) \div (9x + 1)$

33. $(10x^2 + 49x - 25) \div (x + 5)$ **34.** $(15x^2 - 37x + 12) \div (5x - 4)$

   55   Developing Skills in Algebra   Book B

Quotients of Polynomials

Name _____

Date _____ Period _____

Divide.

1. $(x^2 - 20x + 121) \div (x - 11)$

$$x - 9 + \frac{22}{x-11}$$

2. $(x^2 + x - 15) \div (x - 2)$

3. $(x^2 + 28x + 125) \div (x + 7)$

4. $(x^2 + 28x + 150) \div (x + 11)$

5. $(x^2 + 12x - 200) \div (x - 10)$

6. $(x^2 - 22x + 120) \div (x - 9)$

7. $(x^2 + 20x + 60) \div (x + 3)$

8. $(x^2 + 18x + 65) \div (x + 3)$

9. $(x^2 - 28x + 180) \div (x - 7)$

10. $(x^2 - 39x + 360) \div (x - 18)$

11. $(x^2 + 19x + 50) \div (x + 8)$

12. $(x^2 - 5x - 85) \div (x + 8)$

13. $(x^2 + 52x + 75) \div (x + 2)$

14. $(x^2 - 40x + 210) \div (x - 10)$

15. $(x^2 - 34x + 200) \div (x - 11)$

16. $(x^2 - 27x - 75) \div (x + 2)$

17. $(12x^2 + 5x - 10) \div (4x - 1)$

18. $(24x^2 - 58x - 40) \div (3x - 8)$

19. $(15x^2 - 44x + 50) \div (5x - 8)$

20. $(14x^2 - 26x - 42) \div (7x + 1)$

21. $(8x^2 - 58x - 20) \div (4x - 1)$

22. $(50x^2 - 35x - 10) \div (5x - 4)$

23. $(6x^2 + 7x - 45) \div (2x - 5)$

24. $(72x^2 + 74x - 40) \div (9x - 2)$

25. $(16x^2 - 20) \div (4x - 3)$

26. $(25x^2 - 80) \div (5x + 9)$

27. $(25x^2 - 12) \div (5x - 2)$

28. $(196x^2 - 121) \div (14x - 11)$

29. $(21x^2 + 23x + 25) \div (3x + 2)$

30. $(45x^2 - 7x - 30) \div (5x - 3)$

31. $(33x^2 - 67x + 50) \div (3x - 5)$

32. $(70x^2 + 59x + 5) \div (5x + 6)$

33. $(20x^2 - 130x + 180) \div (4x - 10)$

34. $(21x^2 + 37x + 135) \div (3x + 10)$

Developing Skills in Algebra   Book B

Divide.

1. $(x^3 + x^2 - 11x + 13) \div (x - 2)$ $x^2 + 3x - 5 + \dfrac{3}{x-2}$

2. $(x^3 - 2x^2 - 13x + 13) \div (x + 3)$

3. $(x^3 - 2x^2 - 13x - 15) \div (x - 5)$

4. $(x^3 + 2x^2 - 28x + 51) \div (x + 7)$

5. $(2x^3 - 5x^2 + 5x + 3) \div (2x + 1)$

6. $(3x^3 - 17x^2 + 13x - 10) \div (3x - 2)$

7. $(3x^3 + 14x^2 - 40x - 17) \div (3x - 7)$

8. $(x^3 - 18x - 42) \div (x - 5)$

9. $(x^3 - 5x + 16) \div (x + 3)$

10. $(4x^3 + x + 7) \div (2x + 3)$

11. $(9x^3 + 5x - 3) \div (3x + 1)$

12. $(x^4 - 22x^2 - 13x - 5) \div (x - 5)$

13. $(x^4 - 16x^2 + 3x + 19) \div (x + 4)$

14. $(4x^4 - 8x^3 - 21x^2 + 10x + 13) \div (2x + 3)$

15. $(4x^4 + 11x^3 - 19x^2 - 4x + 3) \div (4x - 1)$

16. $(2x^4 + x^3 - 4x^2 - 8x + 2) \div (2x + 1)$

17. $(3x^4 - 2x^3 - 9x^2 + 6x - 9) \div (3x - 2)$

       Developing Skills in Algebra   Book B

Quotients of Polynomials

Name _____

Date _____ Period _____

Divide.

1. $(x^3 + 3x^2 + 7x - 1) \div (x - 1)$ $x^2 + 4x + 11 + \dfrac{10}{x - 1}$

2. $(x^3 - 3x^2 - 29x - 10) \div (x + 4)$

3. $(x^3 - 9x^2 + 21x - 4) \div (x - 3)$

4. $(x^3 + x^2 - 19x + 8) \div (x + 5)$

5. $(2x^3 - 11x^2 - 17x + 12) \div (2x + 3)$

6. $(3x^3 - 13x^2 + 13x - 10) \div (3x - 1)$

7. $(x^3 - 34x - 7) \div (x - 6)$

8. $(x^3 - 15x + 7) \div (x + 4)$

9. $(4x^3 + 7x + 1) \div (2x + 1)$

10. $(9x^3 + 2x + 1) \div (3x - 1)$

11. $(x^4 - 14x^2 - 7x) \div (x - 4)$

12. $(x^4 - 36x^2 + x + 8) \div (x + 6)$

13. $(4x^4 - 25x^2 + 2x + 10) \div (2x + 5)$

14. $(9x^4 - 13x^2 - 3x + 8) \div (3x + 2)$

15. $(5x^4 - 8x^3 - 19x^2 - 6x + 5) \div (5x + 2)$

16. $(2x^4 + 3x^3 - 2x^2 - x - 1) \div (2x + 3)$

17. $(3x^4 - x^3 - 6x^2 + 11x - 8) \div (3x - 1)$

Greatest Common Factors

Name _____

Date _____ Period _____

Factor using prime numbers.

1. 10   _____2·5_____   2. 15 _____

3. 12 _____   4. 21 _____

5. 18 _____   6. 16 _____

7. 24 _____   8. 30 _____

9. 36 _____   10. 40 _____

11. 25 _____   12. 39 _____

13. 45 _____   14. 51 _____

15. 68 _____   16. 65 _____

17. 98 _____   18. 64 _____

Find the greatest common factor for each pair of numbers.

19. (15, 25)   _____5_____   20. (16, 36) _____

21. (40, 44) _____   22. (18, 45) _____

23. (4, 25) _____   24. (25, 50) _____

25. (24, 36) _____   26. (81, 99) _____

27. (150, 90) _____   28. (30, 77) _____

29. (16, 32) _____   30. (30, 70) _____

31. (26, 65) _____   32. (28, 98) _____

Developing Skills in Algebra   Book B

Name _____

Date _____ Period _____

Factor using prime numbers.

1. 24 _____2·2·2·3_____   **2.** 35 _____

3. 22 _____   **4.** 49 _____

5. 91 _____   **6.** 27 _____

7. 33 _____   **8.** 72 _____

9. 48 _____   **10.** 63 _____

11. 75 _____   **12.** 38 _____

13. 80 _____   **14.** 100 _____

15. 110 _____   **16.** 81 _____

17. 125 _____   **18.** 85 _____

Find the greatest common factor for each pair of numbers.

19. (18, 45) _____9_____   **20.** (20, 28) _____

21. (39, 65) _____   **22.** (32, 80) _____

23. (20, 21) _____   **24.** (63, 35) _____

25. (24, 72) _____   **26.** (27, 105) _____

27. (42, 70) _____   **28.** (35, 44) _____

29. (18, 48) _____   **30.** (58, 87) _____

31. (34, 85) _____   **32.** (28, 84) _____

Name _____

Date _____ Period _____

Find the greatest common factor for each pair.

1. $(3x, 6)$ 2

2. $(3a, a)$

3. $(4c^2, 2c)$

4. $(72ab, 36b)$

5. $(42y^2, y)$

6. $(8x^3, x)$

7. $(24mn, 31pq)$

8. $(23ab, 46a^3b^2)$

9. $(15x^4y, 60xy^4)$

10. $(150xy^2, 90x)$

11. $(43xy, 13pq)$

12. $(11a^5b, 30rst)$

13. $(21a^5b^3, 18a^2b^3)$

14. $(21az, 105uz^3)$

15. $(16mn^2, 48m^3n^2)$

16. $(18a^5b^2, 54a^2b^3)$

17. $(40rs, 16s^3t)$

18. $(48a^4b^3, 80a^2b^7)$

19. $[9(a + b)^2, 3(a + b)]$

20. $(27rs, 35ab)$

21. $(15x^7y^4, 40x^9y^6z)$

22. $(33u^5z^2c, 121u^3z^3c^2)$

23. $(15a^3b, 26xy^4)$

24. $(25rst, 100r^3s^2t^3)$

25. $[2(a + b)^3, 8(a + b)^2]$

26. $[(x + y)^2(x - y), (y + x)]$

27. $(16x^4y^2, 48x^3y^4)$

28. $(33mn^3, 12r^3s)$

29. $(11a^3b^2, 44a^5b^3)$

30. $(28bc^3, 39de^4)$

31. $(64m^3n^2, 90m^6n^8)$

32. $[6(r + s), 2(r + s)]$

33. $[14(a + b)(a - b), 21(a + b)]$

34. $[6(c - d), 10(c - d)^2]$

Greatest Common Factors

Name _____

Date _____ Period _____

Find the greatest common factor for each pair.

1. $(4y, 8)$ 4

2. $(6x, 9x^2)$

3. $(25x, 35xy)$

4. $(16ab, 20b)$

5. $(35y^5, 15y^3)$

6. $(16a^2, 80a^5)$

7. $(12z^2, 48z)$

8. $(28r^3s^2t, 70r^2s^5t^3)$

9. $(120x^3y, 45xy^3)$

10. $(28a^2b^3, 56a^5b^7)$

11. $(15b^4, 5b^2)$

12. $(38s^3t^2, 87s^3t^5)$

13. $(15r^3s, 33a^5b^2)$

14. $(29mn^2, 58m^3n^5)$

15. $(45a^{10}b^5c^3, 60a^2b^7c^5)$

16. $(28a^5b^3, 35a^2b^9)$

17. $(43rst, 81abc)$

18. $(19m^3n, 25a^4b)$

19. $(46p^3q^2r^4, 69p^2q^4r)$

20. $(42a^5b^2c, 56a^2b^2c^5)$

21. $(40m^4n^2r, 100m^2n^3r^5)$

22. $(25mn^4, 35m^3n^2)$

23. $[3(a-b)^2(a+b), (a+b)^4]$

24. $(75x^3y^3z^4, 125x^4y^2z^2)$

25. $[8(r+s)^3, 24(r+s)^2]$

26. $(55mnp, 61abc)$

27. $(22m^4n^2, 110mn^6)$

28. $[6(x+y)^3, 15(x+y)]$

29. $[12(x-y)(y+z), 25(y+z)]$

30. $(24a^2z^4, 36a^4z^2)$

31. $(72x^3y^2z, 40x^2y^4z^3)$

32. $[13(a+b)^2(a+c), 27(a+c)]$

33. $(92m^2n^4, 123mn^2)$

34. $[35(m-n), 40(m-n)(s+t)]$

Factoring

Name _____

Date _____ Period _____

Factor.

1. $2x^2 - 10x$ $2x(x-5)$

2. $5x - 20x^2$

3. $x^2y - 3x^2$

4. $ab^2 + 4b^2$

5. $x^2z + y^2z^2$

6. $c^4d^2 + c^2d^3$

7. $8x - 16y$

8. $15a + 25b$

9. $4a + 20b$

10. $6m - 12n$

11. $3x - 6y + 12$

12. $4a - 8b + 16c$

13. $5 + 15n + 45m$

14. $7 + 28a - 35b$

15. $13a^2 - 169a$

16. $15a + 225a^3$

17. $8x - 56x^3$

18. $3a^2 + 12a^4$

19. $14u^2 + 35u^4$

20. $23x^5 - 46x^2$

21. $u^3 - 3u^2 + 17u^4$

22. $x^4 - 3x^3 + 17x^2$

23. $3x^3 + 3x^2 + 6x$

24. $5a^4 - 5a^2 + 25a$

25. $x^3 + 3x^2y + 3xy$

26. $x^4 + 3x^3y^2 + 12x^2y^3$

27. $4a^4b - 16a^2b^2 + 4ab^4$

28. $6a^3b^2 - 12a^2b^3 + 18ab$

29. $15x^2y^2 + 225x^3y^3 + 15x^4y^4$

30. $13a^3b^2 + 39a^2b - 26ab^4$

31. $15x^3 + 24x^2 + 36x$

32. $7c^3 - 28c^2d + 35cd^3$

33. $a^3y^3 + a^2y^2 + ay$

34. $mn + 5m^2n^2 - 12m^2n^3$

Factoring

Factor.

1. $3x^2 - 6x$ $3x(x - 2)$

2. $7b + 14c$

3. $10a - 18b$

4. $6x + 24y$

5. $a^4b^2 - a^2b$

6. $x^3y^2 + x^2y^3$

7. $14x - 18y$

8. $3 - 12a + 15c$

9. $3a + 24b$

10. $13x^3 - 26x$

11. $2x - 8y + 14$

12. $3a + 12b + 15$

13. $7 - 21m + 35n$

14. $24x^4 - 12y$

15. $16a^3 - 12a^2$

16. $13x^3 + 39x^2$

17. $12x^3 + 144x^2$

18. $8r^4 - 24r^3$

19. $a^3 + 2a^2b - ab^4$

20. $15a^3b^2 - 30a^2b^3 + 5ab$

21. $5x^3 + 5x^2 - 10x$

22. $m^3n^2 - m^2n + 5m^4n^3$

23. $a^4 - 3a^3c + 9a^2c^3$

24. $5 + 20r - 25s$

25. $4ab - 2a^2b^2 + 10a^3b^3$

26. $8rst^3 - 4r^2s^2t + 24r^3st^4$

27. $13x^4y^2 + 26x^2y^2 + 13xy$

28. $28a^3b^2 + 7a^2b^2 - 35a^2b^3$

29. $a^3b^2c + 3a^2b^2 + 10abc$

30. $x^3y^2z^5 - 5x^2y^2z^2 + 12x^5y^2z^2$

31. $x^3y^2z - 10xyz + 5x^4y^3$

32. $3a^3b^2c + 6a^6b^3c^2 - 9a^4b^2c^2$

33. $12x^3y + 144x^2y^2 + 60xy^3$

34. $22a^3b - 44a^2b^3 + 66ab^4$

Factoring

Name _____

Date _____ Period _____

Factor.

1. $(m + n) - 5(m + n)$ $-4\,(m+n)$

2. $3(r + s) + (r + s)$

3. $6(a + b) + b(a + b)$

4. $5(m - n) - m(m - n)$

5. $(a + b) + a(a + b) - b(a + b)$

6. $3(x + y) + x(x + y) + y(x + y)$

7. $(x + y)(x - y) + (x + y)(y + z) - (x + y)(y - z)$

8. $(a - b)(2a + 3b) + (a - b)(3a + b)$

9. $(2r + s)(2r - s) + (2r + s)(r - s)$

10. $(a + b)^2(a - b) - (a + b)(a - b)^2$

11. $a^2(b + c)(2b + c) + a(b + c)$

12. $t^3(2r + s)(3r + 2s) + t^2(3r + 2s)$

13. $(2a + 1)(a + 3) - (2a + 1)(a - 3)$

14. $(3x + 2y)(x + 2y) + (3x + 2y)(x - 2y)$

15. $3a(5a + 2b)(3a - 5b) - 9a^2(5a + 2b)(4a - b)$

16. $6m(3n - 2m)(n + m) + 8m^2(3n - 2m)(n + m)$

17. $5x^2y(3x + 2y) + 15xy(3x + 2y)(x - 3y)$

Factoring

Name _____

Date _____ Period _____

Factor.

1. $4(p + q) - (p + q)$ $3(p + q)$

2. $8(r - s) + s(r - s)$

3. $12(a + b) + a(a + b)$

4. $20(x + y) - x(x + y)$

5. $(m - n) + 3(m - n) - n(m - n)$

6. $(r + s) - r(r + s) + s(r + s)$

7. $(a + b)(a - b) + (a + b)(a + c) - (a + b)(a - c)$

8. $(r + s)(s + t) - (r + s)(s - t) + (r + s)(s + t)$

9. $(2x - y)(x + y) + (2x - y)(x - y)$

10. $(3a + b)(2a - b)^2 - (3a + 2b)(2a - b)^3$

11. $x^2(a - b)(2a + 3b) + x(a - b)$

12. $a^4(3b + c)(b + 2c) - a^2(b + 2c)$

13. $(3x + 2)(3x - 1) + (3x + 2)(3x - 5)$

14. $(m - 2n)(m + 3n) - (m - 2n)(m - 3n)$

15. $7x(3x + 10)(3x - 5) + 14x^2(2x + 1)(3x - 5)^2$

16. $3r(7r + 3s)^2 - 15r^2(7r + 3s)$

17. $12a^3b^2(2a + 3b) - 30ab(2a + 3b)(2a - 3b)$

66

Factoring

Name _____

Date _____ Period _____

Factor.

1. $x^2 - 81$ $(x - 9)(x + 9)$

2. $4x^2 - 25$

3. $9x^2 - 25$

4. $x^2 - 64$

5. $4x^2 - 81$

6. $25x^2 - 9$

7. $16 - 25x^2$

8. $16x^2 - 1$

9. $25 - x^2$

10. $9 - 49x^2$

11. $100x^2 - 1$

12. $49 - x^2$

13. $4a^2 - b^2$

14. $4x^2y^2 - 9$

15. $9r^2 - 4t^2$

16. $144a^4 - b^2$

17. $x^2y^2 - 9z^2$

18. $9x^2 - 16y^2$

19. $400a^2 - 9b^2$

20. $x^2y^2z^2 - 4$

21. $9x^2 - 49y^2$

22. $x^6y^4 - 64z^2$

23. $400x^2 - 49y^2$

24. $361a^2b^2 - 9c^2$

25. $4r^2 - 49t^2$

26. $225a^6 - 16b^2$

27. $256x^4 - 9y^2$

28. $169x^4 - 16y^2$

29. $289x^6y^2 - z^2$

30. $225a^6 - 16b^2$

31. $(a - b)^2 - c^2$

32. $(c - d)^2 - z^2$

33. $r^2 - (p + q)^2$

34. $z^2 - (x + y)^2$

67

Factoring

Factor.

1. $x^2 - 1$ $(x - 1)(x + 1)$

2. $x^2 - 4$

3. $x^2 - 16$

4. $4x^2 - 1$

5. $x^2 - 49$

6. $x^2 - 36$

7. $9x^2 - 1$

8. $4x^2 - 9$

9. $x^2 - 25$

10. $x^2 - 9$

11. $9x^2 - 16$

12. $9x^2 - 4$

13. $x^2 - 81y^2$

14. $x^2 - 64y^2$

15. $4x^2 - 25y^2$

16. $9x^2 - 25y^2$

17. $25x^2 - 9y^2$

18. $4x^2 - 49y^2$

19. $36x^2 - 49y^2$

20. $16x^2 - y^2$

21. $4x^2 - 81y^2$

22. $16x^4 - 25y^2$

23. $16a^4b^2 - 49$

24. $9a^2b^2 - 49$

25. $16a^2b^2 - 9c^6d^4$

26. $16a^2b^2 - 81c^4d^6$

27. $25a^2 - c^2d^2$

28. $49a^6 - c^2d^2$

29. $64m^2n^2 - 9$

30. $81r^2s^2 - 4$

31. $(a + b)^2 - c^2$

32. $(r + s)^2 - t^2$

33. $z^2 - (x - y)^2$

34. $m^2 - (n - r)^2$

68

Name _____

Date _____ Period _____

Factor.

1. $x^2 + 2x + 1$ $(x + 1)^2$

2. $x^2 + 6x + 9$

3. $x^2 + 10x + 25$

4. $4x^2 + 28x + 49$

5. $9x^2 - 6x + 1$

6. $4x^2 - 12x + 9$

7. $16x^2 - 40x + 25$

8. $x^2 - 14x + 49$

9. $36x^2 + 12x + 1$

10. $16x^2 - 8x + 1$

11. $x^2 - 18x + 81$

12. $25x^2 + 70x + 49$

13. $100x^2 + 20x + 1$

14. $16x^2 + 72x + 81$

15. $9a^2 - 42ab + 49b^2$

16. $9a^2 + 24ab + 16b^2$

17. $64x^2 - 16xy + y^2$

18. $25x^2 - 20xy + 4y^2$

19. $144r^2 - 24rs + s^2$

20. $49m^2 - 28mn + 4n^2$

21. $25x^4 - 40x^2y + 16y^2$

22. $64a^4 - 80a^2b + 25b^2$

23. $36x^2y^2 - 84xy + 49$

24. $81m^2n^2 + 18mn + 1$

25. $256r^4 + 32r^2 + 1$

26. $169s^4 - 52s^2 + 4$

27. $25p^2 - 80pq + 64q^2$

28. $364r^2 + 36rs^2 + s^4$

29. $49t^2 - 56st + 16s^2$

30. $900x^4 - 60x^2 + 1$

31. $(a + b)^2 + 2(a + b) + 1$

32. $(c - d)^2 + 2(c - d) + 1$

33. $(r - s)^2 - 2(r - s) + 1$

34. $(m + n)^2 - 2(m + n) + 1$

Factoring

Factor.

1. $x^2 + 4x + 4$ $(x + 2)^2$

2. $4x^2 + 4x + 1$

3. $25x^2 + 10x + 1$

4. $x^2 + 8x + 16$

5. $4x^2 - 20x + 25$

6. $49x^2 - 14x + 1$

7. $100x^2 - 140x + 49$

8. $16x^2 + 24x + 9$

9. $x^2 + 12x + 36$

10. $4x^2 - 36x + 81$

11. $100x^2 - 60x + 9$

12. $36x^2 - 60x + 25$

13. $169x^2 + 104x + 16$

14. $49x^2 + 42x + 9$

15. $9a^2 + 12ab + 4b^2$

16. $x^2 - 16xy + 64y^2$

17. $64r^2 - 48rs + 9s^2$

18. $16a^2 + 56ab + 49b^2$

19. $81c^4 + 36c^2 + 4$

20. $49r^4 - 70r^2 + 25$

21. $100x^4y^2 - 180x^2y + 81$

22. $9p^4 - 30p^2 + 25$

23. $9r^4 - 48r^2t + 64t^2$

24. $25a^4 + 30a^2b + 9b^2$

25. $225t^{10} + 30t^5 + 1$

26. $64x^8 - 112x^4 + 49$

27. $25r^4 + 90r^2s + 81s^2$

28. $81m^6 - 72m^3n + 16n^2$

29. $400a^8 - 40a^4 + 1$

30. $25x^4y^2 + 60x^2yz + 36z^2$

31. $(p + q)^2 + 2(p + q) + 1$

32. $(x - y)^2 + 2(x - y) + 1$

33. $(g - h)^2 - 2(g - h) + 1$

34. $(v + w)^2 - 2(v + w) + 1$

Factoring

Name _____

Date _____ Period _____

Factor.

1. $x^2 + 5x + 6$ $(x + 2)(x + 3)$

2. $x^2 + 9x + 20$

3. $x^2 + 7x + 6$

4. $x^2 + 10x + 21$

5. $x^2 + 15x + 56$

6. $x^2 + 3x + 2$

7. $x^2 + 8x + 16$

8. $x^2 + 2x + 1$

9. $x^2 + 7x + 12$

10. $x^2 + 13x + 42$

11. $x^2 + 5x + 4$

12. $x^2 + 14x + 45$

13. $x^2 + 6x + 9$

14. $x^2 + 6x + 5$

15. $x^2 + 10x + 24$

16. $x^2 + 4x + 4$

17. $x^2 + 8x + 7$

18. $x^2 + 12x + 36$

19. $x^2 + 9x + 18$

20. $x^2 + 16x + 63$

21. $x^2 + 10x + 16$

22. $x^2 + 12x + 27$

23. $x^2 - 6x + 8$

24. $x^2 - 11x + 30$

25. $x^2 - 3x + 2$

26. $x^2 - 9x + 8$

27. $x^2 - 13x + 36$

28. $x^2 - 15x + 56$

29. $x^2 - 8x + 16$

30. $x^2 - 8x + 12$

31. $x^2 - 12x + 27$

32. $x^2 - 17x + 72$

33. $x^2 - 11x + 28$

34. $x^2 - 6x + 9$

Developing Skills in Algebra   Book B

Factoring

Name _____

Date _____ Period _____

Factor.

1. $x^2 + 7x + 10$ $(x + 2)(x + 5)$

2. $x^2 + 13x + 40$

3. $x^2 + 4x + 3$

4. $x^2 + 6x + 8$

5. $x^2 + 10x + 25$

6. $x^2 + 10x + 9$

7. $x^2 + 8x + 12$

8. $x^2 + 14x + 49$

9. $x^2 + 15x + 54$

10. $x^2 + 11x + 28$

11. $x^2 + 16x + 64$

12. $x^2 + 8x + 15$

13. $x^2 + 18x + 81$

14. $x^2 + 11x + 24$

15. $x^2 + 11x + 30$

16. $x^2 + 9x + 14$

17. $x^2 + 11x + 18$

18. $x^2 + 12x + 35$

19. $x^2 + 9x + 8$

20. $x^2 + 14x + 48$

21. $x^2 + 13x + 36$

22. $x^2 + 17x + 72$

23. $x^2 - 12x + 32$

24. $x^2 - 8x + 15$

25. $x^2 - 15x + 54$

26. $x^2 - 6x + 5$

27. $x^2 - 12x + 36$

28. $x^2 - 4x + 4$

29. $x^2 - 9x + 14$

30. $x^2 - 13x + 40$

31. $x^2 - 10x + 9$

32. $x^2 - 4x + 3$

33. $x^2 - 14x + 49$

34. $x^2 - 10x + 24$

Factoring

Factor.

1. $x^2 + 2x - 3$ $\quad (x + 3)(x - 1)$

2. $x^2 + 2x - 8$

3. $x^2 + 3x - 40$

4. $x^2 + 3x - 54$

5. $x^2 + 2x - 48$

6. $x^2 + 3x - 28$

7. $x^2 + x - 30$

8. $x^2 + 2x - 15$

9. $x^2 + 8x - 9$

10. $x^2 + 5x - 36$

11. $x^2 + 5x - 24$

12. $x^2 + 7x - 18$

13. $x^2 + 5x - 14$

14. $x^2 + 2x - 35$

15. $x^2 + 3x - 10$

16. $x^2 + x - 72$

17. $x^2 + 7x - 8$

18. $x^2 + 4x - 12$

19. $x^2 - 7x - 18$

20. $x^2 - x - 30$

21. $x^2 - 3x - 40$

22. $x^2 - 2x - 48$

23. $x^2 - 3x - 10$

24. $x^2 - 2x - 3$

25. $x^2 - 8x - 9$

26. $x^2 - 7x - 8$

27. $x^2 - 5x - 36$

28. $x^2 - 3x - 54$

29. $x^2 - 4x - 12$

30. $x^2 - x - 6$

31. $x^2 - 2x - 15$

32. $x^2 - 3x - 28$

33. $x^2 - x - 72$

34. $x^2 - 5x - 14$

Factoring

Factor.

1. $x^2 + 6x - 7$ $(x + 7)(x - 1)$

2. $x^2 + x - 56$

3. $x^2 + 2x - 63$

4. $x^2 + x - 20$

5. $x^2 + x - 2$

6. $x^2 + x - 6$

7. $x^2 + 5x - 6$

8. $x^2 + 3x - 18$

9. $x^2 + 2x - 24$

10. $x^2 + 4x - 45$

11. $x^2 + 4x - 5$

12. $x^2 + 4x - 21$

13. $x^2 + 2x - 8$

14. $x^2 + x - 12$

15. $x^2 + 5x - 36$

16. $x^2 + 6x - 16$

17. $x^2 + 7x - 98$

18. $x^2 + x - 42$

19. $x^2 + 6x - 27$

20. $x^2 + 3x - 4$

21. $x^2 - x - 30$

22. $x^2 - 6x - 27$

23. $x^2 - x - 72$

24. $x^2 - 7x - 8$

25. $x^2 - 9x - 36$

26. $x^2 - 4x - 12$

27. $x^2 - 18x - 40$

28. $x^2 - 10x - 56$

29. $x^2 - 8x - 65$

30. $x^2 - 3x - 28$

31. $x^2 - 7x - 120$

32. $x^2 - x - 56$

33. $x^2 - 8x - 84$

34. $x^2 - 14x - 120$

Factoring

Factor.

1. $2x^2 + 7x + 6$ $(2x + 3)(x + 2)$

2. $2x^2 + 13x + 21$

3. $2x^2 + 3x + 1$

4. $2x^2 + 13x + 20$

5. $2x^2 + 13x + 18$

6. $2x^2 + 21x + 54$

7. $2x^2 + 15x + 7$

8. $2x^2 + 10x + 12$

9. $3x^2 + 10x + 3$

10. $3x^2 + 17x + 20$

11. $3x^2 + 26x + 16$

12. $4x^2 + 11x + 6$

13. $4x^2 + 27x + 18$

14. $4x^2 + 19x + 21$

15. $2x^2 + 15x + 18$

16. $2x^2 + 17x + 36$

17. $3x^2 + 14x + 8$

18. $4x^2 + 9x + 5$

19. $2x^2 + 21x + 49$

20. $3x^2 + 20x + 12$

21. $4x^2 + 19x + 12$

22. $2x^2 + 11x + 15$

23. $3x^2 - 10x + 8$

24. $4x^2 - 35x + 49$

25. $3x^2 - 26x + 35$

26. $2x^2 - 21x + 40$

27. $3x^2 - 13x + 14$

28. $2x^2 - 9x + 7$

29. $4x^2 - 17x + 18$

30. $3x^2 - 22x + 35$

31. $2x^2 - 23x + 63$

32. $3x^2 - 16x + 5$

33. $4x^2 - 27x + 35$

34. $3x^2 - 34x + 63$

Factoring

Name _____

Date _____ Period _____

Factor.

1. $3x^2 + 13x + 12$ $(3x + 4)(x + 3)$

2. $2x^2 + 11x + 14$

3. $4x^2 + 17x + 15$

4. $2x^2 + 15x + 28$

5. $3x^2 + 19x + 28$

6. $5x^2 + 17x + 6$

7. $6x^2 + 11x + 5$

8. $2x^2 + 9x + 10$

9. $3x^2 + 8x + 4$

10. $4x^2 + 13x + 10$

11. $5x^2 + 28x + 15$

12. $2x^2 + 11x + 9$

13. $3x^2 + 16x + 21$

14. $5x^2 + 26x + 5$

15. $5x^2 + 37x + 42$

16. $6x^2 + 23x + 15$

17. $4x^2 + 13x + 3$

18. $2x^2 + 9x + 9$

19. $2x^2 + 23x + 63$

20. $5x^2 + 42x + 16$

21. $6x^2 + 53x + 40$

22. $2x^2 + 13x + 20$

23. $3x^2 - 22x + 24$

24. $5x^2 - 38x + 21$

25. $4x^2 - 25x + 25$

26. $6x^2 - 47x + 35$

27. $2x^2 - 19x + 42$

28. $6x^2 - 31x + 28$

29. $5x^2 - 49x + 36$

30. $3x^2 - 19x + 20$

31. $4x^2 - 5x + 1$

32. $2x^2 - 7x + 5$

33. $5x^2 - 47x + 18$

34. $3x^2 - 31x + 36$

Factoring

Name _____

Date _____ Period _____

Factor.

1. $3x^2 + 20x - 7$ $(3x - 1)(x + 7)$ **2.** $2x^2 - 5x + 3$

3. $4x^2 + 21x + 5$ **4.** $5x^2 - 28x - 12$

5. $2x^2 - 7x + 3$ **6.** $5x^2 + 32x - 64$

7. $4x^2 - 3x - 7$ **8.** $3x^2 + 4x + 1$

9. $2x^2 + 19x + 45$ **10.** $3x^2 - 13x - 56$

11. $4x^2 - 25x - 21$ **12.** $5x^2 - 39x - 54$

13. $6x^2 - 41x + 30$ **14.** $2x^2 - 3x - 27$

15. $3x^2 + 8x + 5$ **16.** $4x^2 + 7x - 2$

17. $4x^2 - 11x - 45$ **18.** $5x^2 + 31x + 30$

19. $2x^2 - 3x - 35$ **20.** $3x^2 - 11x - 42$

21. $5x^2 - 39x + 28$ **22.** $4x^2 - 13x + 9$

23. $3x^2 + 17x - 6$ **24.** $5x^2 + 52x + 63$

25. $6x^2 - 55x + 9$ **26.** $2x^2 - 7x - 72$

27. $3x^2 + 28x + 49$ **28.** $5x^2 + 39x - 8$

29. $4x^2 - 9x - 28$ **30.** $3x^2 - 23x + 30$

31. $2x^2 + 13x + 15$ **32.** $5x^2 - 11x - 12$

33. $4x^2 - x - 3$ **34.** $3x^2 + 28x + 9$

Factoring

Name _____

Date _____ Period _____

Factor.

1. $2x^2 + 17x + 30$ $(2x + 5)(x + 6)$

2. $3x^2 - 5x + 2$

3. $4x^2 - 17x - 15$

4. $3x^2 + 28x + 32$

5. $5x^2 + 23x - 10$

6. $6x^2 - 37x + 35$

7. $2x^2 - 9x + 4$

8. $3x^2 - 11x - 4$

9. $4x^2 + 27x - 7$

10. $5x^2 - 37x - 24$

11. $6x^2 + 25x + 4$

12. $5x^2 + 22x + 21$

13. $5x^2 + 17x + 14$

14. $3x^2 + 5x + 2$

15. $5x^2 - 32x - 21$

16. $5x^2 - 34x - 48$

17. $6x^2 + 35x - 49$

18. $4x^2 - 17x + 4$

19. $2x^2 - 3x - 2$

20. $3x^2 + x - 10$

21. $5x^2 + 32x + 35$

22. $6x^2 - 47x - 63$

23. $4x^2 - 9x - 9$

24. $3x^2 - 7x - 6$

25. $6x^2 + 37x + 6$

26. $5x^2 - 24x - 36$

27. $7x^2 - 22x + 3$

28. $2x^2 - 9x + 35$

29. $5x^2 + 49x + 36$

30. $6x^2 - 41x - 7$

31. $5x^2 - 16x - 16$

32. $7x^2 + 31x + 12$

33. $2x^2 + 23x + 45$

34. $3x^2 - 19x - 40$

Developing Skills in Algebra   Book B

Factor.

1. $4x^2 - 8x - 45$ $(2x - 9)(2x + 5)$ **2.** $12x^2 - 25x - 7$

3. $12x^2 + 13x - 14$ **4.** $15x^2 - 26x + 7$

5. $25x^2 + 15x + 2$ **6.** $35x^2 + 37x - 6$

7. $12x^2 - 44x + 7$ **8.** $21x^2 - 46x - 7$

9. $35x^2 - 27x - 18$ **10.** $14x^2 + 3x - 27$

11. $28x^2 + 15x - 25$ **12.** $24x^2 + 34x + 5$

13. $12x^2 - 28x - 49$ **14.** $4x^2 - 24x + 35$

15. $35x^2 - 27x + 4$ **16.** $15x^2 + 53x + 42$

17. $10x^2 + 27x + 18$ **18.** $36x^2 - 12x - 35$

19. $70x^2 + 41x + 6$ **20.** $36x^2 - 3x - 5$

21. $14x^2 - 11x + 2$ **22.** $15x^2 + 29x + 12$

23. $14x^2 - 55x - 36$ **24.** $8x^2 + 10x - 25$

25. $9x^2 + 18x - 7$ **26.** $49x^2 - 14x - 3$

27. $60x^2 + 29x + 2$ **28.** $26x^2 - 19x + 3$

29. $20x^2 + 21x - 27$ **30.** $15x^2 + 51x + 18$

31. $18x^2 - 27x + 10$ **32.** $14x^2 + 15x - 9$

33. $12x^2 - 18x - 21$ **34.** $14x^2 - 19x - 3$

          Developing Skills in Algebra   Book B

Factoring

Name _____

Date _____ Period _____

Factor.

1. $6x^2 - 25x - 9$ $(2x - 9)(3x + 1)$

2. $15x^2 - 38x + 7$

3. $21x^2 + x - 2$

4. $15x^2 + 8x + 1$

5. $25x^2 + 55x + 18$

6. $25x^2 - 30x - 16$

7. $6x^2 - 11x - 10$

8. $10x^2 - 3x - 27$

9. $24x^2 - 2x - 15$

10. $42x^2 + 5x - 25$

11. $21x^2 + 11x - 6$

12. $4x^2 + 20x + 9$

13. $12x^2 + 20x + 7$

14. $35x^2 - 58x - 9$

15. $28x^2 - 37x + 12$

16. $20x^2 - 9x - 18$

17. $25x^2 - 10x - 63$

18. $49x^2 + 21x - 4$

19. $21x^2 + 19x - 12$

20. $25x^2 - 35x + 12$

21. $16x^2 + 32x + 15$

22. $6x^2 + 11x + 3$

23. $10x^2 - 43x + 28$

24. $35x^2 - 6x - 8$

25. $20x^2 - 23x + 6$

26. $14x^2 - 45x - 14$

27. $4x^2 - 4x - 3$

28. $28x^2 + 15x + 2$

29. $12x^2 + x - 63$

30. $49x^2 - 42x - 16$

31. $18x^2 + 15x + 2$

32. $24x^2 + 26x - 63$

33. $30x^2 + 73x + 7$

34. $50x^2 - 45x - 18$

80

Developing Skills in Algebra   Book B

Factoring   Name _____

                                       Date _____ Period _____

Factor.

1. $3x - xy$ $x(3 - y)$ **2.** $2x + xy$

3. $4x + 4y$ **4.** $3x + xy$

5. $b + bc$ **6.** $nx - ny$

7. $6x + 21$ **8.** $27y - 81$

9. $3a^2bm - a^2bn$ **10.** $3xmn^2 - 2mn^2$

11. $15x^4y^2 + 6x^3y^3$ **12.** $15a^3b + 10a^2b^2$

13. $42x^3y^4 + 18x^2y^6$ **14.** $27m^2n^5 - 63mn^7$

15. $5a^2 - 25a$ **16.** $10bx - 30by$

17. $30x^2y^2 - 20x^2y$ **18.** $120a^3b^2n - 75a^3b^2m$

19. $12abx^2 + 6abx - 30ab$ **20.** $36m^2nx^2 + 84m^2nx - 24m^2n$

21. $r^2 - 3r - 10$ **22.** $m^2 + 5m - 24$

23. $2p^2 - pq - 3q^2$ **24.** $3a^2 - 5a - 2$

25. $m^2 - 4n^2$ **26.** $9x^2 - 4y^2$

27. $49x^2 - 9$ **28.** $36r^2 - 49t^2$

29. $m^2 - 4mn + 4n^2$ **30.** $9x^2 + 12xy + 4y^2$

31. $a^2 - ab - 6b^2$ **32.** $x^2 - xy - 12y^2$

33. $3b^2 + 5ab - 2a^2$ **34.** $4y^2 + 19xy - 5x^2$

81   Developing Skills in Algebra   Book B

Factoring

Name _____

Date _____ Period _____

Factor.

1. $5m - 5n$ $5(m - n)$

2. $3y + y^2$

3. $10x + xy$

4. $5a + 5b$

5. $ab + ac$

6. $mx - my$

7. $8x + 28$

8. $15y - 45$

9. $2a^2bm + a^2bn$

10. $3xmn^2 + 2mn^2$

11. $6x^4y^2 - 15x^3y^3$

12. $10a^3b - 25a^2b^2$

13. $18x^3y^4 - 12x^2y^6$

14. $18m^2n^5 + 27mn^7$

15. $35a - 7a^2$

16. $27by - 9bx$

17. $14xy^2 - 21xy^3$

18. $40abm - 48abn$

19. $36a^2bx^2 - 12a^2bx + 108a^2b$

20. $18mn^2x^2 - 81mn^2x + 27mn^2$

21. $r^2 - r - 6$

22. $m^2 + 3m - 40$

23. $6p^2 - 11pq + 3q^2$

24. $3a^2 - 14a - 5$

25. $16a^2 - 81b^2$

26. $25a^2 - 169y^2$

27. $a^2 - 10ab + 25b^2$

28. $25x^2 - 20xy + 4y^2$

29. $x^2 - 3xy - 28y^2$

30. $x^2 - 5xy - 14y^2$

31. $7x^2 + 13xy - 2y^2$

32. $15x^2 + 13xy + 2y^2$

33. $25 - 81x^2$

34. $169x^2 - 144y^2$

82

Developing Skills in Algebra   Book B

Factoring

Name _____

Date _____ Period _____

Factor.

1. $15x^2 + 36x + 12$ $3(5x + 2)(x + 2)$

2. $60 - 190cd - 70c^2d^2$

3. $180a^2 - 125b^2$

4. $448x^2 + 112x + 7$

5. $6a^3 + 36a^2 + 48a$

6. $9x^3 + 117x^2 + 324x$

7. $28x^3 - 84x^2 + 63x$

8. $48x^2y - 27y$

9. $5x^3y - 17x^2y - 40xy$

10. $2p^3q^3 + 13p^2q^2 - 24pq$

11. $9ab - 49a^3b^3$

12. $12r^3s^3 - 13r^2s^2 + 11rs$

13. $10x^4y^2 - 29x^3y^3 + 10x^2y^4$

14. $81a^2b^3 - 36a^3b^4 + 4a^4b^5$

15. $x^5y + 8x^4y + 7x^3y$

16. $24a^3c + 26a^2c^2 + 5ac$

17. $48a^4b + 24a^2b + 3b$

18. $125m^3n^3 - 20mn$

19. $70c^4d - 45c^3d - 90c^2d$

20. $11a^3b - 22a^4b^2 - 165a^5b^3$

21. $72x^3y^2 - 576x^2y^3 + 504xy^4$

22. $60a^4b - 200a^3b^2 + 140a^2b^3$

23. $27a^3b^2 + 36a^4b^3 - 81a^3b^4$

24. $21m^5n^4 - 39m^3n^4 - 45mn^4$

25. $140c^3d^3 - 135c^2d^3 - 50cd^3$

26. $12a^3b^2 - 84a^2b^2 - 216ab^2$

27. $-75x^5 + 27x^3$

28. $-700c^9 + 420c^8 - 63c^7$

29. $-5x^4 - 10x^3 + 240x^2$

30. $480b^4 - 352b^3 - 40b^2$

31. $63x^5y^4 - 294x^4y^3 + 343x^3y^2$

32. $-48m^3n^3 + 588m^5n^5$

33. $25a^5b + 25ab^5$

34. $105cd - 280c^2d^2 + 560c^3d^3$

Factoring

Factor.

1. $8x^2 + 44x + 20$ $4(2x+1)(x+5)$

2. $36a^4 + 90a^2b^2 + 99b^4$

3. $14a^4 + 49a^3b - 21a^4b^2$

4. $180a^2 - 300a + 125$

5. $36x^3 - 81x$

6. $3y^3 + 33y^2 + 84y$

7. $27a^3 - 90a^2 + 75a$

8. $40d^5 + 10d^3 - 105d$

9. $a^3b + 8a^2b + 12ab$

10. $64p^3q - pq^3$

11. $10p^3q^3 - p^2q^2 - 21pq$

12. $3s^3t - 13s^2t - 10st$

13. $19r^3s^3 - 3r^3s^2 + 10r^3s^2t$

14. $25m^4n + 16m^2n^3$

15. $49x^3y^4 - xy^4$

16. $c^3d^3 - 6c^2d^3 - 16cd^3$

17. $-14x^3y - 105x^2y + 189xy$

18. $16r^3s^3t^3 - 25rst$

19. $3m^2n^3 - 9m^2n^2 - 162m^2n$

20. $-28p^2q - 172p^2q^2 - 24p^2q^3$

21. $128a^3b^3 + 192a^2b^3 + 72ab^3$

22. $98z^5 + 245z^4 + 175z^3$

23. $36m^4n^2 - 168m^3n^3 + 27m^2n^4$

24. $539v^4w^4 + 462v^3w^3 + 99v^2w^2$

25. $375r^3s^3t^3 - 540rst$

26. $48z^3a^3 - 372z^2a^2 - 96za$

27. $175p^3q^4 - 40p^2q^4 - 15pq^4$

28. $-160m^3n + 608m^2n - 168mn$

29. $-2r^4t^3 + 10r^3t^3 - 12r^2t^3$

30. $5r^5t^2 - 320r^3t^2$

31. $9a^4b^3 + 21a^4b^2 + 12a^4b$

32. $567m^3n^3 - 252m^3n^2 + 28m^3n$

33. $63x^3y^4 + 42x^2y^4 + 7xy^4$

34. $5a^3w^2 + 10a^2w^2 - 315aw^2$

Factoring

Name _____

Date _____ Period _____

Factor.

1. $x^2 - ax + cx - ac$ $(x + c)(x - a)$

2. $c^2 + cd - ce - de$

3. $2a^2 + ab + 2ac + bc$

4. $3x^2 + xy - 3xz - yz$

5. $6x^2 + 3xy + 2xz + yz$

6. $10a^2 + 2ab + 5ad + bd$

7. $x^2 + 2xy + y^2 - z^2$

8. $a^2 + 2ab + b^2 - 9c^2$

9. $m^2 + 2mn + n^2 - 16p^2$

10. $r^2 + 2rs + s^2 - 36t^2$

11. $s^2 - m^2 + 2mn - n^2$

12. $a^2 - b^2 + 2bc - c^2$

13. $3a^3 + 3a^2b + 4a^2 + 4ab + a + b$

14. $x^3 + x^2y + 5x^2 + 5xy + 6x + 6y$

15. $x^2 + 2xy + y^2 + 4x + 4y + 4$

16. $a^2 + 2ab + b^2 + 6a + 6b + 9$

17. $16 + 8r + 8s + r^2 + 2rs + s^2$

18. $25 + 10m + 10n + m^2 + 2mn + n^2$

19. $6x^3 + 2x^2y + 21x^2 + 7xy + 15x + 5y$

20. $20a^3 + 5a^2b - 68a^2 - 17ab + 24a + 6b$

21. $8a^3 + 12a^2b - 24a^2 - 36ab + 18a + 27b$

22. $9x^3 + 6x^2y - 45x^2 - 30xy + 36x + 24y$

23. $6x^3 - 2x^2 - 21x^2y + 7xy - 45xy^2 + 15y^2$

24. $15x^2 + 30xy + 15y^2 - 7x - 7y - 2$

25. $8a^2 + 16ab + 8b^2 + 18a + 18b + 9$

26. $28c^2 + 56cd + 28d^2 - c - d - 2$

    85   Developing Skills in Algebra   Book B

Factoring

Name _____

Date _____ Period _____

Factor.

1. $ac + bc - ad - bd$ $(c - d)(a + b)$

2. $rt + st + ru + su$

3. $2a^2 + 3ab - 2ac - 3bc$

4. $6x^2 + 2xy - 3xz - yz$

5. $6m^2 + 4m - 9mn - 6n$

6. $10x^2 + 6x - 25xy - 15y$

7. $x^2 + 2xy + y^2 - 4z^2$

8. $a^2 + 2ab + b^2 - 16c^2$

9. $r^2 + 2rs + s^2 - 64t^2$

10. $c^2 + 2cd + d^2 - 81$

11. $x^2 - y^2 - 2yz - z^2$

12. $16a^2 - b^2 - 2bc - c^2$

13. $a^2 + 2ab + b^2 + 2a + 2b + 1$

14. $c^2 + 2cd + d^2 + 6c + 6d + 9$

15. $16 + 8r + 8s + r^2 + 2rs + s^2$

16. $25 + 10m + 10n + m^2 + 2mn + n^2$

17. $6x^3 + 2x^2 + 21x^2y + 7xy + 9xy^2 + 3y^2$

18. $6x^3 + 3x^2 + 14x^2y + 7xy + 8xy^2 + 4y^2$

19. $10x^2 + 2x^2y + 35x^2 + 7xy + 30x + 6y$

20. $12x^3 + 9x^2 - 52x^2y - 39xy - 40xy^2 - 30y^2$

21. $10m^3 - 25m^2 - 26m^2n + 65mn - 12mn^2 + 30n^2$

22. $6c^3 + 21c^2 - 18c^2d - 63cd - 24cd^2 - 84d^2$

23. $14r^3 + 7r^2t - 32r^2 - 16rt - 30r - 15t$

24. $35x^2 + 70xy + 35y^2 - 3x - 3y - 2$

25. $6x^2 + 12xy + 6y^2 - 7x - 7y - 5$

Developing Skills in Algebra   Book B

Factoring

Name _____

Date _____ Period _____

Factor.

1. $20ax^2 + 60ax + 45a$ $5a(2x+3)^2$

2. $p^2 + pq + tp + tq$

3. $5x^3 - 5cx^2 + 10x^2 - 10xc$

4. $54x^2y + 63xy + 9y$

5. $x^4 - 256$

6. $8x^4 + 88x^3 + 240x^2$

7. $13x^4 - 13x^3 - 260x^2$

8. $90a^2x^2 - 6a^2x - 12a^2$

9. $96mx^2 + 232mx + 120m$

10. $x^2 + 6xy + 9y^2 - 1$

11. $27a^3 - 48a$

12. $16 - x^4$

13. $a^2 - 4ab + 4b^2 - 4$

14. $6a^3 + 6a^2b - 18a^2 - 18ab$

15. $54x^2y^2 - 63xy^2 - 27y^2$

16. $63x^3 - 42x^2 + 7x$

17. $r^2 - rt - 5r + 5t$

18. $24p^3 - 24p^2q + 56p^2 - 56pq$

19. $12am^2 + 6amn - 30am - 15an$

20. $28x^4 - 175x^2$

21. $5x^3 - 15x^2y - 90xy^2$

22. $48tx^2 - 32tx - 60t$

23. $16a^4 - 81b^4$

24. $5x^5 + 50x^4 + 105x^3$

25. $72ax^2 - 84ax - 60a$

26. $14xyz + 21yz + 14xzt + 21zt$

27. $84x^4y^2 - 4x^3y^3 - 8x^2y^4$

28. $60a^3b - 78a^2b^2 - 18ab^3$

29. $2a^3z + 6a^2z^2 + 10a^2z + 30az^2$

30. $625 - 16a^4$

31. $a^2 + 2ab + b^2 + 3a + 3b + 2$

32. $x^2 + 2xy + y^2 - 5x - 5y - 14$

33. $a^2 + 2ab + b^2 - 3a - 3b - 10$

34. $x^2 + 2xy + y^2 + 11x + 11y + 28$

Factoring

Name _____

Date _____ Period _____

Factor.

1. $x^4 - 625y^4$ $(x-5y)(x+5y)(x^2+25y^2)$

2. $x^2 + 8xy + 16y^2 - 25$

3. $7r^3 - 14r^2 - 105r$

4. $7a^4 + 70a^3 + 147a^2$

5. $8ax^2 + 12ax + 4axy + 6ay$

6. $6p^2m - 6mpq + 21mp - 21mq$

7. $60a^2t^3 - 4at^3 - 8t^3$

8. $15x^3 + 10x^2 - 15x^2y - 10xy$

9. $27x^3 + 90x^2 + 75x$

10. $24a^3 + 90a^2 + 21a$

11. $10x^2z + 5xyz + 30xz + 15yz$

12. $13r^3 - 325r$

13. $120m^2n - 32mn - 24n$

14. $256 - 81r^4$

15. $x^2 - 10xy + 25y^2 - 16$

16. $c^2 + vc + 7c + 7v$

17. $18a^2r + 87ar + 84r$

18. $2401 - x^4$

19. $16x^4 - 625y^4$

20. $135z^2 - 63z^3 - 18z^4$

21. $a^2 - 2at + ab - 2bt$

22. $4a^6 + 36a^5 + 56a^4$

23. $175a^2x - 112x$

24. $18ab^2 + 3b^2 + 18abc + 3bc$

25. $48c^3 + 156c^2 + 90c$

26. $192r^3 - 288r^2 + 108r$

27. $6xyr + 9yr - 6xrz - 9rz$

28. $36a^5 - 15a^4 - 6a^3$

29. $5x^2m^2 - 15xm^2 - 50m^2$

30. $189r^4 - 261r^3 - 90r^2$

31. $16a^2 + 8ab + b^2 + 60a + 15b + 6$

32. $4a^2 - 4ab + b^2 + 16a - 8b + 15$

33. $9a^2 + 6ab + b^2 + 6a + 2b - 3$

34. $25a^2 + 10ab + b^2 + 25a + 5b + 4$

Polynomial Equations

Name _____

Date _____ Period _____

Solve.

1. $x^2 - 2x - 5 = 30$ $x = 7 \text{ or } -5$

2. $x^2 + 19x + 12 = -48$

3. $6x^2 + 53x - 50 = -12$

4. $10x^2 - 69x + 100 = -19$

5. $24x^2 - 2x = 15$

6. $14x^2 + 33x = 5$

7. $(x + 4)(x - 3) = 18$

8. $(x + 9)(x - 8) = 38$

9. $(2x + 5)(x + 7) = 180$

10. $(3x + 2)(x + 5) = 170$

11. $40x^2 + 25 = -67x - 3$

12. $21x^2 - 11 = 44x + 21$

13. $22x^2 + 81x + 14 = 0$

14. $39x^2 + 55x + 4 = 0$

15. $x^2 - 63 = 2x + 132$

16. $x^2 - 44 = 496 + 7x$

17. $63x^2 + 4x - 99 = 0$

18. $50x^2 - 55x + 12 = 0$

19. $(2x + 9)(3x - 11) = -8$

20. $(4x + 3)(7x - 4) = 38$

21. $4x^2 - 32x = -55$

22. $9x^2 - 48x = -63$

23. $90x^2 = 6 - 12x$

24. $91x^2 = 10 + 51x$

25. $3x^2 + 33x - 126 = 0$

26. $4x^2 + 40x - 96 = 0$

27. $20x^2 = 22x + 70$

28. $48x^2 = -54x - 15$ $12x^2 + 29x + 14$

29. $(2x + 11)(2x + 5) = 40$

30. $(3x + 2)(4x + 7) = -1$

31. $14x^2 + 197x + 14 = 0$

32. $13x^2 + 170x + 13 = 0$

33. $63x^2 + 20x - 12 = 20$

34. $35x^2 - 24x - 7 = 20$

    89   Developing Skills in Algebra   Book B

Polynomial Equations

Solve.

1. $x^2 - 8x - 50 = 55$ $x = 15 \text{ or } -7$

2. $x^2 - 6x - 72 = 40$

3. $3x^2 - 8x = 35$

4. $2x^2 - 3x = 54$

5. $14x^2 = 56$

6. $24x^2 = 6$

7. $35x^2 + 114x + 91 = 0$

8. $40x^2 + 133x + 99 = 0$

9. $(2x + 9)(x - 5) = 108$

10. $(3x - 11)(x + 2) = 28$

11. $77x^2 = 12 - 5x$

12. $108x^2 = 10 + 21x$

13. $18x^2 + 48x + 24 = 0$

14. $10x^2 + 55x + 75 = 0$

15. $140x^2 = 182x - 56$

16. $180x^2 = 210x - 60$

17. $7x^2 - 73x - 132 = 0$

18. $8x^2 - 79x - 99 = 0$

19. $(3x - 4)(2x + 5) = 323$

20. $(2x - 5)(3x + 7) = 35$

21. $44x^2 + 27x = 35$

22. $63x^2 + x = 12$

23. $48x^2 + 125x - 4 = 4$

24. $75x^2 + 50x - 2 = 6$

25. $28x^2 = 10 - 6x$

26. $30x^2 = 3 - 9x$

27. $10x^2 - 59x + 63 = 0$

28. $21x^2 - 73x + 56 = 0$

29. $(x + 8)(x - 4) = 288$

30. $(x + 11)(x - 7) = 448$

31. $14x^2 - 101x - 30 = 0$

32. $15x^2 + 32x - 28 = 0$

33. $48x^2 = 24 - 84x$

34. $45x^2 = 60 - 60x$

Polynomial Word Problems

Name _____

Date _____ Period _____

Show a complete solution for each problem.

1. A number and the square of that same number add to 42. Find the number.

n = the number $n + n^2 = 42$ The number is
                   $n^2 + n - 42 = 0$ either 6 or -7.
                   $(n - 6)(n + 7) = 0$
                   $n = 6$ or -7

2. The length of a rectangle is 11 cm more than its width. The area of the rectangle is 2040 cm^2. Find the dimensions of the rectangle.

3. The sum of two numbers is 28. The sum of the squares of the two numbers is 490. Find the numbers.

4. A rectangular lawn is 14 m long and 10 m wide. A strip of uniform width is mowed around the outside of the lawn. How wide is the strip when the area of the unmowed portion of the lawn is 12 m^2.

5. A rectangle is formed from a square by adding 6 m to one side and 3 m to the other side. The area of the rectangle is 238 m^2. Find the dimensions of the original square.

6. The formula $h = 300t - 6t^2$ gives the height, h, in meters, of a rocket t seconds after take-off. The maximum height reached by the rocket is 3750 m. How long will it take the rocket to reach this maximum height?

7. A rectangular garden is fenced on three sides with a wall forming the fourth side. The total length of the fence is 30 m. The area of the garden is 112 m^2. Find the dimensions of the garden.

8. The edge of one cube is 2 cm shorter than the edge of a second cube. The volumes of the two cubes differ by 386 cm^3. Find the edge of the smaller cube.

9. The square of the largest of three consecutive integers is 140 less than the sum of the squares of the two smaller integers. Find the three integers.

Polynomial Word Problems

Show a complete solution for each problem.

1. A number subtracted from its square is 110. Find the number.

    n = the number $n^2 - n = 110$ The number is
                        $(n - 11)(n + 10) = 0$ either 11 or -10.
                            $n = 11$ or -10

2. The width of a rectangle is 55 cm less than three times its length. The area of the rectangle is 100 cm^2. Find the dimensions of the rectangle.

3. The sum of two numbers is 32. The sum of the squares of the two numbers is 544. Find the numbers.

4. A picture that measures 8 cm × 10 cm has a border of uniform width surrounding it. The area of the picture and the border together is 224 cm^2. Find the width of the border.

5. A rectangle has length 40 cm and width 21 cm. If a new rectangle is formed by adding the same amount to both the length and the width, the new area is 2262 cm^2. Find the dimensions of the new rectangle.

6. The formula $h = 300t - 5t^2$ gives the height, h, in meters, of a rocket t seconds after take-off. The maximum height reached by the rocket is 4500 m. How long will it take the rocket to reach this maximum height?

7. A rectangular garden is fenced on three sides with a wall forming the fourth side. The total length of the fence is 80 m. The area of the garden is 750 m^2. Find the dimensions of the garden.

8. The edge of one cube is 3 cm shorter than the edge of a second cube. The volumes of the two cubes differ by 513 cm^3. Find the edge of the smaller cube.

9. The square of the largest of three consecutive integers is 320 less than the sum of the squares of the two smaller integers. Find the three integers.

          Developing Skills in Algebra   Book B

Polynomial Word Problems

Show a complete solution for each problem.

1. The square of a number is 81 less than 18 times the number. Find the number.

n = the number $n^2 = 18n - 81$ *The number is 9.*

$n^2 - 18n + 81 = 0$

$(n - 9)^2 = 0$

$n = 9$

2. A rectangle whose perimeter is 80 m has an area of 384 m². Find the dimensions of the rectangle.

3. The sum of two numbers is 23. The sum of the squares of the two numbers is 325. Find the numbers.

4. A swimming pool 20 m long and 10 m wide is surrounded by a deck of uniform width. The total area of the swimming pool and the deck is 704 m². Find the width of the deck.

5. If the radius of a circle is increased by 6 cm, the new area is 121π cm². Find the radius of the original circle.

6. The formula $h = 240t - 6t^2$ gives the height, h, in meters, of a rocket t seconds after take-off. The maximum height reached by the rocket is 2400 m. How long will it take the rocket to reach this maximum height?

7. A rectangular garden is fenced on three sides with a wall forming the fourth side. The total length of the fence is 70 m. The area of the garden is 600 m². Find the dimensions of the garden.

8. The edge of one cube is 4 m shorter than the edge of a second cube. The volumes of the two cubes differ by 1216 m³. Find the edge of the smaller cube.

9. The sum of the squares of the two larger of three consecutive even integers is 12 less than 4 times the square of the smaller one. Find the integers.

Polynomial Word Problems

Show a complete solution for each problem.

1. The sum of the squares of two consecutive positive integers is 365. Find the integers.

n = first integer $n^2 + (n+1)^2 = 365$ The integers
$n + 1$ = next integer $2n^2 + 2n - 364 = 0$ are 13 and 14.
                 $2(n - 13)(n - 14) = 0$
                     $n = 13$ or 14

2. The dimensions of a rectangle are 6 cm × 10 cm. A new rectangle is formed by increasing each dimension by the same amount. The area of the new rectangle is 80 cm² more than the area of the original rectangle. Find the dimensions of the new rectangle.

3. The sum of two numbers is 35. The sum of the squares of the two numbers is 613. Find the numbers.

4. A rectangular garden was 16 m wide and 30 m long. The area of the garden was increased to 912 m² by digging a uniform border around the garden. Find the width of the border.

5. A rectangle was 25 cm longer than it was wide. A new rectangle was formed by decreasing the length by 6 cm and decreasing the width 5 cm. The area of the new rectangle was 585 cm². Find the dimensions of the original rectangle.

6. The formula $h = 280t - 7t^2$ gives the height, h, in meters, of a rocket t seconds after take-off. The maximum height reached by the rocket is 2800 m. How long will it take the rocket to reach this maximum height?

7. A rectangular garden is fenced on three sides with a wall forming the fourth side. The total length of the fence is 120 m. The area of the garden is 1600 m². Find the dimensions of the garden.

8. The edge of one cube is 5 cm shorter than the edge of a second cube. The volumes of the two cubes differ by 875 cm³. Find the edge of the smaller cube.

9. The sum of the squares of the largest and smallest of three consecutive odd integers is 353 less than three times the square of the middle one. Find the integers.

         94   Developing Skills in Algebra   Book B

Fractions   Name _____

                                             Date _____ Period _____

Reduce each fraction to lowest terms. Assume no denominator is 0.

1. $\dfrac{r(t+2)}{r(t-7)}$ $\dfrac{t+2}{t-7}$

2. $\dfrac{a(b+1)}{a(b-1)}$

3. $\dfrac{m(n+t)}{n(n+t)}$

4. $\dfrac{c(r+s)}{d(r+s)}$

5. $\dfrac{3x+xy}{4x+xy}$

6. $\dfrac{2y+xy}{3y+xy}$

7. $\dfrac{ab+ac}{b^2+bc}$

8. $\dfrac{mx-my}{nx-ny}$

9. $\dfrac{6x+21}{8x+28}$

10. $\dfrac{27y-81}{15y-45}$

11. $\dfrac{3a^2bm-a^2bn}{2a^2bm+a^2bn}$

12. $\dfrac{3xmn^2-2mn^2}{3xmn^2+2mn^2}$

13. $\dfrac{15x^4y^2+6x^3y^2}{6x^4y^2-15x^3y^3}$

14. $\dfrac{15a^3b+10a^2b^2}{10a^3b-25a^2b^2}$

15. $\dfrac{42x^3y^4+18x^2y^6}{18x^3y^4-12x^2y^6}$

16. $\dfrac{27m^2n^5-63mn^7}{18m^2n^5+27mn^7}$

17. $\dfrac{5a^2-25a}{35a-7a^2}$

18. $\dfrac{10bx-30by}{27by-9bx}$

19. $\dfrac{30x^2y^2-20x^2y}{14xy^2-21xy^3}$

20. $\dfrac{120a^3b^2n-75a^3b^2m}{40abm-64abn}$

21. $\dfrac{12abx^2+6abx-30ab}{36a^2bx^2-12a^2bx+108a^2b}$

22. $\dfrac{36m^2nx^2+84m^2nx-24m^2n}{18mn^2x^2-81mn^2x+27mn^2}$

23. $\dfrac{r^2-3r-10}{r^2-r-6}$

24. $\dfrac{m^2+5m-24}{m^2+3m-40}$

25. $\dfrac{2p^2-pq-3q^2}{6p^2-11p+3q^2}$

26. $\dfrac{3a^2-5a-2}{3a^2-14a-5}$

Fractions

Reduce each fraction to lowest terms. Assume no denominator is 0.

1. $\dfrac{a(b-5)}{a(b+3)}$ $(b-5)/(b+3)$

2. $\dfrac{c(t+2)}{c(t+3)}$

3. $\dfrac{x(r+m)}{y(r+m)}$

4. $\dfrac{a(c+d)}{b(c+d)}$

5. $\dfrac{3y-3r}{3y+3r}$

6. $\dfrac{2c+7cm}{4c+7cm}$

7. $\dfrac{mx+nx}{ym+yn}$

8. $\dfrac{tr+ts}{rv+sv}$

9. $\dfrac{4x+20}{5x+25}$

10. $\dfrac{36x-90}{30x-75}$

11. $\dfrac{2x^2yz-5x^2y}{2x^2yz+3x^2y}$

12. $\dfrac{5rt^2x+3rt^2}{5xrt^2-3rt^2}$

13. $\dfrac{8a^3b^3-12a^3b^2}{12a^3b^3+18a^3b^2}$

14. $\dfrac{12a^2x+18abx}{16a^2x-24abx}$

15. $\dfrac{40x^4y+16x^2y^3}{60x^2y^2-36xy^3}$

16. $\dfrac{21r^2s^2+14rs^3}{28r^2s^2+42rs^3}$

17. $\dfrac{9r^2-27r}{8r^2-24r}$

18. $\dfrac{30ab-45ac}{40b^2-60bc}$

19. $\dfrac{60a^2b^2-48a^3b}{75ab^2-60a^2b}$

20. $\dfrac{80a^3b^2-60a^2bc}{120a^2b^3-90ab^2c}$

21. $\dfrac{12acx^2+8acx+36ac}{30acx^2-6acx+42ac}$

22. $\dfrac{45r^3s+27r^2s+108rs}{90r^3s+30r^2s+105rs}$

23. $\dfrac{x^2-3x-10}{x^2-2x-15}$

24. $\dfrac{m^2-m-6}{m^2-8m+15}$

25. $\dfrac{4x^2-9y^2}{4x^2+4xy-15y^2}$

26. $\dfrac{3r^2+r-10}{2r^2+3r-2}$

Fractions

Name _____

Date _____ Period _____

Multiply. Answers must be reduced to lowest terms. Assume no denominator is 0.

1. $\dfrac{a^3}{3b} \cdot \dfrac{9b^3}{a}$ $3a^2b^2$

2. $\dfrac{b^2}{5c} \cdot \dfrac{15c^3}{b^4}$

3. $\dfrac{m^2}{2n} \cdot \dfrac{16n^4}{5m^5}$

4. $\dfrac{3z^4}{10y^4} \cdot \dfrac{20y^2}{9z}$

5. $\dfrac{8xy^4}{5z^3} \cdot \dfrac{15z}{28x^3y}$

6. $\dfrac{12x^3y^4}{35ab^3} \cdot \dfrac{21a^3b}{36xy^2}$

7. $\dfrac{9m^4n^3}{8r^4} \cdot \dfrac{28r^2}{27m^2n^5}$

8. $\dfrac{42a^7b}{25r^2t} \cdot \dfrac{35r^3t}{36a^5b^4}$

9. $\dfrac{x-2}{3a+1} \cdot \dfrac{6a+2}{x+2}$

10. $\dfrac{a-b}{a+3b} \cdot \dfrac{a+2b}{3a-3b}$

11. $\dfrac{m+n}{m+2n} \cdot \dfrac{2m+4n}{5m+5n}$

12. $\dfrac{3x+y}{x+y} \cdot \dfrac{2x+2y}{15x+5y}$

13. $\dfrac{2m+2n}{b-a} \cdot \dfrac{a-b}{3n+3m}$

14. $\dfrac{4x+2y}{x-y} \cdot \dfrac{y-x}{6x+3y}$

15. $\dfrac{5r+15s}{2x-1} \cdot \dfrac{1-2x}{5s+10r}$

16. $\dfrac{4b+2c}{3b-2c} \cdot \dfrac{2c-3b}{2b-2c}$

17. $\dfrac{x+y}{x-y} \cdot \dfrac{x^2-y^2}{3x+3y}$

18. $\dfrac{2r+s}{r-s} \cdot \dfrac{r^2-s^2}{2r-s}$

19. $\dfrac{6b-3a}{a+b} \cdot \dfrac{b^2-a^2}{8b-4a}$

20. $\dfrac{2x+3}{2x+1} \cdot \dfrac{1-4x^2}{2x+5}$

21. $\dfrac{3xy+3y^2}{8x^2y} \cdot \dfrac{10x}{x^2-y^2}$

22. $\dfrac{4a^2-4ab}{9a^2b} \cdot \dfrac{21a^3b}{a^2-b^2}$

23. $\dfrac{10rs+25r}{8r^2s^2} \cdot \dfrac{12r^3s^3}{4s^2-25}$

24. $\dfrac{25a^3b^3}{3ab-3} \cdot \dfrac{a^2b^2-1}{35a^2b}$

25. $\dfrac{3x^2-3y^2}{15x+5y} \cdot \dfrac{5x^3y}{6y-6x}$

26. $\dfrac{7a+14b}{6b+3a} \cdot \dfrac{12ab}{4b^2-a^2}$

Developing Skills in Algebra   Book B

Fractions

Multiply. Answers must be reduced to lowest terms. Assume no denominator is 0.

1. $\dfrac{x^5}{4y} \cdot \dfrac{16y^3}{x^2}$ $4x^3y^2$

2. $\dfrac{7c^3}{d^4} \cdot \dfrac{d^2}{21c^2}$

3. $\dfrac{12r^5}{t^2} \cdot \dfrac{t^5}{15r^2}$

4. $\dfrac{a^7}{10b^3} \cdot \dfrac{15b}{a^2}$

5. $\dfrac{13a^2b^3}{9cd^2} \cdot \dfrac{12c^3d}{26ab^3}$

6. $\dfrac{25m^2n^3}{8rt^3} \cdot \dfrac{20r^3t}{15mn^4}$

7. $\dfrac{39x^3y}{44z^5} \cdot \dfrac{55z^3}{26xy^2}$

8. $\dfrac{12c^4}{25ab^3} \cdot \dfrac{35a^2b^5}{16c^2}$

9. $\dfrac{a-3}{b+3} \cdot \dfrac{b-3}{2a-6}$

10. $\dfrac{r+s}{2r-s} \cdot \dfrac{6r-3s}{2r+s}$

11. $\dfrac{3x+1}{10x+5} \cdot \dfrac{2x+1}{2x+3}$

12. $\dfrac{r+2}{3r-1} \cdot \dfrac{3r+1}{4r+8}$

13. $\dfrac{3a-3b}{2a+1} \cdot \dfrac{4a+2}{2b-3a}$

14. $\dfrac{5r+5s}{2r-3s} \cdot \dfrac{3s-2r}{5r+10y}$

15. $\dfrac{2x-3y}{5x+15y} \cdot \dfrac{10x+15y}{3y-2x}$

16. $\dfrac{14x+6y}{3x-y} \cdot \dfrac{y-3x}{21x+9y}$

17. $\dfrac{5a+5b}{a-b} \cdot \dfrac{a^2-b^2}{6a+6b}$

18. $\dfrac{x^2-y^2}{2y+4x} \cdot \dfrac{6x+3y}{y-x}$

19. $\dfrac{2r+3}{4r^2-1} \cdot \dfrac{1-2r}{6+4r}$

20. $\dfrac{4x-3y}{6x+3y} \cdot \dfrac{10x+5y}{16x^2-9y^2}$

21. $\dfrac{5a+10b}{14ab} \cdot \dfrac{21a^3}{a^2-4b^2}$

22. $\dfrac{2a+3}{9a^2-16} \cdot \dfrac{3a+4}{6a+9}$

23. $\dfrac{25r^3s}{16r^2-25s^2} \cdot \dfrac{4r-5s}{15rs^3}$

24. $\dfrac{100a^2-81b^2}{14a^2b^2} \cdot \dfrac{21a^3b^4}{10a+9b}$

25. $\dfrac{5t+15s}{49t^2-25s^2} \cdot \dfrac{5s-7t}{12s+8t}$

26. $\dfrac{64m^2-1}{6m+9} \cdot \dfrac{10m+15}{8m+1}$

    98   Developing Skills in Algebra   Book B

Fractions

Name _____

Date _____ Period _____

Multiply. Answers must be reduced to lowest terms. Assume no denominator is 0.

1. $\dfrac{x+5}{(x+3)(x+2)} \cdot \dfrac{3(x+2)}{x^2-25}$ $\dfrac{3}{(x+3)(x-5)}$

2. $\dfrac{a^2-9}{(a+4)(a-2)} \cdot \dfrac{5(a+4)}{a+3}$

3. $\dfrac{(x+7)(x-3)}{4x^2-1} \cdot \dfrac{2x-1}{x+7}$

4. $\dfrac{a+5}{5a+3} \cdot \dfrac{25a^2-9}{(a+5)(a+3)}$

5. $\dfrac{(x+1)(x+4)}{x-3} \cdot \dfrac{x(x-3)}{x+4}$

6. $\dfrac{(x-2)(x-5)}{(x+5)} \cdot \dfrac{x(x+5)}{x-2}$

7. $\dfrac{r^3+3r}{r+2} \cdot \dfrac{r^2-5r-14}{r^4+3r^3}$

8. $\dfrac{p+5q}{p^2-pq-6q^2} \cdot \dfrac{p-3q}{q^2p+5q^3}$

9. $\dfrac{x^2+y^2}{2x^2-xy-21y^2} \cdot \dfrac{x^2+2xy-3y^2}{x^4-y^4}$

10. $\dfrac{4a^2+9}{4a^2+8a+3} \cdot \dfrac{4a^2-9}{16a^4-81}$

11. $\dfrac{r^2+rs-6s^2}{r^2+s^2} \cdot \dfrac{r^4-s^4}{r^2-3rs+2s^2}$

12. $\dfrac{r^2-s^2}{2r^2+rs-3s^2} \cdot \dfrac{2r^2+13rs+15s^2}{r+s}$

13. $\dfrac{3x^2+16x+5}{2x^2-5x-12} \cdot \dfrac{2x^2-9x+4}{3x^2+7x+2}$

14. $\dfrac{4a^2+6a-4}{a^2-12a+35} \cdot \dfrac{2a^2-17a+35}{4a^2+2a-12}$

15. $\dfrac{4m^2-5mn-6n^2}{m^2+3n+2n^2} \cdot \dfrac{m^2+mn-2n^2}{4m^2-mn-3n^2}$

16. $\dfrac{2r^2+rs-3s^2}{2r^2-5rs+3s^2} \cdot \dfrac{2r^2+rs-s^2}{2r^2-3rs+s^2}$

17. $\dfrac{3x-3}{2x^2-7x-15} \cdot \dfrac{2x^2-5x-12}{1-x^2}$

18. $\dfrac{y^2-xy-12x^2}{x^2-y^2} \cdot \dfrac{5y-5x}{y^2+xy-6x^2}$

19. $\dfrac{a^2-2a-15}{16-9a^2} \cdot \dfrac{6a-8}{2a^2-9a-5}$

20. $\dfrac{100-169a^2}{10a^2+11a+3} \cdot \dfrac{10a^2+a-3}{26a-20}$

21. $\dfrac{3r^2+7rt+2t^2}{7r^2t} \cdot \dfrac{14t^2+14tr}{3r^2+4rt+t^2}$

22. $\dfrac{2x^2-3xy-9y^2}{21x^2y} \cdot \dfrac{14x^2+7xy}{2x^2-5xy-3y^2}$

23. $\dfrac{6m^2+5mn+n^2}{12m^2-24mn} \cdot \dfrac{3m^2-21mn+30n^2}{2m^2-9mn-5n^2}$

24. $\dfrac{6x^2+xy-y^2}{8x^2-40xy} \cdot \dfrac{6x-30y}{12x^2-64xy+20y^2}$

25. $\dfrac{9a+18b}{12a^2-3b^2} \cdot \dfrac{5b-10a}{5a^2+15ab+10b^2}$

26. $\dfrac{15-20a}{3a^2+3a-6} \cdot \dfrac{12a-12}{80a^2-45}$

Fractions

Name _____

Date _____ Period _____

Multiply. Answers must be reduced to lowest terms. Assume no denominator is 0.

1. $\dfrac{5(x-1)}{x^2-49} \cdot \dfrac{x+7}{(x+2)(x-1)}$ $\quad \dfrac{5}{(x-7)(x+2)}$

2. $\dfrac{4(a+2b)}{9a^2-b^2} \cdot \dfrac{(3a+b)(2a-b)}{(a+2b)(a-b)}$

3. $\dfrac{6(x+2)}{3(4x-1)} \cdot \dfrac{16x^2-1}{(x+2)(x-3)}$

4. $\dfrac{10(5x+3)}{2x+3} \cdot \dfrac{(2x+1)(2x+3)}{25x^2-9}$

5. $\dfrac{(x+3)(x-5)}{x-4} \cdot \dfrac{x(x-4)}{x-5}$

6. $\dfrac{a(a-3b)}{a^2(a+2b)} \cdot \dfrac{a+2b}{(a-3b)(a+4b)}$

7. $\dfrac{x^2-4x-21}{2x+1} \cdot \dfrac{2x^3+x^2}{x^2-7x}$

8. $\dfrac{m^3-2m^2n}{m^2+mn} \cdot \dfrac{m+n}{m^2+mn-6n^2}$

9. $\dfrac{16a^4-1}{2a^2+5a-3} \cdot \dfrac{2a^2+9a+9}{4a^2+1}$

10. $\dfrac{x^2+16}{x^2+2x-3} \cdot \dfrac{x^2-x-12}{x^4-256}$

11. $\dfrac{15x-10}{81x^4-16} \cdot \dfrac{9x^2+4}{30x+10}$

12. $\dfrac{45-18a}{75+3a^2} \cdot \dfrac{625-a^4}{25-5a-2a^2}$

13. $\dfrac{2x^2+13x+15}{5x^2-13x-6} \cdot \dfrac{5x^2-3x-2}{4x^2+4x-3}$

14. $\dfrac{3a^2-16a+5}{a^2+a-30} \cdot \dfrac{2a^2+15a+18}{3a^2+5a-2}$

15. $\dfrac{5r^2+7r+2}{6r^2-r-1} \cdot \dfrac{3r^2-2r-1}{5r^2-3r-2}$

16. $\dfrac{14a^2+13a+3}{4a^2+9a+2} \cdot \dfrac{2a^2+3a-2}{14a^2-15a-9}$

17. $\dfrac{4a-4b}{4a^2+4ab-3b^2} \cdot \dfrac{2a^2+5ab+3b^2}{b^2-a^2}$

18. $\dfrac{2x^2+xy-y^2}{5x-5y} \cdot \dfrac{y^2-x^2}{x^2-2xy-3y^2}$

19. $\dfrac{2r^2+3rs+s^2}{4s^2-r^2} \cdot \dfrac{3r+6s}{2r^2-rs-s^2}$

20. $\dfrac{9y^2-4x^2}{y^2+xy-6x^2} \cdot \dfrac{x^2+5xy+6y^2}{10x-15y}$

21. $\dfrac{3x^3-9x^2-30x}{x^2+x-2} \cdot \dfrac{x^2+2x-3}{6x^4-12x^3-90x^2}$

22. $\dfrac{10y^2-20y-80}{y^2+4y-21} \cdot \dfrac{y^2+2y-35}{5y^2-45y+100}$

23. $\dfrac{x^2-2x-15}{10x^3-20x^2-80x} \cdot \dfrac{5x^2+5x-10}{x^2-6x+5}$

24. $\dfrac{2y^2-4y-30}{2y^2+y-3} \cdot \dfrac{y^2+y-2}{4y^4+20y^3+24y^2}$

25. $\dfrac{x^2+4xy+3y^2}{10x^2-10y^2} \cdot \dfrac{15y-15x}{x^2+xy-6y^2}$

26. $\dfrac{b^2+ab-6a^2}{15b-15a} \cdot \dfrac{12a^2-12b^2}{b^2-5ab+6a^2}$

Developing Skills in Algebra   Book B

Name _____

Date _____ Period _____

Divide. Answers must be reduced to lowest terms. Assume no denominator is 0.

1. $\dfrac{y+6}{y^2} \div \dfrac{1}{y^5}$ $y^3(y+6)$

2. $\dfrac{2x+5}{y^4} \div \dfrac{1}{y^3}$

3. $\dfrac{8x^4}{4y} \div 2x^3y^2$

4. $\dfrac{12x^7}{3y^2} \div 4x^2y$

5. $\dfrac{x-y}{x^2y^2} \div \dfrac{x-y}{xy^3}$

6. $\dfrac{2x-y}{2xy^3} \div \dfrac{2x-y}{2x^2y^3}$

7. $\dfrac{x+y}{3x-y} \div \dfrac{1}{9x^2-6xy+y^2}$

8. $\dfrac{x-y}{2x+3y} \div \dfrac{1}{4x^2+12xy+9y^2}$

9. $\dfrac{x}{8-4y} \div \dfrac{x^2}{6-3y}$

10. $\dfrac{x^2}{10-4y} \div \dfrac{x^2}{50-20y}$

11. $\dfrac{x^2-81}{9x-81} \div \dfrac{x^2+16x+63}{x^3+7x^2}$

12. $\dfrac{x^2-49}{7x-49} \div \dfrac{x^2+13x+42}{x^3+6x^2}$

13. $\dfrac{x^2+12x+32}{x^2+15x+44} \div \dfrac{x^2+11x+24}{x^2+8x+15}$

14. $\dfrac{x^2+12x+27}{x^2+6x-7} \div \dfrac{x^2+16x+63}{x^2-13x+12}$

15. $\dfrac{2x^2-17x-30}{x^2-7x-18} \div \dfrac{2x^2+7x+6}{x^2-6x-40}$

16. $\dfrac{3x^2-28x+9}{x^2-3x-54} \div \dfrac{3x^2+35x-12}{x^2+19x+84}$

17. $\dfrac{20x^2+37x+15}{4x^2+x-5} \div \dfrac{10x^2-9x-9}{2x^2-5x+3}$

18. $\dfrac{21x^2+29x-10}{3x^2+8x+5} \div \dfrac{7x^2+40x-12}{x^2+5x-6}$

19. $\dfrac{20x^2+48x-5}{3x^2+7x-40} \div \dfrac{8x^2+34x+35}{12x^2-11x-56}$

20. $\dfrac{16x^2-46x+15}{6x^2-11x-10} \div \dfrac{96x^2-68x+12}{9x^2+3x-2}$

21. $\dfrac{10x^2+29x+10}{2x^2-9x-35} \div \dfrac{15x^2-14x-8}{6x^2+7x-20}$

22. $\dfrac{42x^2+85x+42}{6x^2+61x+63} \div \dfrac{35x^2+44x+12}{5x^2+47x+18}$

23. $\dfrac{56x^2+56x+14}{2x^2-3x-2} \div \dfrac{4x^2-1}{2x^2+5x-3}$

24. $\dfrac{96x^2+96x+24}{7x^2-9x+2} \div \dfrac{4x^2+4x+1}{21x^2+22x-8}$

25. $\dfrac{36x^2+63x+20}{6x^2-7x-20} \div \dfrac{12x^2-103x-45}{x^2-81}$

26. $\dfrac{26x^2+73x+20}{39x^2-x-4} \div \dfrac{16x^2+34x-15}{16x^2-14x+3}$

Developing Skills in Algebra   Book B

Fractions

Name _____

Date _____ Period _____

Divide. Answers must be reduced to lowest terms. Assume no denominator is 0.

1. $\dfrac{y-5}{y^3} \div \dfrac{1}{y^2}$ $\dfrac{y-5}{y}$

2. $\dfrac{3y-2}{y^3} \div \dfrac{1}{y^7}$

3. $\dfrac{8x^6}{2y^2} \div 2x^2y^4$

4. $\dfrac{15x^5}{5y^4} \div 9x^3y^3$

5. $\dfrac{x+y}{x^3y^3} \div \dfrac{x+y}{x^2y}$

6. $\dfrac{3x-2y}{3x^4y^5} \div \dfrac{3x-2y}{3x^5y^4}$

7. $\dfrac{x-y}{4x+2y} \div \dfrac{1}{4x^2+4xy+y^2}$

8. $\dfrac{2x+5y}{5x+2y} \div \dfrac{1}{25x^2+20x+4y^2}$

9. $\dfrac{4x}{5x-15} \div \dfrac{8x^2}{7x-21}$

10. $\dfrac{3x^3}{4x+16} \div \dfrac{15x^2}{11x+44}$

11. $\dfrac{4x^2-1}{6x-6} \div \dfrac{2x^2+5x-3}{3x^3+9x^2}$

12. $\dfrac{9x^2-4}{15x+10} \div \dfrac{3x^2+7x-6}{7x^2+21x}$

13. $\dfrac{2x^2+x-21}{x^2+x-12} \div \dfrac{2x^2+5x-7}{x^2+9x+20}$

14. $\dfrac{3x^2+x-10}{2x^2+3x-2} \div \dfrac{3x^2+7x-20}{x^2+x-12}$

15. $\dfrac{7x^2-27x-4}{x^2-2x-15} \div \dfrac{7x^2+22x+3}{2x^2-9x-5}$

16. $\dfrac{5x^2+17x+6}{x^2+7x+12} \div \dfrac{5x^2-33x-14}{x^2-10x+21}$

17. $\dfrac{6x^2+x-1}{6x^2+7x+2} \div \dfrac{3x^2-16x+5}{x^2-x-20}$

18. $\dfrac{6x^2-5x-25}{6x^2-11x-35} \div \dfrac{2x^2+11x-40}{x^2+11x+24}$

19. $\dfrac{16x^2-18x-9}{8x^2-59x+21} \div \dfrac{2x^2-7x-15}{x^2+4x-45}$

20. $\dfrac{12x^2+5x-2}{16x^2-1} \div \dfrac{9x^2+3x-2}{3x^2+14x-5}$

21. $\dfrac{20x^2-64x-21}{6x^2-13x-28} \div \dfrac{30x^2+49x+12}{5x^2-7x-6}$

22. $\dfrac{15x^2+x-2}{20x^2-7x-6} \div \dfrac{4x^2+25x-21}{4x^2+31x+21}$

23. $\dfrac{24x^2+44x-28}{2x^2-7x+3} \div \dfrac{9x^2-49}{x^2+2x-15}$

24. $\dfrac{45x^2+57x+18}{20x^2+7x-3} \div \dfrac{12x^2+11x+2}{20x^2+17x+3}$

25. $\dfrac{35x^2+3x-2}{35x^2+31x+6} \div \dfrac{10x^2+13x-3}{5x^2+28x+15}$

26. $\dfrac{6x^2+17x+7}{3x^2+22x+35} \div \dfrac{2x^2-17x-9}{x^2-25}$

© 1984 by Dale Seymour Publications   102   Developing Skills in Algebra   Book B

Name _____

Date _____ Period _____

Simplify. Assume no denominator is 0.

1. $\dfrac{2x^2}{3y^2} \cdot \dfrac{12a^2}{5y} \div \dfrac{4ab}{25y}$ $\dfrac{10ax^2}{by^2}$

2. $\dfrac{16a^2b}{33xy} \div \dfrac{14b}{11y} \div \dfrac{7a}{3}$

3. $\dfrac{2(a+b)^2}{3(x+y)^2} \cdot \dfrac{4(x+y)}{9(a+b)} \div \dfrac{7(a+b)}{3(x+y)}$

4. $\dfrac{3x}{4x-5} \div \dfrac{2x+5}{25-20x} \cdot \dfrac{1}{6x}$

5. $\dfrac{a-b}{4a^2b} \div \dfrac{a^2-b^2}{3ab} \cdot \dfrac{2b}{2a+1}$

6. $\dfrac{2x-3y}{9x-6} \div \dfrac{x+1}{6x-4} \cdot \dfrac{2x+2}{3y-2x}$

7. $\dfrac{3xy^2}{x^2+y^2} \cdot \dfrac{x^2+y^2}{6} \div \dfrac{x^2-y^2}{x+y}$

8. $\dfrac{n^2+n-2}{n+2} \div \dfrac{n-1}{5n^2} \cdot \dfrac{1}{n-1}$

9. $\dfrac{2x+y}{3x^2} \cdot \dfrac{x-1}{6xy} \div \dfrac{6x+3y}{x+1}$

10. $\dfrac{2x-y}{x+y} \div \dfrac{6x-3y}{3y} \cdot \dfrac{4x+4y}{xy}$

11. $\dfrac{3x-1}{1-2x} \div \dfrac{x+y}{2xy} \div \dfrac{4-12x}{x+2y}$

12. $\dfrac{2x^2-5xy-3y^2}{25x^2+15xy+2y^2} \div \dfrac{2x^2+7xy+3y^2}{5x^2-18xy-8y^2} \cdot \dfrac{x-4y}{3y^2-4xy+x^2}$

13. $\dfrac{9a^2+6ab+b^2}{6a^2+5ab+b^2} \cdot \dfrac{a^2+10ab+25b^2}{3a^2+7ab+2b^2} \div \dfrac{3a^2+16ab+5b^2}{2a^2+5ab+2b^2}$

Developing Skills in Algebra   Book B

Name _____

Date _____ Period _____

Simplify. Assume no denominator is 0.

1. $\dfrac{5x^3}{7y^2} \cdot \dfrac{16y^3}{15xy} \div \dfrac{8x}{21y}$ *2xy*

2. $\dfrac{28rs^3}{25mn} \div \dfrac{7r^3s}{5ab} \div \dfrac{6ab^2}{5mn}$

3. $\dfrac{5(r + s)^2}{9(t + u)^2} \div \dfrac{3(t + u)}{8(r + s)} \div \dfrac{10(t + u)}{4(r + s)}$

4. $\dfrac{5x}{2x - 1} \div \dfrac{2x + 3}{12x - 6} \cdot \dfrac{1}{15x^2}$

5. $\dfrac{x^2 - y^2}{5x^2y} \cdot \dfrac{x - y}{3xy} \div \dfrac{x + y}{10xy^2}$

6. $\dfrac{4a - 5b}{3a + 2} \cdot \dfrac{6a + 4}{2a + 1} \cdot \dfrac{2a + 1}{8a - 10b}$

7. $\dfrac{4ab^3}{16a^2 - 9b^2} \cdot \dfrac{8a + 6b}{2a + b} \div \dfrac{10a^2b^2}{4a - 3b}$

8. $\dfrac{r^2 - r - 6}{r - 4} \div \dfrac{r - 3}{r + 2} \cdot \dfrac{r - 4}{r + 2}$

9. $\dfrac{5x - 2y}{4x^2} \cdot \dfrac{10xy^2}{15x - 6y} \div \dfrac{2x + 3y}{3x}$

10. $\dfrac{8x - 3y}{5x - 2} \div \dfrac{2x - 3y}{2x - 5} \cdot \dfrac{4x - 6y}{9y - 24x}$

11. $\dfrac{3x - 12y}{10x + 15y} \cdot \dfrac{x + 3y}{4y - x} \div \dfrac{x + 6y}{2x + 3y}$

12. $\dfrac{8a^2 + 6ab + b^2}{5a^2 - 6ab + b^2} \cdot \dfrac{5a^2 + 9ab - 2b^2}{12a^2 + 7ab + b^2} \div \dfrac{2a^2 + 5ab + 2b^2}{b^2 - a^2}$

13. $\dfrac{m^2 + mn - 12n^2}{m^2 + 3mn + 2n^2} \cdot \dfrac{m^2 + 4mn + 3n^2}{3m^2 - 2mn - n^2} \div \dfrac{m^2 + 7mn + 12n^2}{m^2 + mn - 2n^2}$

         Developing Skills in Algebra   Book B

Name _____

Date _____ Period _____

Find the least common multiple for each pair.

1. $(4ac, 12ab)$ $12\,abc$

2. $(3xy, 9yz)$

3. $(15mn, 5nt)$

4. $(20bc, 10cd)$

5. $(8r^2s, 12rs^2)$

6. $(15x^2y, 20x^2y^2)$

7. $(15ab^2, 25a^2b^3)$

8. $(30m^2n, 35mn^3)$

9. $[(x-y)(x+y), (x-y)(x+y)^2]$

10. $[(r-2s)(r+3s), (r-2s)^2(r+3s)]$

11. $[(2x+1)(2x-1)^2, (2x+1)^2(2x-1)]$

12. $[(a+3b)(a+2b)^2, (a+3b)^2(a+2b)]$

13. $[(x+3)(x+4), (x+3)(x-4)]$

14. $[(2a+3)(2a-1), (2a-1)(3a+2)]$

15. $[(x+5)(x-1), (x-1)(x+3)]$

16. $[(3a+2)(3a-1), (3a+2)(2a+1)]$

17. $(x^2-y^2, x^2+xy-2y^2)$

18. $(a^2-b^2, 2a^2+3ab+b^2)$

19. $(4a^2-9b^2, 4a^2+12ab+9b^2)$

20. $(2a^2+11a+5, a^2-25)$

21. $(a^2-2a-15, a^2+a-6)$

22. $(x^2-2xy-3y^2, x^2-xy-2y^2)$

23. $(2a^2+7a+3, 2a^2+5a-3)$

24. $(4a^2-b^2, b^2+ab-6a^2)$

25. $(m^2-9n^2, 6n^2-5mn+m^2)$

26. $(y^2-8xy+15x^2, 25x^2-y^2)$

27. $(x^2-y^2, y^2+xy-2x^2)$

28. $(x^2+x-20, x^2+2x-24)$

29. $(9x^2-9x-10, 6x^2-x-15)$

30. $(4x^2+8x+3, 6x^2+7x-3)$

31. $(4r^2+12rs+5s^2, 8r^3+20r^2s-2rs^2-5s^3)$

32. $(25x^2-5xy-6y^2, 125x^3-50x^2y-45xy^2-18y^3)$

Developing Skills in Algebra   Book B

Name _____

Date _____ Period _____

Find the least common multiple for each pair

1. $(3mn, 12nt)$ $12\,m\,n\,t$

2. $(25xy, 5xz)$

3. $(20rs, 4st)$

4. $(7ab, 14bc)$

5. $(15rs^3, 20r^2s)$

6. $(12m^2n^2, 20m^3n)$

7. $(12a^3b, 18ab^3)$

8. $(21xy^3, 35x^2y)$

9. $[(x - 5)(x - 1)^2, (x - 5)(x - 1)]$

10. $[(3x + 2)(2x - 1), (2x - 1)^2(3x + 2)]$

11. $[(x + 2)^2(x + 3), (x + 2)(x + 3)]$

12. $[(x - 7)(x - 3)^2, (x - 7)(x - 3)]$

13. $[(x - 5)(x + 2), (x - 5)(x + 3)]$

14. $[(2x + 1)(2x + 3), (2x + 3)(2x - 5)]$

15. $[(2x + 1)(x + 3), (2x + 1)(x + 4)]$

16. $[(3x - 1)(x + 2), (3x - 1)(x + 3)]$

17. $(p^2 - q^2, p^2 + pq - 2q^2)$

18. $(r^2 + 5rs + 6s^2, r^2 - 4s^2)$

19. $(m^2 + 5mn + 6n^2, m^2 - 9n^2)$

20. $(4x^2 - 9y^2, 4x^2 + 8xy + 3y^2)$

21. $(x^2 - xy - 6y^2, x^2 - 2xy - 8y^2)$

22. $(6a^2 - a - 1, 3a^2 - 5a - 2)$

23. $(8r^2 - 16rs + 6s^2, 4r^2 + 4rs - 3s^2)$

24. $(4m^2 + 8mn + 3n^2, 4m^2 - 18mn - 10n^2)$

25. $(x^2 - 4y^2, 2y^2 - 7xy + 3x^2)$

26. $(3a^2 + 7ab - 6b^2, 4b^2 - 9a^2)$

27. $(2x^2 + xy - 15y^2, 25y^2 - 4x^2)$

28. $(16m^2 - n^2, n^2 - 2mn - 8m^2)$

29. $(25x^2 + 5xy - 6y^2, 10x^2 + xy - 3y^2)$

30. $(2r^2 - 5rs - 12s^2, 3r^2 - 10rs - 8s^2)$

31. $(r^3 + 3r^2s - rs^2 - 3s^3, r^2 - 2rs - 15s^2)$

32. $(4x^2 + 8x + 3, 12x^3 - 4x^2 - 27x + 9)$

Developing Skills in Algebra   Book B

Name _____

Date _____ Period _____

Complete. Assume no denominator is 0.

1. $\dfrac{4}{5a} = \dfrac{?}{10a^2}$ **8a**

2. $\dfrac{3}{10b} = \dfrac{?}{30bc}$

3. $\dfrac{6a}{11b^2c} = \dfrac{?}{55b^3c^2}$

4. $\dfrac{7m}{25xy^2} = \dfrac{?}{75x^3y^3}$

5. $\dfrac{9x}{x-y} = \dfrac{?}{(x-y)(2x+1)}$

6. $\dfrac{3r}{r+t} = \dfrac{?}{(r+t)(r-3t)}$

7. $\dfrac{4t}{3t+2} = \dfrac{?}{(3t+2)(t-1)}$

8. $\dfrac{8a}{5-3a} = \dfrac{?}{(5-3a)(3+2a)}$

9. $\dfrac{x+3}{x-2} = \dfrac{?}{x^2-7x+10}$

10. $\dfrac{2x+1}{x+4} = \dfrac{?}{x^2+2x-8}$

11. $\dfrac{2a-5}{a+7} = \dfrac{?}{a^2+10a+21}$

12. $\dfrac{4a+2b}{3a-b} = \dfrac{?}{6a^2+7ab-3b^2}$

13. $\dfrac{3m+n}{m-5} = \dfrac{?}{m^2-3m-10}$

14. $\dfrac{a+2m}{7a-m} = \dfrac{?}{7a^2+20am-3m^2}$

15. $\dfrac{5r+t}{2r-t} = \dfrac{?}{2r^2+5rt-3t^2}$

16. $\dfrac{2r+t}{r-t} = \dfrac{?}{r^2-t^2}$

17. $\dfrac{3x+2y}{x+y} = \dfrac{?}{x^2-y^2}$

18. $\dfrac{4x+y}{5x+2y} = \dfrac{?}{25x^2-4y^2}$

19. $\dfrac{3a-5b}{2a-3b} = \dfrac{?}{4a^2-9b^2}$

20. $\dfrac{2x+3y}{4x-y} = \dfrac{?}{4x^2+7xy-2y^2}$

21. $\dfrac{3+2t}{5-3t} = \dfrac{?}{3t^2-14t+15}$

22. $\dfrac{7x-y}{2x-3y} = \dfrac{?}{15y^2-16xy+4x^2}$

23. $\dfrac{2m+5n}{3m-n} = \dfrac{?}{n^2-mn-6m^2}$

24. $\dfrac{6x+1}{3x-2} = \dfrac{?}{6-7x-3x^2}$

25. $\dfrac{5x-3y}{x+y} = \dfrac{?}{x^4-y^4}$

26. $\dfrac{2b+c}{b-c} = \dfrac{?}{b^4-c^4}$

Developing Skills in Algebra   Book B

Name _____

Date _____ Period _____

Complete. Assume no denominator is 0.

1. $\dfrac{3}{2x} = \dfrac{?}{8x^2}$ *12x*

2. $\dfrac{7}{9b} = \dfrac{?}{27b^2}$

3. $\dfrac{4a}{13bc^2} = \dfrac{?}{52b^2c^3}$

4. $\dfrac{7d}{15x^2y} = \dfrac{?}{60x^3y^3}$

5. $\dfrac{3m}{m-n} = \dfrac{?}{(m-n)(3m+n)}$

6. $\dfrac{5b}{h+2t} = \dfrac{?}{(h+2t)(h+3t)}$

7. $\dfrac{5x}{5x+2y} = \dfrac{?}{(5x+2y)(x-3y)}$

8. $\dfrac{7c}{3a+b} = \dfrac{?}{(5a-3b)(3a+b)}$

9. $\dfrac{x+7}{x-5} = \dfrac{?}{3x^2-13x-10}$

10. $\dfrac{2a+9}{a+3} = \dfrac{?}{2a^2+a-15}$

11. $\dfrac{3m-5}{m+7} = \dfrac{?}{3m^2+23m+2}$

12. $\dfrac{c+d}{c-2d} = \dfrac{?}{3c^2-10c+8}$

13. $\dfrac{2r+3t}{2r-5t} = \dfrac{?}{10r^2-27r+5}$

14. $\dfrac{3x+y}{5x-y} = \dfrac{?}{5x^2-21xy+4y^2}$

15. $\dfrac{3r-1}{5r+7} = \dfrac{?}{10r^2-r-21}$

16. $\dfrac{4a-b}{3a-2b} = \dfrac{?}{6a^2-31ab+18b^2}$

17. $\dfrac{7a-3b}{a+2b} = \dfrac{?}{a^2-4b^2}$

18. $\dfrac{a+3b}{3a-5b} = \dfrac{?}{9a^2-25b^2}$

19. $\dfrac{x+2y}{5x-4y} = \dfrac{?}{25x^2-16y^2}$

20. $\dfrac{6r+5t}{3r+7t} = \dfrac{?}{9r^2-49t^2}$

21. $\dfrac{7-3t}{2-5t} = \dfrac{?}{15t^2-26t+8}$

22. $\dfrac{a+b}{2a-7b} = \dfrac{?}{35b^2+11ab-6a^2}$

23. $\dfrac{r+2t}{3r-5t} = \dfrac{?}{25t^2-10rt-3r^2}$

24. $\dfrac{7-3x}{5-2x} = \dfrac{?}{6x^2-17x+5}$

25. $\dfrac{3m+1}{m+2} = \dfrac{?}{m^4-16}$

26. $\dfrac{2a+3}{a-3} = \dfrac{?}{a^4-81}$

     Developing Skills in Algebra   Book B

Addition of Fractions

Simplify. Assume no denominator is 0.

1. $\dfrac{3x}{4} + \dfrac{5}{12}$ $\dfrac{9x + 5}{12}$

2. $\dfrac{4x}{3} + \dfrac{7}{15}$

3. $\dfrac{1}{18} + \dfrac{5a}{54}$

4. $\dfrac{3}{32} + \dfrac{a}{8}$

5. $\dfrac{5x}{72} + \dfrac{7y}{162}$

6. $\dfrac{7x}{84} + \dfrac{5y}{126}$

7. $\dfrac{2a}{15} + \dfrac{1}{25}$

8. $\dfrac{5a}{16} + \dfrac{3}{64}$

9. $\dfrac{3x}{20} + \dfrac{7y^2}{50}$

10. $\dfrac{2x}{15} + \dfrac{3y^2}{20}$

11. $\dfrac{2y}{5x} + \dfrac{3}{20y}$

12. $\dfrac{11y}{3x} + \dfrac{7}{18y}$

13. $\dfrac{4x}{3z} + \dfrac{5z}{6x}$

14. $\dfrac{3x}{5z} + \dfrac{3t}{8x}$

15. $\dfrac{a}{3b} + \dfrac{2b}{9a}$

16. $\dfrac{3a}{8b} + \dfrac{b}{4a}$

17. $\dfrac{5x}{24} + \dfrac{3y}{16x}$

18. $\dfrac{9x}{26} + \dfrac{5y}{39x}$

19. $\dfrac{3}{28x} + \dfrac{5}{98x^2}$

20. $\dfrac{3}{40x^2} + \dfrac{7}{72x^3}$

21. $\dfrac{3}{8x} + \dfrac{5}{18xy^2}$

22. $\dfrac{5}{10x^2} + \dfrac{6}{35x^2y^2}$

23. $\dfrac{9}{12ab^3} + \dfrac{8}{40a^2b^2}$

24. $\dfrac{7}{14a^2b^3} + \dfrac{14}{42a^2b}$

25. $\dfrac{21}{28xy^2} + \dfrac{36}{84x^2y}$

26. $\dfrac{18}{24x^2y^2} + \dfrac{28}{56xy}$

Addition of Fractions

Name _____

Date _____ Period _____

Simplify. Assume no denominator is 0.

1. $\dfrac{8x}{3} + \dfrac{2}{9}$ $\dfrac{2x+2}{9}$

2. $\dfrac{7x}{8} + \dfrac{11}{32}$

3. $\dfrac{11}{28} + \dfrac{4b}{49}$

4. $\dfrac{7}{24} + \dfrac{9b}{64}$

5. $\dfrac{2y}{21} + \dfrac{6x}{63}$

6. $\dfrac{y}{20} + \dfrac{3x}{56}$

7. $\dfrac{3x}{16} + \dfrac{9}{80}$

8. $\dfrac{13x}{38} + \dfrac{26}{76}$

9. $\dfrac{4x^2}{25} + \dfrac{y}{15}$

10. $\dfrac{3x^3}{55} + \dfrac{y^2}{11}$

11. $\dfrac{7b}{6a} + \dfrac{14}{24b}$

12. $\dfrac{3b}{9a} + \dfrac{28}{36b}$

13. $\dfrac{5y}{4x} + \dfrac{5x}{6y}$

14. $\dfrac{5y}{3x} + \dfrac{3x}{2y}$

15. $\dfrac{12y}{5x} + \dfrac{45}{15y}$

16. $\dfrac{18y}{13x} + \dfrac{27x}{39y}$

17. $\dfrac{11a}{18} + \dfrac{11b}{45a}$

18. $\dfrac{13a}{34} + \dfrac{26b}{85x}$

19. $\dfrac{15}{26a^2} + \dfrac{55}{78a^3}$

20. $\dfrac{12}{23a^2} + \dfrac{6}{46a^3}$

21. $\dfrac{3}{6a^2} + \dfrac{24}{21a^2b^3}$

22. $\dfrac{12}{14a^3} + \dfrac{28}{42a^3b^3}$

23. $\dfrac{16}{15x^2y^2} + \dfrac{12}{25x^2y}$

24. $\dfrac{7}{16xy^3} + \dfrac{15}{64x^2y^2}$

25. $\dfrac{20}{29x^2y^2} + \dfrac{28}{87x^2y^3}$

26. $\dfrac{14}{27x^2y^2} + \dfrac{25}{84x^2y^3}$

110   Developing Skills in Algebra   Book B

Simplify. Assume no denominator is 0.

1. $\dfrac{9x}{10} - \dfrac{5x}{12}$ $\dfrac{29x}{60}$

2. $\dfrac{7x}{15} - \dfrac{x}{10}$

3. $\dfrac{11x}{36} - \dfrac{4y}{45}$

4. $\dfrac{14a}{25} - \dfrac{3y}{35}$

5. $\dfrac{xy}{21} - \dfrac{x^2}{35}$

6. $\dfrac{ab}{18} - \dfrac{bc}{24}$

7. $\dfrac{3z}{10} - \dfrac{6z^2}{35}$

8. $\dfrac{4x}{15} - \dfrac{3x^2}{20}$

9. $\dfrac{u^2}{22} - \dfrac{2u}{33}$

10. $\dfrac{x^2}{32} - \dfrac{3x}{40}$

11. $\dfrac{a}{3c} - \dfrac{b}{5c^2}$

12. $\dfrac{m}{4n} - \dfrac{n}{6m}$

13. $\dfrac{2b}{9a} - \dfrac{5a}{12b}$

14. $\dfrac{7c}{15x} - \dfrac{3d}{20y}$

15. $\dfrac{2y}{9x} - \dfrac{7x}{12y^2}$

16. $\dfrac{4r}{15t} - \dfrac{7s}{25t^2}$

17. $\dfrac{2}{15t} - \dfrac{5}{6z^2}$

18. $\dfrac{15}{13x} - \dfrac{11}{26x}$

19. $\dfrac{5}{28x^2} - \dfrac{5}{24x}$

20. $\dfrac{7}{4a^2} - \dfrac{7}{14a}$

21. $\dfrac{y}{30x^2} - \dfrac{x}{60x^2}$

22. $\dfrac{2y}{14x^2} - \dfrac{3x}{35y^2}$

23. $\dfrac{1}{x^2} - \dfrac{1}{x(x+1)}$

24. $\dfrac{1}{x^2-1} + \dfrac{x}{x+1}$

25. $\dfrac{x}{x-1} - \dfrac{2x}{x+1}$

26. $\dfrac{x+1}{2x} - \dfrac{x}{x-1}$

Name _____

Date _____ Period _____

Simplify. Assume no denominator is 0.

1. $\dfrac{3a}{16} - \dfrac{7a}{24}$ $\dfrac{-5a}{48}$

2. $\dfrac{5a}{12} - \dfrac{11a}{14}$

3. $\dfrac{13b}{24} - \dfrac{17c}{30}$

4. $\dfrac{16m}{25} - \dfrac{13n}{30}$

5. $\dfrac{3x}{28} - \dfrac{9x}{42}$

6. $\dfrac{mn}{20} - \dfrac{n^2}{35}$

7. $\dfrac{rt}{18} - \dfrac{t^2}{24}$

8. $\dfrac{7a}{12} - \dfrac{9b^2}{15}$

9. $\dfrac{m}{30} - \dfrac{5m}{42}$

10. $\dfrac{z^2}{27} - \dfrac{5z}{36}$

11. $\dfrac{p}{10t} - \dfrac{q}{15t}$

12. $\dfrac{r}{3s} - \dfrac{t}{15s}$

13. $\dfrac{9z}{14a} - \dfrac{12a}{35z}$

14. $\dfrac{3a}{16z} - \dfrac{11a}{24z^2}$

15. $\dfrac{3r}{26x} - \dfrac{7s}{39t}$

16. $\dfrac{7x}{12m} - \dfrac{10y}{28n}$

17. $\dfrac{4}{19z} - \dfrac{8}{57z^2}$

18. $\dfrac{23}{17x} - \dfrac{15}{34xy}$

19. $\dfrac{15}{15x^3} - \dfrac{12}{25x^2}$

20. $\dfrac{19}{33a^2} - \dfrac{7}{22b^2}$

21. $\dfrac{7x}{15a^2} - \dfrac{12y}{25b^2}$

22. $\dfrac{3c}{16a^2} - \dfrac{7c}{20b^2}$

23. $\dfrac{1}{r(r+2)} - \dfrac{1}{r^2}$

24. $\dfrac{1}{r^2 - 3r} - \dfrac{1}{r}$

25. $\dfrac{a}{a-2} - \dfrac{3a}{a+1}$

26. $\dfrac{b+2}{3b} - \dfrac{b}{b-2}$

---

    112   Developing Skills in Algebra   Book B

Addition and Subtraction of Fractions

Name _____

Date _____ Period _____

Simplify. Assume no denominator is 0.

1. $\dfrac{1}{a} + \dfrac{1}{2a} - \dfrac{1}{3a}$ $\dfrac{7}{6a}$

2. $\dfrac{1}{2a} + \dfrac{1}{3a} - \dfrac{1}{4a}$

3. $\dfrac{2}{a} + \dfrac{5}{a} - \dfrac{3}{2a}$

4. $\dfrac{3}{a^2} + \dfrac{7}{a^2} - \dfrac{5}{3a^2}$

5. $\dfrac{1}{a} + \dfrac{1}{b} - \dfrac{1}{c}$

6. $\dfrac{2}{a^2} + \dfrac{2}{b^2} - \dfrac{2}{c^2}$

7. $\dfrac{b}{a} + \dfrac{a}{b} - \dfrac{1}{c}$

8. $\dfrac{b}{a^2} + \dfrac{a}{b^2} - \dfrac{1}{c^2}$

9. $\dfrac{2x}{y} + \dfrac{2z}{y^2} - \dfrac{xz}{2y}$

10. $\dfrac{3x}{y^2} + \dfrac{3z}{y^3} - \dfrac{2xz}{2y^2}$

11. $\dfrac{x}{y} + \dfrac{2x}{3y} - \dfrac{3x}{4y^2}$

12. $\dfrac{2x}{y^2} + \dfrac{4x}{3y^2} - \dfrac{5x}{4y^3}$

13. $\dfrac{2x}{3z} + \dfrac{1}{6} - \dfrac{4x}{z^2}$

14. $\dfrac{3x}{5z} + \dfrac{1}{10} - \dfrac{6x}{z^2}$

15. $\dfrac{z}{z-1} + \dfrac{z}{z+1} - \dfrac{2z^2}{z^2-1}$

16. $\dfrac{2z}{z-1} + \dfrac{2z}{z+1} - \dfrac{5z^2}{z^2-1}$

17. $\dfrac{1}{x-1} + \dfrac{x}{x-1} - \dfrac{2}{x}$

18. $\dfrac{3}{x-2} + \dfrac{2x}{x-2} - \dfrac{1}{x}$

19. $\dfrac{1}{x} + \dfrac{1}{y} - \dfrac{1}{xy}$

20. $\dfrac{2}{a} + \dfrac{2}{b} - \dfrac{2}{ab}$

21. $\dfrac{2x}{y} + \dfrac{3y}{x} - \dfrac{2x^2+3y^2}{xy}$

22. $\dfrac{5x}{2y} + \dfrac{4y}{2x} - \dfrac{10x^2+5y^2}{4xy}$

23. $\dfrac{3y}{2x} + \dfrac{2x}{3y} - \dfrac{7y^2}{6xy}$

24. $\dfrac{2y}{3x} + \dfrac{5x}{7y} - \dfrac{11y^2}{21xy}$

25. $\dfrac{z}{4x} + \dfrac{2x}{3z} - \dfrac{4z}{x}$

26. $\dfrac{2z}{5x} - \dfrac{3x}{7z} - \dfrac{5z}{2x}$

Addition and Subtraction of Fractions

Name _____

Date _____ Period _____

Simplify. Assume no denominator is 0.

1. $\dfrac{1}{xy} + \dfrac{1}{3xy} - \dfrac{1}{5x}$ $\dfrac{20-3y}{15xy}$

2. $\dfrac{1}{2xy} + \dfrac{1}{6xy} - \dfrac{1}{10x}$

3. $\dfrac{5}{x} + \dfrac{7}{x} - \dfrac{11}{3x}$

4. $\dfrac{3}{x^2} + \dfrac{5}{x^2} - \dfrac{7}{5x^2}$

5. $\dfrac{5}{2x^2} + \dfrac{5}{2y^2} - \dfrac{5}{2z^2}$

6. $\dfrac{2}{x^2} + \dfrac{3}{2y^2} - \dfrac{1}{3z^2}$

7. $\dfrac{2x}{3y} + \dfrac{3y}{2x} - \dfrac{1}{6z}$

8. $\dfrac{4x^2}{5y^2} + \dfrac{2y^2}{x^2} - \dfrac{2}{3z^2}$

9. $\dfrac{5a}{2b} + \dfrac{5z}{4b^2} - \dfrac{3az}{4b}$

10. $\dfrac{8a^2}{3b^2} + \dfrac{2c}{5b^3} - \dfrac{4a^2c}{6b^2}$

11. $\dfrac{11a}{7b} + \dfrac{22a}{21b} - \dfrac{33a}{28b^2}$

12. $\dfrac{9a}{5b^2} + \dfrac{16a}{17b^2} - \dfrac{24a}{85b^2}$

13. $\dfrac{12a}{17b} + \dfrac{3}{34} - \dfrac{22a}{b^2}$

14. $\dfrac{15a^2}{22b} + \dfrac{5}{44} - \dfrac{11a^2}{b^2}$

15. $\dfrac{x}{2x-3} + \dfrac{2x}{2x+3} - \dfrac{3x^2}{4x^2-9}$

16. $\dfrac{x}{3x-2} + \dfrac{3x}{3x+2} - \dfrac{5x^2}{9x^2-4}$

17. $\dfrac{3x}{5x-2} + \dfrac{2x}{5x-2} - \dfrac{5}{x}$

18. $\dfrac{5x}{3x-1} + \dfrac{7x}{3x-1} - \dfrac{4}{x}$

19. $\dfrac{7}{x-1} + \dfrac{7}{y-1} - \dfrac{1}{xy-x-y+1}$

20. $\dfrac{11}{2x-3} + \dfrac{11}{2y-3} - \dfrac{1}{4xy-6x-6y+9}$

21. $\dfrac{5a}{2b} + \dfrac{4b}{3a} - \dfrac{a^2+2b^2}{6ab}$

22. $\dfrac{4a^2}{3b^2} + \dfrac{7b^2}{5a^2} - \dfrac{2a^2+3b^2}{15a^2b^2}$

23. $\dfrac{7a}{3b} + \dfrac{5b}{4a} - \dfrac{13a^2}{12ab}$

24. $\dfrac{5a}{7b^3} + \dfrac{9b^3}{11a} - \dfrac{12a^2}{77ab^3}$

25. $\dfrac{2x}{5y} + \dfrac{11y}{7x} - \dfrac{4x}{y^2}$

26. $\dfrac{4x}{3y} - \dfrac{3y}{4x} - \dfrac{12y}{x^2}$

114

Simplify. Assume no denominator is 0.

1. $\dfrac{1}{a-b} + \dfrac{1}{a+b}$ $\dfrac{2a}{a^2-b^2}$

2. $\dfrac{1}{a+b} - \dfrac{1}{a-b}$

3. $\dfrac{a}{a+b} + \dfrac{b}{a-b}$

4. $\dfrac{a}{a+b} - \dfrac{a}{a-b}$

5. $\dfrac{a^2}{a^2-b^2} - \dfrac{b}{a+b}$

6. $\dfrac{x}{(x-1)^2} - \dfrac{x+1}{x-1}$

7. $\dfrac{2}{(x+1)^2} - \dfrac{1}{x}$

8. $\dfrac{x}{(x+1)^2} + \dfrac{1}{x+1}$

9. $\dfrac{2}{(x-1)^3} - \dfrac{x^2}{(x-1)^2}$

10. $\dfrac{2x}{(x-1)^4} + \dfrac{1}{(x-1)^2}$

11. $\dfrac{1}{x^2} - \dfrac{1}{(x-1)^2}$

12. $\dfrac{2}{x^2} + \dfrac{(x-1)^2}{x^3}$

13. $\dfrac{1}{2x} + \dfrac{x+1}{3x^2}$

14. $\dfrac{1}{3x} + \dfrac{x-1}{2x^2}$

15. $\dfrac{1}{x(x+1)} - \dfrac{1}{x-1}$

16. $\dfrac{x-1}{x+1} + \dfrac{x+1}{x-1}$

17. $\dfrac{1}{(x+1)(x+2)} + \dfrac{1}{(x+1)^2}$

18. $\dfrac{1}{(x-3)(x+1)} - \dfrac{1}{x(x-3)}$

19. $\dfrac{1}{(x-2)(x+3)} - \dfrac{2}{(x+3)^2}$

20. $\dfrac{1}{(x+1)(x-5)} + \dfrac{1}{(x-5)(x+2)}$

21. $\dfrac{1}{(x-1)^2} - \dfrac{1}{(x-2)^2}$

22. $\dfrac{1}{x-2} - \dfrac{1}{(x+3)^2}$

23. $\dfrac{1}{(x+3)(x+4)} + \dfrac{1}{x+4}$

24. $\dfrac{1}{3x+2} - \dfrac{1}{(3x-2)(3x+2)}$

25. $\dfrac{10}{(2x-5)(2x+5)} + \dfrac{1}{2x+5}$

26. $\dfrac{1}{3x-4} - \dfrac{1}{(3x+4)(3x-4)}$

Addition and Subtraction of Fractions

Name _____

Date _____ Period _____

Simplify. Assume no denominator is 0.

1. $\dfrac{1}{2x-y} + \dfrac{1}{2x+y}$ $\dfrac{4x}{4x^2-y^2}$

2. $\dfrac{1}{2x+y} - \dfrac{1}{2x-y}$

3. $\dfrac{x}{x+2y} + \dfrac{y}{x-2y}$

4. $\dfrac{x}{x+2y} - \dfrac{y}{x-2y}$

5. $\dfrac{3x^2}{4x^2-9y^2} - \dfrac{3y^2}{2x+3y}$

6. $\dfrac{2a}{(2a-3)^2} - \dfrac{2a+3}{2a-3}$

7. $\dfrac{4}{(3x+2)^2} - \dfrac{2}{3x}$

8. $\dfrac{5x}{(4x-1)^2} + \dfrac{2}{4x-1}$

9. $\dfrac{5}{(x-5)^3} - \dfrac{x}{(x-5)^2}$

10. $\dfrac{x}{(3x+7)^2} + \dfrac{3}{(3x+7)^4}$

11. $\dfrac{11}{a^3} - \dfrac{1}{(2a-3)^2}$

12. $\dfrac{1}{a^2} + \dfrac{(2a+5)^2}{a^3}$

13. $\dfrac{3}{5x^2} - \dfrac{2+x}{3x^3}$

14. $\dfrac{4}{7x^2} + \dfrac{1+x}{5x}$

15. $\dfrac{1}{x^2(x-3)} - \dfrac{1}{x+3}$

16. $\dfrac{2x-3}{2x+3} + \dfrac{5x+1}{5x-1}$

17. $\dfrac{1}{(x-2)(x+3)} + \dfrac{3}{(x-2)^2}$

18. $\dfrac{1}{(x+5)(x-2)} - \dfrac{1}{x(x-2)}$

19. $\dfrac{1}{(x+8)(x+1)} - \dfrac{1}{(x+8)^2}$

20. $\dfrac{1}{(x-3)(x-9)} + \dfrac{1}{(x-9)(x+2)}$

21. $\dfrac{1}{(x+2)^2} - \dfrac{1}{(x-3)^2}$

22. $\dfrac{1}{x+5} - \dfrac{2x}{(x-1)^2}$

23. $\dfrac{1}{(x-4)(x-7)} + \dfrac{1}{x-7}$

24. $\dfrac{1}{5x-1} - \dfrac{1}{(5x-1)(5x+1)}$

25. $\dfrac{8}{(6x-1)(6x+1)} + \dfrac{1}{6x-1}$

26. $\dfrac{1}{8x-7} - \dfrac{1}{(8x+7)(8x-7)}$

Name _____

Date _____ Period _____

Simplify. Assume no denominator is 0.

1. $\dfrac{x}{x^2 - 5x - 36} + \dfrac{1}{x^2 + 3x - 4}$

$$\dfrac{x^2 - 9}{(x - 9)(x + 4)(x - 1)}$$

2. $\dfrac{2x}{x^2 - 4x - 5} - \dfrac{3}{x^2 - 2x - 3}$

3. $\dfrac{2}{x + 1} + \dfrac{x^2 - 1}{x^2 - 2x + 1}$

4. $\dfrac{x - 2}{x^2 - 11x + 28} - \dfrac{3x - 2}{3x^2 - 39x + 108}$

5. $\dfrac{1}{x^2 + 9x + 8} + \dfrac{1}{x^2 - 5x - 6}$

6. $\dfrac{x - 2}{x^2 + 5x - 14} - \dfrac{2x + 11}{x^2 + 11x + 28}$

7. $\dfrac{x}{x^2 + 9x + 14} - \dfrac{6}{x^2 - 10x + 16}$

8. $\dfrac{x - 3}{x^2 - 6x - 16} + \dfrac{2 - x}{x^2 - 4x - 12}$

9. $\dfrac{x - 14}{x^2 - 10x + 16} - \dfrac{x - 21}{x^2 - 3x - 40}$

10. $\dfrac{3x - 7}{6x^2 - 5x + 1} - \dfrac{9x + 15}{18x^2 - 9x + 1}$

11. $\dfrac{x - 1}{2x^2 - 7x + 3} - \dfrac{x + 3}{2x^2 + 3x - 27}$

12. $\dfrac{8x - 4}{24x^2 - 38x + 15} + \dfrac{1 - 6x}{18x^2 - 27x + 10}$

13. $\dfrac{3x - 1}{27x^2 - 21x + 4} - \dfrac{4x + 2}{36x^2 - 43x + 12}$

Addition and Subtraction of Fractions

Name _____

Date _____ Period _____

Simplify. Assume no denominator is 0.

1. $\dfrac{x}{x^2 - 6x + 8} + \dfrac{1}{x^2 - 5x + 6}$ $\dfrac{x^2 - 2x - 4}{(x-4)(x-2)(x-3)}$

2. $\dfrac{x^2 - 1}{(x - 1)^2} - \dfrac{1}{x - 1}$

3. $\dfrac{3}{x - 1} - \dfrac{x^2 - 1}{x^2 + 2x + 1}$

4. $\dfrac{x + 25}{x^2 - 5x - 24} - \dfrac{x - 3}{x^2 + 9x + 18}$

5. $\dfrac{3}{x^2 - 7x + 10} + \dfrac{4}{x^2 - 14x + 45}$

6. $\dfrac{x - 4}{x^2 - 5x + 6} + \dfrac{1 - x}{x^2 - 8x + 15}$

7. $\dfrac{x + 4}{x^2 + 8x + 15} - \dfrac{x + 6}{x^2 + 12x + 35}$

8. $\dfrac{6x - 3}{6x^2 - 7x + 2} - \dfrac{8x - 8}{8x^2 - 10x + 3}$

9. $\dfrac{3x - 8}{2x^2 - 7x + 6} - \dfrac{3x + 20}{2x^2 - 13x + 15}$

10. $\dfrac{2x - 3}{6x^2 - 11x - 10} - \dfrac{3x - 8}{3x^2 - 19x - 14}$

11. $\dfrac{5x - 2}{28x^2 + 31x - 5} - \dfrac{6x - 1}{7x^2 + 20x - 3}$

12. $\dfrac{x - 1}{12x^2 + 5x - 25} + \dfrac{4x + 5}{9x^2 - 25}$

13. $\dfrac{5x - 7}{10x^2 + 27x - 28} - \dfrac{x - 11}{5x^2 - 19x + 12}$

Name _____

Date _____ Period _____

Simplify. Assume no denominator is 0.

1. $2 + \dfrac{1}{x}$ $\dfrac{2x + 1}{x}$

2. $3 - \dfrac{1}{x^2}$

3. $x + \dfrac{2}{x}$

4. $2x - \dfrac{3}{x}$

5. $2x - \dfrac{2}{x - 1}$

6. $2x + \dfrac{1}{x + 1}$

7. $3x - 1 - \dfrac{1}{x - 1}$

8. $2x + 1 + \dfrac{1}{x + 1}$

9. $\dfrac{x^2}{x + 2} - x$

10. $\dfrac{2x^2}{x - 2} + x^2$

11. $x - \dfrac{y - x}{2} + 2y$

12. $2x + \dfrac{x - y}{3} - 3y$

13. $\dfrac{2x - 3}{(x - 2)^2} + 1$

14. $\dfrac{x + 5}{(x + 1)^2} - 2$

15. $\dfrac{a + b}{a - b} - \dfrac{a - b}{a + b} + 1$

16. $\dfrac{2a - 3b}{2a + 3b} + \dfrac{2a + 3b}{2a - 3b} - 1$

17. $a - b + \dfrac{1}{a} + \dfrac{1}{b}$

18. $a + b + \dfrac{1}{2a} - \dfrac{1}{2b}$

19. $\dfrac{1}{x} - \dfrac{1}{y} + \dfrac{y}{x} + 1$

20. $\dfrac{2}{x} + \dfrac{2}{y} - \dfrac{x}{y} - 1$

21. $a - \dfrac{x}{b} - b - x$

22. $\dfrac{a}{b} + x + \dfrac{b}{a} - \dfrac{x}{b}$

23. $\dfrac{x}{y} + \dfrac{y}{x} + \dfrac{1}{2} + 3$

24. $\dfrac{2x}{y} - \dfrac{3y}{x} + \dfrac{1}{3} - 2$

25. $\dfrac{a^2}{b^2} - 1 + \dfrac{b^2}{a^2} - \dfrac{1}{2}$

26. $\dfrac{2a^2}{b^2} - 2 + \dfrac{2b^2}{a^2} + \dfrac{1}{3}$

Mixed Expressions

Name _____

Date _____ Period _____

Simplify. Assume no denominator is 0.

1. $-5 - \dfrac{1}{x^2}$ $\dfrac{-5x^2 - 1}{x^2}$

2. $-4 + \dfrac{1}{2x^2}$

3. $4x - \dfrac{3}{x}$

4. $5x + \dfrac{2}{3x}$

5. $x - 1 + \dfrac{1}{x + 1}$

6. $2x + 3 - \dfrac{1}{x - 1}$

7. $\dfrac{x}{x + 1} - 3$

8. $\dfrac{2x}{2x + 1} - 4$

9. $\dfrac{x - 1}{x + 1} - x$

10. $\dfrac{2x - 1}{2x + 1} + 3x$

11. $1 + \dfrac{4x}{x^2 + 4}$

12. $2 - \dfrac{3x}{x^2 - 4}$

13. $\dfrac{a - 1}{b} + \dfrac{b + 1}{a} - 2$

14. $\dfrac{a + 2}{2b} - \dfrac{2b - 3}{2a} - 3$

15. $\dfrac{1}{a} - 1 + \dfrac{1}{a} + \dfrac{3}{a^2}$

16. $1 - \dfrac{5a - 2b}{5a + 2b} + \dfrac{2}{a}$

17. $\dfrac{a - b}{a} - (a + b) + \dfrac{a + b}{b^2}$

18. $\dfrac{2a - b}{2a} + (a - b) - \dfrac{2a + b}{2b}$

19. $\dfrac{x}{y} - 1 - \dfrac{y}{x} + \dfrac{1}{3}$

20. $\dfrac{2x}{3y} - \dfrac{1}{4} - \dfrac{3y}{2x} + \dfrac{1}{3}$

21. $1 - \dfrac{a + b}{2b} + \dfrac{2b}{a} + \dfrac{1}{b}$

22. $2 + \dfrac{a - b}{3a} + \dfrac{3a}{2b} - \dfrac{1}{a}$

23. $\dfrac{a + b}{a} + \dfrac{a + b}{b} - \dfrac{1}{ab}$

24. $\dfrac{a - b}{b} - \dfrac{a - b}{a} - \dfrac{a}{b}$

25. $\dfrac{a - b}{3a} - 3a - \dfrac{4b}{a^2}$

26. $\dfrac{2a - b}{5b} - 4b - \dfrac{a + b}{2ab}$

Complex Fractions

Simplify. Assume no denominator is 0.

1. $\dfrac{\dfrac{x}{5}}{\dfrac{4x}{5}}$ $\dfrac{1}{4}$

2. $\dfrac{\dfrac{6x}{7}}{\dfrac{9x}{14}}$

3. $\dfrac{\dfrac{1}{2} - \dfrac{1}{12}}{\dfrac{1}{2} + \dfrac{1}{12}}$

4. $\dfrac{\dfrac{2}{3} + \dfrac{1}{6}}{\dfrac{3}{4} + \dfrac{1}{12}}$

5. $\dfrac{\dfrac{2a}{3b^2}}{\dfrac{a}{b}}$

6. $\dfrac{1 + \dfrac{5}{x^2}}{x + 3}$

7. $\dfrac{2x + \dfrac{4x}{x-1}}{2x - \dfrac{4x}{x+1}}$

8. $\dfrac{x + \dfrac{2x}{x^2 + 2}}{x - \dfrac{2x + 2}{x^2 + 2}}$

9. $\dfrac{\dfrac{2a}{2a+b} + \dfrac{2b}{2a-b}}{\dfrac{2a}{2a-b} - \dfrac{2b}{2a+b}}$

10. $\dfrac{\dfrac{x}{x+1} + \dfrac{x^2}{x^2-1}}{\dfrac{3x}{x-1} - \dfrac{2x^2}{x+1}}$

11. $\dfrac{\dfrac{x}{y} + \dfrac{x-y}{x+y}}{\dfrac{x}{y} - \dfrac{x-y}{x+y}}$

12. $\dfrac{3 + \dfrac{x-3}{9-x^2}}{3 - \dfrac{4}{x+3}}$

13. $\dfrac{\dfrac{1}{x} - \dfrac{1}{x^2-4}}{x + \dfrac{1}{2-x}}$

14. $\dfrac{x + \dfrac{x^2 + 5x + 6}{(x+3)^2}}{\dfrac{1}{x} - \dfrac{x+2}{x^2-9}}$

Complex Fractions

Simplify. Assume no denominator is 0.

1. $\dfrac{\dfrac{2x}{11}}{\dfrac{5x}{11}}$ $\dfrac{2}{5}$

2. $\dfrac{\dfrac{5x}{9}}{\dfrac{15x^2}{18}}$

3. $\dfrac{\dfrac{1}{4} - \dfrac{3}{16}}{\dfrac{1}{3} + \dfrac{1}{2}}$

4. $\dfrac{\dfrac{3}{5} + \dfrac{5}{8}}{\dfrac{3}{4} - \dfrac{1}{10}}$

5. $\dfrac{\dfrac{3x}{4y^2}}{\dfrac{2x}{y}}$

6. $\dfrac{2 - \dfrac{4}{x^2}}{x - 2}$

7. $\dfrac{3x - \dfrac{5x}{2x - 3}}{3x + \dfrac{5x}{2x + 3}}$

8. $\dfrac{5x - \dfrac{x}{x^2 + 4}}{5 + \dfrac{x + 2}{x^2 + 4}}$

9. $\dfrac{\dfrac{3x}{x - y} - \dfrac{3y}{x + y}}{\dfrac{3x}{x + y} + \dfrac{3y}{x - y}}$

10. $\dfrac{\dfrac{2a}{2a + 3} + \dfrac{a^3}{4a^2 - 9}}{\dfrac{5a}{2a - 3} - \dfrac{a^3}{2a + 3}}$

11. $\dfrac{\dfrac{2a}{3b} - \dfrac{a - b}{2a - b}}{\dfrac{2a}{3b} + \dfrac{a - b}{2a - b}}$

12. $\dfrac{5 + \dfrac{x - 2}{25 - 4x^2}}{5 - \dfrac{5}{2x + 5}}$

13. $\dfrac{\dfrac{2}{x} + \dfrac{2}{4x^2 - 1}}{2x - \dfrac{1}{1 - 2x}}$

14. $\dfrac{3x + \dfrac{2x^2 + 7x - 7}{(2x + 1)^2}}{3x - \dfrac{x + 7}{2x - 1}}$

ANSWERS

Page 1 Using Exponents

1. a^5 **2.** b^3 **3.** x^2y^3 **4.** m^5 **5.** $3a^3c^3$ **6.** $6x^3y^2$
7. $(x - y)^2$ **8.** $(r + t)^3$ **9.** $5m^3n^3$ **10.** $11a^2b^2c^2$
11. $5(4 + x)^2$ **12.** $13(x - 8)^3$ **13.** $xxxxx$ **14.** $yyyyyyy$
15. $xxxyy$ **16.** $mmmmnnn$ **17.** $(m + n)(m + n)(m + n)$
18. $(a + b)(a + b)(a + b)(a + b)(a + b)$ **19.** $3rrrrtttt$
20. $9bbbcccddd$ **21.** 100 **22.** 8 **23.** 125 **24.** 49
25. 27 **26.** 100 **27.** 216 **28.** 1000 **29.** 256 **30.** 32

Page 2 Using Exponents

1. x^5 **2.** c^2 **3.** a^4b **4.** x^3y^2 **5.** $4m^3n^2$ **6.** $9p^2q^4$
7. $(2a - 3)^2$ **8.** $(x + 2)^3$ **9.** $3a^4c^4$ **10.** $8r^3s^3t^3$
11. $3(a + 2b)^2$ **12.** $7(3x - 5)^2$ **13.** $4yyy$ **14.** $ppqqqq$
15. $rrssst$ **16.** $5xxxy$ **17.** $(5a - 3b)(5a - 3b)$
18. $(2x + 7y)(2x + 7y)(2x + 7y)$ **19.** $7vvvwww$
20. $3mmnnpp$ **21.** 64 **22.** 81 **23.** 36 **24.** 64 **25.** 64
26. 192 **27.** 10000 **28.** 324 **29.** 121 **30.** 1331

Page 3 Classifying Polynomials

1. 2; 4 **2.** 1; 17 **3.** 1; 3 **4.** 4; -8 **5.** 0; 7 **6.** 4; 15
7. 4; -5 **8.** 4; -21 **9.** 6; -8 **10.** 0; 28 **11.** $3x^3y$
12. $-5x^3y^2$ **13.** $3x^3y^2z$ **14.** $2xyz$ **15.** $2x^2y^2z^2$ **16.** $3xy^3z$
17. 3 **18.** 4 **19.** 2 **20.** 4 **21.** 5 **22.** 5
23. $5x^3 - 3x^2 + 14x + 2$ **24.** $-9z^3 + 8z^2 - 2z + 7$
25. $-5y^5 + 3y^2 + 2y + 2$ **26.** $7x^5 + x^3 - 2x^2 + 4$

Page 4 Classifying Polynomials

1. 3; 5 **2.** 4; 13 **3.** 0; 10 **4.** 7; 13 **5.** 6; 9 **6.** 6; -2
7. 6; 13 **8.** 0; 25 **9.** 4; 18 **10.** 7; 8 **11.** $2ab^4$
12. $2m^3n^3$ **13.** $x^3y^2z^2$ **14.** $14abc^4$ **15.** $2a^3b^2c^3$
16. $5x^3y^2z$ **17.** 4 **18.** 5 **19.** 5 **20.** 5 **21.** 3 **22.** 4
23. $-4y^4 + 7y^2 + 4y + 23$ **24.** $8x^3 + 2x^2 - 3x - 5$
25. $-6z^4 + 7z^2 + z + 2$ **26.** $2y^5 + 10y^2 + 16y - 1$

Page 5 Addition of Polynomials

1. $x^2y, 3x^2y, -2x^2y$ **2.** $46xy, -6xy$ **3.** $4x^3h, -12hx^3$
4. $3x^3p, -4px^3, 13px^3$ **5.** $7ha, 8ah$ **6.** $ut^2x, 2xt^2u, -7xut^2$
7. mn^2r, mn^2r **8.** $-11pq^2s, 13pq^2s$ **9.** 17, -72
10. $\pi r^2, 5\pi r^2$ **11.** $5a + 2$ **12.** $8x + 1$ **13.** $5m + 10n$
14. $-3r + 2u - 87$ **15.** $x - 2y - 8$ **16.** $c + 13d - 1$
17. $p + 14r + 7$ **18.** $7x + y + 1$ **19.** $6k - 3kn$
20. $4ax + 13by + 9$ **21.** $4u^2 - 12r + 8$ **22.** $3a^3 + 7a^2b + 8b^3$
23. $4x^2 + 7x - 7$ **24.** $-4a^2 + 5a + 1$ **25.** $3a^2b + 5abc - 3$
26. $10x^3y + x^2y^2z^2 + 2$ **27.** $-3mn + 10a + 7d$
28. $-3r^2t + 14rt^2$ **29.** $17a + 2b + 11c$ **30.** $8x + 7y - 8z$
31. $5ab - 2ac - 4bc$ **32.** $9a^2x - 10b^2x$

Page 6 Addition of Polynomials

1. $ab^3, -2ab^3$ **2.** 25, 13 **3.** $x^3y, 7x^3y, 3x^3y$ **4.** $10rst, -3rst$
5. $5mn, 2mn, 14mn$ **6.** $cy, 3cy, -5cy$ **7.** $ph, 3hp, 11ph$
8. $9q^3p^2r^2, 13p^2r^2q^3$ **9.** $4x^2z, 16x^2z$ **10.** $a^3h, -7a^3h$
11. $8x - 4$ **12.** $-3a$ **13.** $-b + 8c$ **14.** $15d$ **15.** $5a + b + 3$
16. $12x - y - 4$ **17.** $10n + r - 5$ **18.** $12a + 5b - 7$
19. $2ax + 11by$ **20.** $8x + 11y - 7$ **21.** $6a^3 - 12b^3 + 1$
22. $2x - y + 6z$ **23.** $4r^2 - 5r + 1$ **24.** $8x^2 + 5$
25. $mn^3 + 3m^2n + 4mn$ **26.** $-2a^2x + b^2y^2 + 7$
27. $5rc + 12r - 7c + 1$ **28.** $8m^3n^2 - 2$ **29.** $13b^2 - 4b + 2$
30. $3x^4 + 12x^3y^2 - 2x$ **31.** $8rst + 3rs - 10$
32. $27m^2n^3 - 3x^2y - 2$

Page 7 Addition of Polynomials

1. $3a - b$ **2.** $20x - 2y$ **3.** $12z + 2$ **4.** $3s + 7p + 3$
5. $5q + 2h + 1$ **6.** $10b + 5a + c$ **7.** $9m + 2n - 3$ **8.** $-2x^2 + 2x$
9. $8y^2 - 2y$ **10.** $13z^2 - 2z + 4$ **11.** $-2u^2 + 2u + 6$
12. $-3h^3 - 3h^2 + 4h$ **13.** $2x^2 + x - 8$ **14.** $x^2 + x - 14$
15. $2x^2 + 2x - 9$ **16.** $x^3 - 3x^2 + x + 5$ **17.** $2x^2 - 7x - 4$
18. $-2x^3 - 4x^2 - 16$ **19.** $x^3 + x^2 - 2x - 1$

Page 8 Addition of Polynomials

1. $-a - 16b$ **2.** $-14x - 7y$ **3.** $-3z - 7$ **4.** $5s + 4p - 5$
5. $5q - 5h - 4$ **6.** $20b - 19a + 4c$ **7.** $11m - 6n + 1$
8. $-5x^2 + 4x$ **9.** $9y^2 + 7y + 7$ **10.** $z^2 + 3z + 4$
11. $7u^2 - 4u + 8$ **12.** $-13h^3 + h^2 + 4h - 5$ **13.** $11x^2 + 12x - 11$
14. $7x^2 + x + 5$ **15.** $-2x^2 - 28x + 24$ **16.** $10x^3 + 4x^2 + 6x - 12$
17. $2x^3 - 7x^2 - 2x - 2$ **18.** $12x^4 - 15x^3 + 3x^2 - 19$
19. $10x^2 - 4x + 4$

Page 9 Subtraction of Polynomials

1. $-a - 8b$ **2.** $-x + 3c$ **3.** $15z - 13$
4. $15p - 10q + 1$ **5.** $4x - 4y - c$ **6.** $-u^2 + 2u - 1$ **7.** $z^2 + 2z + 9$
8. $h^2 - h - 20$ **9.** $-2x - 18$ **10.** $4x^2 - 8x - 7$ **11.** $2x$
12. $-2x^2 + x - 1$ **13.** $5x^3 - 3x^2 + 5x - 2$ **14.** $-7x^3 + 4x + 5$
15. $a - 16b + 3$ **16.** $2x - y - 3$ **17.** $6r - 4n + 2$
18. $12c - 4d - 11$ **19.** $4mn - 14rs$ **20.** $5x - 15y + 4$
21. $21s - 16t - 13$ **22.** $5x - 4y - 7z$ **23.** $-4x^2 + 7x - 16$
24. $8z^2 + 9z - 11$ **25.** $pq + rs - 15mn$ **26.** $7b^2 + 2b - 7$
27. $12m^2 + 9m - 9$ **28.** $-7c^2d^2 + 13$ **29.** $12x^2 - 9x - 22$
30. $11x^3y^2 - 5x^2 - 7x$ **31.** $9m^2n + 9mn + 19$
32. $18a^2 + 5a - 16$

Page 10 Subtraction of Polynomials

1. $-6x$ **2.** $16a - 14b$ **3.** $5a - 12$ **4.** $9r - 23s - 8$
5. $-n^2 - 5n + 5$ **6.** $5x^2 - 2x$ **7.** $-4r^2 + 5r + 13$
8. $10y^2 - 15y - 3$ **9.** $9x^2 + 4x + 9$ **10.** $-7b^2 + 1$
11. $-5r - 6$ **12.** $-x^2 - 9x + 5$ **13.** $3y^2 - 4y + 1$
14. $-4x^2 + 2x + 4$ **15.** $-2m - 10n + 7$
16. $8z^2 - 4z - 13$ **17.** $5a - 15b + 7$
18. $-x - 18y - 11$ **19.** $7cd - 11pq$ **20.** $-8x^2 + 2x - 10$
21. $14z^2 - 20z - 15$ **22.** $-a + 4b + 1$ **23.** $-23xy + 4rst$
24. $2m^2 - 8m + 12$ **25.** $st + 4pq - 5$ **26.** $3r - 4s - 8$
27. $17ab - 15cd$ **28.** $-3m^2n + 13mn^2$
29. $-12x^3 + 3x^2 - 14$ **30.** $-3rt + zy - 4$
31. $8cq - 4q + 17$ **32.** $-5b^2 + 3b + 14$

Page 11 Subtraction of Polynomials

1. $7x - 5y$ **2.** $7a + 10b$ **3.** $-9c - 6d$ **4.** $11r - t - 6$
5. $-11x + 12$ **6.** $19r - 7s + 2t$ **7.** $32c - 5d + 14$
8. $-11x - 38y$ **9.** $-14m^2 + 3m - 39$ **10.** $28r^2 - 7r + 9$
11. $-9c^2 - c + 27$ **12.** $2x^3 - 2x^2 + 15x - 7$ **13.** $14z^2 + 3z$
14. $11a^2 + 8a + 11$ **15.** $19b^2 - 26b - 37$ **16.** $-2x^3 - 2x + 8$
17. $-3x + 7$ **18.** $-20x^2 + 5x + 16$ **19.** $4x^2 + 5x + 15$

Page 12 Subtraction of Polynomials

1. $15x + 11y$ **2.** $-7r - 2s$ **3.** $14a$ **4.** $15x + 3y + 4$
5. $29m + 7$ **6.** $27z + 9w + 9$ **7.** $41x - 2y - z$ **8.** $b - 6c$
9. $-17r^2 + 7r - 15$ **10.** $27s^2 + 4s + 14$ **11.** $-5z^2 + 4$
12. $34y^3 + 5y^2 + 19y + 4$ **13.** $12a^2 + 6a - 14$ **14.** $23x^2 - 41$
15. $39r^2 - 26r - 42$ **16.** $2m^3 + 6m^2 - m - 31$ **17.** $-z^2 + 6z - 8$
18. $-19y + 5$ **19.** $17x^2 - 43$

Page 13 Addition and Subtraction of Polynomials

1. b **2.** $-5y$ **3.** $3a - 8b$ **4.** $x + 10y$ **5.** $a - 8$ **6.** $5y - 4$
7. $2x + 10$ **8.** $9m - 3$ **9.** $2x - 1$ **10.** $7a^2 - 2a - 1$
11. $-6x^2 - 12x + 14$ **12.** $-5a^3 + 19a^2 - 12a - 2$
13. $46x^2 - 7xy + 11y^2$ **14.** $19a^2 - 16ab + 12b^2$
15. $-14m^2r^2 + 14m^2n - 12mn + 13n + 11m + 2m^2$
16. $16c^2d - 4cd^2 + 21c^2 - 19d^2 - 22$ **17.** $-2r^2 + 20r - 30$
18. $-3k^2 - 11km + 4m^2$ **19.** $15x + 2y - 25z$ **20.** $6x^3 + 24x^2 - 7$
21. $-15mn - 7pq - rs$ **22.** $8xy - 6xz - 17yz$

Page 14 Addition and Subtraction of Polynomials

1. $6x + 5y$ **2.** $14c - 16d$ **3.** $18v - 11w$ **4.** $12a - 11b$
5. $5x - 17$ **6.** $-10c - 11$ **7.** $18x + 2$ **8.** $18r - 5$ **9.** $-4a + 4$
10. $9x^2 - 4x - 9$ **11.** $-4a^2 - 18a + 25$ **12.** $11x^3 + 9x^2 - 2x - 6$
13. $11c^2 - 18cd + 19d^2$ **14.** $25m^2 + 6mn + 23n^2$
15. $6a^3 + 18a^2 + a + 1$ **16.** $14m^4 - 2m^3 - 2m^2 - 2m + 6$
17. $25x^2 + 20x - 24$ **18.** $15r^2 - 20rs + 3s^2$ **19.** $a - 32b + 25c$
20. $24x^3 + 4x^2 + 3x - 14$ **21.** $5ab + 2ac - 13bc$
22. $39mn - 12mp - 11np$

Page 15 Products of Monomials

1. a^5 **2.** b^5 **3.** $3a^5$ **4.** $7b^7$ **5.** $30a^7$ **6.** $6b^7$ **7.** $-864a^6$
8. $63b^6$ **9.** $1225a^4$ **10.** $-288b^5$ **11.** $6x^5y^4$ **12.** $21m^8n^3$
13. $-35x^5y^4$ **14.** $-12m^5n^2$ **15.** a^8 **16.** b^7 **17.** $-a^{11}$
18. $-b^{10}$ **19.** $104x^5y^3$ **20.** $-168m^8n^5$ **21.** $-42a^4b^5$
22. $-120a^6b^3$ **23.** $-432a^7b^3$ **24.** $48m^8n^2$ **25.** 10^5 **26.** 2^7
27. 5^9 **28.** 3^7 **29.** a^{r+2} **30.** b^{m+3} **31.** r^{3+x}
32. x^{4+n} **33.** $-24y^{3+x}$ **34.** $30r^{3+c}$

Page 16 Products of Monomials

1. x^6 **2.** y^5 **3.** $5x^7$ **4.** $4y^7$ **5.** $14x^6$ **6.** $45y^4$ **7.** $147x^7$
8. $160y^9$ **9.** $784x^4$ **10.** $-1323y^5$ **11.** $21a^6b^3$ **12.** $12r^6s^3$
13. $-24a^7b^4$ **14.** $-45r^8s^2$ **15.** c^9 **16.** z^{10} **17.** m^6 **18.** $-t^9$
19. $102a^7b^3$ **20.** $-70s^7t^3$ **21.** $-24x^5y^6$ **22.** $-18m^5n^3$
23. $-30r^6s^3$ **24.** $-110c^6s^3$ **25.** 12^4 **26.** 3^6 **27.** 7^8
28. 2^{11} **29.** c^{r+3} **30.** d^{s+4} **31.** a^{4+x} **32.** r^{4+y}
33. $30x^{4+a}$ **34.** $168d^{3+r}$

Page 17 Powers of Monomials

1. a^6 **2.** x^8 **3.** x^6 **4.** b^{10} **5.** u^{70} **6.** z^{40} **7.** $8x^6$
8. $81y^{12}$ **9.** $9x^4$ **10.** $-125y^9$ **11.** $(1/4)x^8$ **12.** $(1/9)y^6$
13. $0.008x^9$ **14.** $0.0081y^8$ **15.** $54a^6$ **16.** $-32x^9$ **17.** $8x^6$
18. $9t^6$ **19.** $100x^6$ **20.** $10y^6$ **21.** $-x^6$ **22.** $4y^6$
23. $9x^6$ **24.** $-125y^6$ **25.** a^{mn} **26.** b^{xy} **27.** $27b^{3s}$
28. $25x^{2p}$ **29.** $4x^{2m+2n}$ **30.** a^{3r+2s} **31.** x^{8b} **32.** y^{11c}
33. $8x^{5m}$ **34.** $9y^{5r}$

Page 18 Powers of Monomials

1. c^{12} **2.** t^{10} **3.** c^8 **4.** t^6 **5.** m^{25} **6.** y^{24} **7.** $81a^8$
8. $32b^{15}$ **9.** $25a^6$ **10.** $16b^{16}$ **11.** $(1/64)c^9$ **12.** $(1/25)m^6$
13. $0.16x^6$ **14.** $0.001y^{15}$ **15.** $80x^{12}$ **16.** $-189y^6$
17. $72x^6$ **18.** $108t^6$ **19.** $200a^6$ **20.** $10.83b^6$ **21.** a^{12}
22. $-27b^{12}$ **23.** $-32a^{30}$ **24.** $16b^6$ **25.** x^{pq} **26.** y^{rs}
27. 16^{4x} **28.** $81n^{2y}$ **29.** $4a^{3r+2s}$ **30.** c^{2p+3q} **31.** t^{9c}
32. n^{10x} **33.** $9a^{5y}$ **34.** $125b^{7t}$

Page 19 Operations with Monomials

1. $60a^7$ **2.** $138b^5$ **3.** $144c^5$ **4.** $272d^6$ **5.** $4104a^5$
6. $11720x^6$ **7.** $40a^4b^5$ **8.** $249x^5y^5$ **9.** $117x^7$
10. $152y^8$ **11.** $888a^8b^3$ **12.** $1256x^5y^3$ **13.** $-184m^3n^2$
14. $3088r^2s^5$ **15.** $-90a^6b^2$ **16.** $-80a^2c^5$ **17.** $-3x^3y^3z^2$
18. $-63r^3s^3t^2$ **19.** $5a^4b^4x^4$ **20.** $-22t^3u^2v$ **21.** $-a^4b^6c^2$
22. $-7c^3d^3t^3$ **23.** $-118m^4n^4$ **24.** $-69x^5y^5$ **25.** $101u^4p^5$
26. $917r^4s^5$ **27.** $25027a^3b^5$ **28.** $160c^3d^3$ **29.** 0
30. $11a^2b^2c^3$ **31.** $-210a^3x^4$ **32.** $-52m^3r^3$ **33.** $289a^5b^3$
34. 0

Page 20 Operations with Monomials

1. $52b^5$ **2.** $222x^6$ **3.** $5199m^6$ **4.** $2887r^5$ **5.** $711d^7$
6. $2033r^5$ **7.** $66x^5y^5$ **8.** $110m^4n^4$ **9.** $383a^9$ **10.** $1576b^7$
11. $37152x^7y^5$ **12.** $236a^5b^2$ **13.** $724s^2t^4$ **14.** $289c^2d^2$
15. $403x^5y^3$ **16.** $-128m^5r^2$ **17.** $-24p^3q^4r^2$ **18.** $-26a^5b^3c^2$
19. $41x^5y^3z^2$ **20.** $-17m^3r^2t^5$ **21.** $7f^3g^4h$ **22.** $-56p^2q^5r^5$
23. $540x^5y^5$ **24.** $-34a^4b^4$ **25.** $-16g^4t^5$ **26.** $263m^3s^7$
27. $1004x^4y^3$ **28.** $-1291u^5v^3$ **29.** $-13s^3t^2u^4$ **30.** $25d^6e^4f$
31. $11a^3b^3$ **32.** $188r^3s^3$ **33.** $-1094g^4h^3$ **34.** $-495x^3y^4$

Page 21 Multiplication of a Polynomial and a Monomial

1. $3x + 15$ **2.** $10x + 15$ **3.** $x^2 - 3x$ **4.** $y^2 - 5y$ **5.** $3x^2 + 21x$
6. $5y^2 - 45y$ **7.** $2c^2 - 6cd$ **8.** $4m^2 + 28mn$ **9.** $-6a^2 - 9ab$
10. $-35x^2 + 28xy$ **11.** $-21c^2 + 28cd$ **12.** $-28t^2 - 12tu$
13. $2x^3 - 6x^2 + 10x$ **14.** $4y^3 + 28y^2 - 8y$ **15.** $-4c^3 - 24c^2 + 8c$
16. $-9x^3 + 63x^2 - 135x$ **17.** $45s^2t + 27st^2 - 81st$
18. $55p^2q - 77pq^2 + 44pq$ **19.** $-112m^2n + 64mn^2 - 24mn$
20. $-84u^2v - 42uv^2 + 77uv$ **21.** $x^2y^2 - uxy$ **22.** $5p^2q^2 + pqv$
23. $x^5y - x^2y^2$ **24.** $3a^2b^2 + 2ab^3$ **25.** $x^3z^3 - 5x^3z$
26. $r^2s^4 - 7r^2s$ **27.** $3x^3y^2 + 6x^4$ **28.** $8yz^2 + 28z^3$
29. $x^4y^3 - 2x^2y^3$ **30.** $m^5n^3 + 3m^2n^3$ **31.** $a^5x^3 - 8a^4cx$
32. $m^2r^4 + 9mr^3t$ **33.** $8x^5y^2 + 60x^2yz$ **34.** $-21c^5d^2 + 98c^3de$

Page 22 Multiplication of a Polynomial and a Monomial

1. $8y + 32$ **2.** $27a - 45$ **3.** $c^2 - 7c$ **4.** $z^2 + 15z$
5. $2y^2 + 16y$ **6.** $3p^2 - 11p$ **7.** $7a^2 - 28ab$ **8.** $3d^2 + 6dg$
9. $-15yz - 20z^2$ **10.** $-8m^2 + 12mn$ **11.** $-12t^2 - 21tu$
12. $-6rs + 12r^2$ **13.** $7z^3 - 35z^2 + 63z$ **14.** $8a^3 + 24a^2 - 40a$
15. $-4t^3 - 28t^2 + 20t$ **16.** $-3a^3 + 6a^2 - 51a$
17. $7a^2b + 28ab^2 - 42ab$ **18.** $156r^2s + 78rs^2 - 91rs$
19. $-84m^2r + 49mr^2 - 35mr$ **20.** $-108s^2t - 27st^2 + 135st$
21. $p^2q^2 - pqv$ **22.** $7a^2b^2 + abc$ **23.** $a^5b - a^3b$
24. $x^2y^3 + 3xy^4$ **25.** $r^2s^4 - 9r^2s$ **26.** $v^2w^4 - 14v^2w$
27. $7x^5 - 49x^2y$ **28.** $63b^3 + 72b^2c$ **29.** $c^5d^3 - 2c^3d^3$
30. $v^5w^3 + 9v^4w^2$ **31.** $p^4q^3 - 9pq^2r$ **32.** $s^2t^4 + 7st^3u$
33. $-15x^5y^3 - 75x^3yz$ **34.** $24r^3s^2 + 96rst$

Page 23 Multiplication of a Polynomial and a Monomial

1. $8x^4 - 12x^3 + 4x^2$ **2.** $63y^4 + 45y^3 - 27y^2$
3. $21x^4y + 14x^3y^2 - 35x^2y^3$ **4.** $6a^5b - 12a^4b^2 + 21a^3b^3$
5. $x^2y^5 + x^2y^3 + 2x^2y^2$ **6.** $2a^2b^4 - 5a^2b^3 + a^2b^2$
7. $-ax^5 - 5ax^3 - 3x^3$ **8.** $-by^5 + 6by^4 + 9y^4$
9. $a^4b^2 + 2a^3b^2 + a^2b^2$ **10.** $c^2d^4 + 3c^2d^3 - 7c^2d^2$
11. $-a^3 + 2a^2 - 3a$ **12.** $-3c^3 - 4c^2 + 2c$ **13.** $2x^3 + 6x^2 - 4x$
14. $5y^3 - 21y^2 + 3y$ **15.** $3x^4y^3z^3 + 4x^2y^3z^4 + 7x^2y^2z^3$
16. $4p^4q^4r^2 + 2p^2q^4r^3 - 9p^2q^3r^2$ **17.** $3a^5b^3 - 9a^4b^4c + 3a^2b^3c^3$
18. $7r^6s^3 + 6r^5s^4t - 2r^3s^3t$ **19.** $42m^4n^6p^3 - 27m^3n^3p^5$
20. $24r^4u^5v^5 + 38r^3u^2v^7$ **21.** $-18w^2x^2y^5 - 12w^2xy^6 + 42wx^2y^6$
22. $-45r^2s^4t^2 - 18rs^4t^3 + 72r^2s^3t^3$ **23.** $26a^4b^6c^3 + 39a^5b^3c^5$
24. $27m^4n^4r^2 - 18m^3n^3r^4 + 27m^6n^2r^4$
25. $154x^4y^3z - 132xy^4z^2 + 77xy^3z$
26. $-120p^4q^6 + 105p^5r^2q^3 - 30p^2q^3$
27. $115a^6d^4 - 161a^4cd^2 + 92a^4d^2$
28. $96u^5v^5 + 144u^3v^2t - 128u^3v^2$
29. $27x^5z + 36x^3z^3 + 18x^3y^2z^4$ **30.** $28a^5t - 42a^3t^2 + 42a^3t^2u$
31. $126cd^4 - 108c^2d^2 + 27bcd^2$
32. $-28p^6q^2 - 14p^3q^3 + 63p^3q^2r$
33. $-96m^5n^2 - 40m^3nt + 56m^2n^2t^3$
34. $54r^4s^4 - 36r^5s^2t + 30r^2s^3u$

Page 24 Multiplication of a Polynomial and a Monomial

1. $15a^4 - 35a^3 + 20a^2$ **2.** $56c^5 + 14c^4 - 63c^3$
3. $15m^5n - 12m^4n^2 - 24m^3n^3$ **4.** $18x^4y - 30x^3y^2 + 54x^2y^3$
5. $p^2q^4 + p^2q^3 - 5p^2q^2$ **6.** $5m^3n^4 - 7m^3n^3 + 2m^3n^2$
7. $-az^6 + 9az^3 - 5z^3$ **8.** $-ab^4 + 7b^4 - 13b^3$
9. $a^2r^4 + 5a^2r^3 - 7a^2r^2$ **10.** $x^3y^4 - 9x^3y^3 + 14x^3y^2$
11. $-4x^3 + 6x^2 - 2x$ **12.** $-6z^3 - 12z^2 + 9z$ **13.** $6x^3 + 15x^2 - 3x$
14. $10y^3 - 8y^2 + 12y$ **15.** $4a^4b^3c^3 + 9a^2b^3c^4 + 3a^2b^2c^3$

16. $2t^3u^5v^3 - 3t^4u^2v^3 - 11t^3u^2v^2$ 17. $7r^4t^3 - 3r^4t^4q + 5r^2t^4q$
18. $4w^3z^5 + 9w^3y^3z^5 - 5w^2yz^4$ 19. $117u^6v^4w^3 - 72u^4v^2w^3$
20. $77a^5b^4t^4 + 77a^4b^2t^6$ 21. $-35c^2de^5 - 28cd^2e^5 + 56c^2d^2e^4$
22. $-14ab^3c^4 + 6a^2b^2c^4 + 18a^2b^3c^3$ 23. $33m^4n^6r^3 - 77m^2n^6r^5$
24. $10r^4s^5t^2 - 15r^3s^3t^4 - 25r^5s^2t^5$
25. $209c^3d^3e - 228cd^4e^2 + 95cd^3e$
26. $-138r^6t^4 - 69r^6q^2t^2 + 161r^3t^2$
27. $45m^4t^6 - 60m^3nt^3 - 105m^2t^3$
28. $52x^7 z^4 + 78x^5yz^2 - 117x^4z^2$ 29. $15a^6c + 6a^4c^4 - 21a^6c^3$
30. $18b^5q - 30b^3q^2 - 48b^4q^2$ 31. $60r^6t^2 - 44r^3t^3 + 20c^3r^3t^2$
32. $-27y^5z^2 + 18y^2z^4 + 45dy^2z^2$ 33. $-22b^5r^3 - 6ab^4r + 12b^3r^2t$
34. $49 q^3t^6 - 56qt^7x - 28qst^5$

Page 25   Products of Binomials

1. $x^2 + 4x + 3$ 2. $x^2 + 11x + 30$ 3. $2x^2 + 7x + 3$
4. $4x^2 + 20x + 21$ 5. $3x^2 + 17x + 10$ 6. $12x^2 + 15x + 6$
7. $12x^2 + 11x + 2$ 8. $4x^2 + 39x + 56$ 9. $5x^2 + 21x + 4$
10. $10x^2 + 21x + 9$ 11. $5x^2 + 48x + 64$ 12. $6x^2 + 35x + 25$
13. $2x^2 + 5x + 2$ 14. $2x^2 + 17x + 30$ 15. $3x^2 + 25x + 8$
16. $12x^2 + 14x + 6$ 17. $10x^2 + 47x + 9$ 18. $15x^2 + 19x + 6$
19. $10x^2 + 45x + 56$ 20. $14x^2 + 53x + 14$ 21. $7x^2 + 34x + 24$
22. $7x^2 + 31x + 12$ 23. $3x^2 + 16x + 21$ 24. $4x^2 + 29x + 7$
25. $8x^2 + 22x + 15$ 26. $4x^2 + 24x + 27$ 27. $2x^2 + 15x + 18$
28. $3x^2 + 28x + 32$ 29. $3x^2 + 22x + 35$ 30. $4x^2 + 23x + 15$
31. $3x^2 + 25x + 42$ 32. $5x^2 + 23x + 24$ 33. $x^2 + 7x + 12$
34. $2x^2 + 11x + 15$

Page 26   Products of Binomials

1. $x^2 + 11x + 28$ 2. $2x^2 + 15x + 7$ 3. $9x^2 + 18x + 5$
4. $3x^2 + 23x + 30$ 5. $4x^2 + 21x + 20$ 6. $4x^2 + 13x + 9$
7. $10x^2 + 55x + 72$ 8. $8x^2 + 26x + 21$ 9. $20x^2 + 9x + 1$
10. $4x^2 + 39x + 56$ 11. $2x^2 + 15x + 28$ 12. $8x^2 + 26x + 15$
13. $15x^2 + 47x + 28$ 14. $14x^2 + 13x + 3$ 15. $7x^2 + 55x + 42$
16. $5x^2 + 31x + 30$ 17. $6x^2 + 43x + 42$ 18. $4x^2 + 33x + 54$
19. $2x^2 + 9x + 7$ 20. $2x^2 + 19x + 42$ 21. $x^2 + 11x + 24$
22. $4x^2 + 25x + 25$ 23. $12x^2 + 25x + 7$ 24. $6x^2 + 17x + 7$
25. $5x^2 + 24x + 27$ 26. $10x^2 + 27x + 5$ 27. $6x^2 + 11x + 3$
28. $21x^2 + 52x + 7$ 29. $20x^2 + 47x + 24$ 30. $35x^2 + 33x + 4$
31. $21x^2 + 29x + 10$ 32. $28x^2 + 67x + 40$ 33. $5x^2 + 18x + 27$
34. $5x^2 + 9x + 4$

Page 27   Products of Binomials

1. $x^2 - 6x + 5$ 2. $x^2 - 13x + 15$ 3. $2x^2 - 7x + 6$
4. $3x^2 - 7x + 4$ 5. $3x^2 - 26x + 35$ 6. $8x^2 - 38x + 35$
7. $20x^2 - 13x + 2$ 8. $6x^2 - 25x + 21$ 9. $15x^2 - 28x + 12$
10. $7x^2 - 8x + 1$ 11. $8x^2 - 30x + 7$ 12. $6x^2 - 29x + 9$
13. $x^2 - 10x + 21$ 14. $16x^2 - 56x + 45$ 15. $10x^2 - 29x + 21$
16. $14x^2 - 29x + 12$ 17. $7x^2 - 51x + 14$ 18. $9x^2 - 21x + 10$
19. $2x^2 - 23x + 45$ 20. $x^2 - 6x + 8$ 21. $5x^2 - 23x + 12$
22. $2x^2 - 21x + 27$ 23. $3x^2 - 10x + 1$ 24. $4x^2 - 29x + 7$
25. $30x^2 - 11x + 1$ 26. $21x^2 - 13x + 2$ 27. $7x^2 - 15x + 8$
28. $15x^2 - 32x + 16$ 29. $25x^2 - 20x + 3$ 30. $5x^2 - 24x + 16$
31. $6x^2 - 53x + 40$ 32. $2x^2 - 19x + 45$ 33. $6x^2 - 29x + 28$
34. $24x^2 - 46x + 21$

Page 28   Products of Binomials

1. $x^2 - 13x + 40$ 2. $x^2 - 13x + 12$ 3. $15x^2 - 41x + 28$
4. $2x^2 - 21x + 54$ 5. $4x^2 - 7x + 3$ 6. $12x^2 - 43x + 35$
7. $3x^2 - 20x + 25$ 8. $7x^2 - 24x + 9$ 9. $25x^2 - 55x + 24$
10. $16x^2 - 40x + 21$ 11. $6x^2 - 13x + 5$ 12. $3x^2 - 4x + 1$
13. $2x^2 - 25x + 72$ 14. $35x^2 - 46x + 15$ 15. $14x^2 - 23x + 8$
16. $12x^2 - 28x + 15$ 17. $4x^2 - 31x + 21$ 18. $x^2 - 13x + 36$
19. $8x^2 - 30x + 7$ 20. $15x^2 - 28x + 12$ 21. $8x^2 - 22x + 9$
22. $7x^2 - 29x + 4$ 23. $6x^2 - 25x + 25$ 24. $21x^2 - 40x + 16$
25. $4x^2 - 13x + 3$ 26. $7x^2 - 11x + 4$ 27. $7x^2 - 37x + 36$
28. $4x^2 - 43x + 63$ 29. $6x^2 - 35x + 25$ 30. $2x^2 - 15x + 27$
31. $x^2 - 11x + 24$ 32. $12x^2 - 19x + 4$ 33. $20x^2 - 59x + 42$
34. $5x^2 - 43x + 56$

1. $2x^2 - 11x - 40$ 2. $2x^2 - 3x - 54$ 3. $5x^2 + 39x - 8$
4. $10x^2 - 23x - 5$ 5. $12x^2 - 19x - 21$ 6. $10x^2 - 29x - 21$
7. $3x^2 - 14x - 56$ 8. $12x^2 + 28x - 5$ 9. $12x^2 + x - 35$
10. $5x^2 - 38x - 63$ 11. $15x^2 - x - 2$ 12. $x^2 - 4x - 12$
13. $8x^2 + 2x - 1$ 14. $7x^2 - 62x - 9$ 15. $10x^2 + 39x - 27$
16. $21x^2 + 34x - 35$ 17. $35x^2 + 29x - 28$ 18. $20x^2 + 13x - 21$
19. $3x^2 + 25x - 18$ 20. $4x^2 - 16x - 9$ 21. $x^2 - 8x - 9$
22. $x^2 + 8x - 9$ 23. $12x^2 + 5x - 25$ 24. $5x^2 + 13x - 6$
25. $25x^2 - 20x - 21$ 26. $14x^2 + 23x - 30$ 27. $4x^2 - 33x - 27$
28. $6x^2 - 19x - 36$ 29. $7x^2 - 33x - 54$ 30. $3x^2 + 7x - 6$
31. $6x^2 - 5x - 1$ 32. $20x^2 - 9x - 18$ 33. $5x^2 - 31x - 28$
34. $35x^2 + 3x - 2$

Page 30   Products of Binomials

1. $3x^2 - 14x - 24$ 2. $4x^2 - 3x - 27$ 3. $14x^2 - 19x - 3$
4. $5x^2 + 12x - 9$ 5. $6x^2 - 3x - 6$ 6. $5x^2 - 37x - 24$
7. $5x^2 - 28x - 49$ 8. $21x^2 - 8x - 4$ 9. $21x^2 + 22x - 8$
10. $6x^2 + 7x - 49$ 11. $15x^2 + 14x - 16$ 12. $3x^2 - 25x - 18$
13. $4x^2 + 11x - 45$ 14. $7x^2 - 4x - 3$ 15. $6x^2 + 13x - 63$
16. $30x^2 + 19x - 4$ 17. $4x^2 + 8x - 5$ 18. $3x^2 + x - 4$
19. $10x^2 + 37x - 36$ 20. $4x^2 + 23x - 35$ 21. $7x^2 + 27x - 4$
22. $24x^2 + 38x - 7$ 23. $7x^2 + 20x - 32$ 24. $18x^2 - 9x - 5$
25. $4x^2 + 19x - 30$ 26. $4x^2 + 9x - 28$ 27. $x^2 + x - 20$
28. $18x^2 + 15x - 25$ 29. $15x^2 + x - 40$ 30. $3x^2 - 5x - 2$
31. $15x^2 + 22x - 5$ 32. $5x^2 - 27x - 56$ 33. $28x^2 - 25x - 42$
34. $10x^2 - x - 24$

Page 31   Products of Binomials

1. $9x^2 + 24x + 7$ 2. $5x^2 - 14x - 3$ 3. $25x^2 - 80x + 63$
4. $x^2 + 6x + 5$ 5. $3x^2 + 23x - 36$ 6. $4x^2 + 15x - 4$
7. $7x^2 - 53x - 24$ 8. $30x^2 - 17x + 2$ 9. $4x^2 + 23x - 35$
10. $3x^2 + 4x - 7$ 11. $4x^2 + 24x + 27$ 12. $3x^2 + 11x + 10$
13. $5x^2 - 52x + 63$ 14. $7x^2 - 6x - 1$ 15. $10x^2 + 11x - 8$
16. $20x^2 + x - 12$ 17. $3x^2 - 14x - 24$ 18. $42x^2 + 11x - 20$
19. $10x^2 + 43x - 9$ 20. $24x^2 - 58x + 35$ 21. $5x^2 - 37x + 42$
22. $12x^2 - 20x - 25$ 23. $2x^2 + x - 10$ 24. $7x^2 + 32x + 16$
25. $35x^2 + 66x + 16$ 26. $12x^2 - x - 1$ 27. $20x^2 + 33x - 27$
28. $12x^2 - 56x + 49$ 29. $7x^2 - 59x + 24$ 30. $15x^2 - 2x - 8$
31. $3x^2 + 8x - 35$ 32. $4x^2 + 11x + 7$ 33. $18x^2 + 51x + 35$
34. $14x^2 - 33x + 18$

Page 32   Products of Binomials

1. $8x^2 - 18x + 9$ 2. $5x^2 + 44x - 9$ 3. $5x^2 + 12x - 32$
4. $3x^2 + 14x - 5$ 5. $5x^2 + 7x + 2$ 6. $7x^2 + 48x - 7$
7. $12x^2 + x - 35$ 8. $2x^2 + 21x + 40$ 9. $30x^2 + 43x - 8$
10. $20x^2 - 21x + 4$ 11. $5x^2 - 9x - 18$ 12. $12x^2 + 32x + 21$
13. $2x^2 + 15x + 18$ 14. $10x^2 - 17x - 63$ 15. $6x^2 - 19x - 7$
16. $28x^2 + 41x - 14$ 17. $15x^2 + 53x + 42$ 18. $2x^2 - 17x + 8$
19. $16x^2 - 64x + 63$ 20. $6x^2 - 29x - 5$ 21. $7x^2 - 43x - 42$
22. $16x^2 - 24x + 5$ 23. $4x^2 - 7x - 15$ 24. $5x^2 + 38x + 21$
25. $21x^2 - 40x + 16$ 26. $20x^2 - 23x - 7$ 27. $15x^2 + 38x + 24$
28. $2x^2 - 17x + 8$ 29. $35x^2 + 18x - 5$ 30. $30x^2 + 7x - 15$
31. $x^2 + 2x - 63$ 32. $7x^2 + 37x + 10$ 33. $15x^2 - 22x + 8$
34. $5x^2 - 2x - 16$

Page 33   Products of Binomials

1. $81x^2 - 1$ 2. $9x^2 - 1$ 3. $x^2 - 25y^2$ 4. $36 - c^2$ 5. $49a^2 - 1$
6. $4x^2 - 1$ 7. $16r^2s^2 - 9$ 8. $64r^4 - s^4$ 9. $49 - 64d^2$
10. $16a^2 - 36b^2$ 11. $x^2 - y^2$ 12. $81r^2 - 4s^2$ 13. $25p^2 - 16$
14. $9x^2 - 16y^2$ 15. $49 - 25a^2b^2$ 16. $16a^6 - 9$ 17. $4r^2 - 25$
18. $36a^2 - 9b^2$ 19. $9a^2 - b^2$ 20. $r^2 - 9s^2$ 21. $25x^2 - 64y^2$
22. $4b^4 - 81$ 23. $81a^2 - 25b^2$ 24. $1 - 16v^2$ 25. $25c^4 - 4d^4$
26. $64a^2 - 49b^2$ 27. $v^2 - 16$ 28. $9 - 25u^2$ 29. $16r^2s^2 - 1$
30. $25x^2 - 1$ 31. $81x^2 - 49y^2$ 32. $25x^2 - 49y^2$ 33. $36 - c^6$
34. $1 - 81x^2$

Page 34 Products of Binomials

1. $16q^4 - 49$ 2. $25x^2 - 9$ 3. $a^2 - 4b^2$ 4. $49 - 36r^2$
5. $25x^2 - 49y^2$ 6. $16a^2 - 25b^2$ 7. $36 - 25a^2$ 8. $c^4d^4 - 25$
9. $4r^2 - 9s^2$ 10. $9x^2 - 4y^2$ 11. $49c^2 - 4$ 12. $25 - 4a^2$
13. $64 - 9b^2$ 14. $9x^2 - 49y^2$ 15. $16x^2y^2 - 49$ 16. $49c^2 - 9$
17. $25r^2 - 81$ 18. $a^2 - 36b^2$ 19. $1 - d^4$ 20. $4x^4 - 49$
21. $4 - 49t^2$ 22. $64 - x^2y^2$ 23. $49x^2 - 16y^2$ 24. $4 - 81t^2$
25. $a^2 - 9b^2$ 26. $36r^2 - 49s^2$ 27. $a^2b^2 - 49$ 28. $81a^2 - 16b^2$
29. $x^6 - 25$ 30. $81 - 64c^2$ 31. $64x^2 - 81y^2$ 32. $r^2 - 64s^2$
33. $4y^4 - 9$ 34. $9 - 4a^2$

Page 35 Powers of Binomials

1. $25 + 10x + x^2$ 2. $4y^2 + 4y + 1$ 3. $9a^2b^2 - 24ab + 16$
4. $49x^2 - 28x + 4$ 5. $c^2 + 2c + 1$ 6. $64a^2 - 16ab + b^2$
7. $16x^2 - 24xy + 9y^2$ 8. $x^2 + 18xy + 81y^2$ 9. $9 + 12d + 4d^2$
10. $81x^2 + 36xy + 4y^2$ 11. $25r^2 - 80r + 64$ 12. $p^2 - 4p + 4$
13. $16a^2 + 40ab + 25b^2$ 14. $25a^2b^2 - 20ab + 4$
15. $49x^2 - 42xy + 9y^2$ 16. $36 - 60xy + 25x^2y^2$ 17. $q^2 - 6q + 9$
18. $81s^2 + 18s + 1$ 19. $64 - 80t + 25t^2$ 20. $a^2b^2 + 16ab + 64$
21. $81a^2 + 72ab + 16b^2$ 22. $9 - 30m + 25m^2$
23. $25v^2 + 30v + 9$ 24. $25z^2 + 90z + 81$
25. $49c^2 - 56cd + 16d^2$ 26. $36x^2 + 12xy + y^2$
27. $x^3 + 3x^2 + 3x + 1$ 28. $8c^3 - 12c^2 + 6c - 1$
29. $8a^3 - 36a^2b + 54ab^2 - 27b^3$ 30. $r^3 + 12r^2 + 48r + 64$
31. $1 - 4c + 6c^2 - 4c^3 + c^4$ 32. $16a^2 + 32a^3 + 24a^2 + 8a + 1$
33. $81x^4 + 216x^3y + 216x^2y^2 + 96xy^3 + 64y^4$
34. $1 - 16r + 96r^2 - 256r^3 + 256r^4$

Page 36 Powers of Binomials

1. $9a^2 - 6ab + b^2$ 2. $25c^2d^2 + 40cd + 16$ 3. $x^2 - 8x + 16$
4. $16x^2 + 72xy + 81y^2$ 5. $49 + 70a + 25a^2$
6. $49x^2 - 126xy + 81y^2$ 7. $16b^2 + 56b + 49$
8. $49 - 112x + 64x^2$ 9. $25a^2 - 70ab + 49b^2$
10. $m^2 + 10m + 25$ 11. $49 + 14r + r^2$ 12. $81x^2 - 90x + 25$
13. $9 + 42xy + 49x^2y^2$ 14. $4a^2 - 20ab + 25b^2$
15. $49s^2 + 84st + 36t^2$ 16. $4m^2 + 36m + 81$
17. $64a^2 - 144ab + 81b^2$ 18. $16t^2 + 8t + 1$ 19. $v^2 + 12v + 36$
20. $25x^2 - 60xy + 36y^2$ 21. $64x^2y^2 + 48xy + 9$
22. $81a^2 + 126ab + 49b^2$ 23. $4 + 12z + 9z^2$
24. $4y^2 - 28y + 49$ 25. $64 - 112x + 49x^2$ 26. $36a^2 + 84a + 49$
27. $27a^3 - 27a^2b + 9ab^2 - b^3$ 28. $r^3 + 6r^2 + 12r + 8$
29. $27 + 27p + 9p^2 + p^3$ 30. $1 - 30x + 300x^2 - 1000x^3$
31. $81a^4 + 108a^3 + 54a^2 + 12a + 1$
32. $x^4 - 8x^3 + 24x^2 - 32x + 16$
33. $x^4 - 12x^3y + 54x^2y^2 - 108xy^3 + 81y^4$
34. $r^4 + 40r^3 + 600r^2 + 4000r + 10000$

Page 37 Products of Polynomials

1. $2a^3 + 7a^2 - 5a - 4$ 2. $27 + 15x + x^2 + 2x^3$ 3. $4c^3 - 5c^2 + 1$
4. $32r^3 - 64r^2s + 22rs^2 - 2s^3$ 5. $8m^3 - 14m^2n - 7mn^2 + 6n^3$
6. $7c^3 + 48c^2 - 9c - 14$ 7. $3s^3 - 24s^2 - 29s + 42$
8. $12m^3 - 17m^2n - 31mn^2 - 24n^3$ 9. $21 + 17c + 5c^2 + 2c^3$
10. $6a^3 + 11a^2 - a - 5$ 11. $s^3 - 9s^2 + 10s - 16$
12. $12r^3 + 23r^2 - r + 18$ 13. $24x^3 + 11x^2y - 5xy^2 - 2y^3$
14. $48s^3 - 14s^2t - 41st^2 + 7t^3$ 15. $45s^3 - 7s^2 + 8s - 10$
16. $21u^3 - u^2v - 8uv^2 + 2v^3$ 17. $54r^3 - 39r^2s + 32rs^2 - 15s^3$
18. $21c^3 - 38c^2 - 62c - 12$ 19. $15p^3 + 17p^2q + 29pq^2 + 20q^3$
20. $30 + r - 19r^2 + 3r^3$ 21. $49c^3 + 70c^2 - 12c - 27$
22. $3x^3 + 7x^2 - 2x - 6$ 23. $32r^3 - 68r^2 + 22r + 5$
24. $20s^3 + 77s^2 + 82s + 16$ 25. $7u^3 - 53u^2t - 45ut^2 - 9t^3$
26. $18c^3d^3 - 39c^2d^2 - 22cd + 35$ 27. $40 - 77a + 4a^2 + 9a^3$
28. $27r^3 + 42r^2 + 24r + 5$ 29. $5r^3 - 26r^2 + 11r - 30$
30. $3x^3 + 25x^2y + 22xy^2 - 8y^3$ 31. $18c^3 + 11c^2 - 3c - 2$
32. $30a^3 + 42a^2 + 17a + 2$ 33. $24u^3 + 6u^2t - 26ut^2 + 5t^3$
34. $42 - 17c - 9c^2 - 5c^3$

Page 38 Products of Polynomials

1. $20s^3 - s^2 + 3s - 1$ 2. $12u^3 + 38u^2t - t^3$ 3. $2r^3 + 2r^2 - 11r + 3$
4. $7x^3 - 12x^2 - 3x - 2$ 5. $6c^3 - 7c^2d - 39cd^2 - 35d^3$
6. $3x^3 + x^2y + 11xy^2 + 20y^3$ 7. $16 - 38u + u^2 - 15u^3$
8. $20v^3 + 3v^2w - 17vw^2 - 6w^3$ 9. $30r^3 - 5r^2 + 11r + 30$
10. $24 - s + 13s^2 - 6s^3$ 11. $6x^3 + 50x^2 + 15x - 8$
12. $8r^3 + 33r^2s + 9rs^2 + 20r^3$ 13. $15u^3 - 4u^2 - u - 2$
14. $3w^3 + 13w^2 + 5w - 21$ 15. $6c^3 - 29c^2d + 24cd^2 + 14d^3$
16. $15a^3 + 37a^2 + 23a - 4$ 17. $18r^3 + 3r^2 - 31r - 4$
18. $10u^3 + 21u^2t + 29ut^2 + 12t^3$ 19. $2x^3 + 20x^2 + 25x + 63$
20. $20r^3 + 36r^2 - 3r - 1$ 21. $42s^3 - 55s^2 + 31s - 28$
22. $36s^3 + 20s^2t - 7st^2 - 4t^3$ 23. $42a^3 + 62a^2 + 15a + 1$
24. $9x^3 + 9x^2y - 13xy^2 - 5y^3$ 25. $49c^3 + 5cd^2 + 6d^3$
26. $8s^3 - 57s^2 + 30s + 27$ 27. $20x^3 + 3x^2 + 6x - 9$
28. $15r^3 - 38r^2s + 31rs^2 - 56$ 29. $72r^3 - 65r^2 + 43r - 28$
30. $s^3 + 8s^2 + 19s + 42$ 31. $35c^3 - 36c^2d - 27cd^2 - 8d^3$
32. $49x^3 - 49x^2 - 22x + 16$ 33. $18 + 25s - 11s^2 - 12s^3$
34. $27m^3 - 33m^2n - 55mn^2 + 56n^3$

Page 39 Products of Polynomials

1. $15x^3 + 42x^2 - 4x - 1$ 2. $12 - 17r + 18r^2 - 9r^3$
3. $6c^3 - c^2d - 38cd^2 + 5d^3$ 4. $6a + 5a^2 + 13a + 6$
5. $6a^3 - 15a^2 - 10a + 3$ 6. $8x^3 - 10x^2y + 17xy^2 + 5y^3$
7. $49 + 14r - 20r^2 - 3r^3$ 8. $4c^3 + 15c^2 + 11c - 6$
9. $7a^3 + 30a^2 - 24a + 5$ 10. $6x^3 - 17x^2y - 27xy^2 + 30y^3$
11. $9c^3 - 9c^2 - 37c - 8$ 12. $32a^3 + 12a^2 - 27a - 7$
13. $4r^3 - 23r^2 + 40r - 21$ 14. $14s^3 - 15s^2t - 7st^2 - 3t^3$
15. $63x^3 - 22x^2 - x - 4$ 16. $2 - 26c + 69c^2 + 27c^3$
17. $35s^3 + 32s^2 - 19s + 2$ 18. $24m^3 - 4m^2n - 62mn^2 - 35n^3$
19. $2s^3 + 27s^2 + 85s + 18$ 20. $30a^3 - 47a^2b + 2ab^2 + 14b^3$
21. $30c^3 + 19c^2 + 16c + 16$ 22. $30r^3 + 56r^2s + 19rs^2 - 6s^3$
23. $63r^3 + 25r^2 + 20r + 2$ 24. $8x^3 - 14x^2 - 45x + 7$
25. $35x^3 - 58x^2y + 16xy^2 - 45y^3$ 26. $40 + 71c + 13c^2 - 3c^3$
27. $36a^3 - 46a^2b + 59ab^2 - 35b^3$ 28. $45a^3 + 38a^2 - 37a - 20$
29. $40c^3 + 61c^2 + 42c + 49$ 30. $42r^3 - r^2 + 23r - 4$
31. $18x^3 + 39x^2y - 17xy^2 - 5y^3$ 32. $4 + 31x + 14x^2 - 49x^3$
33. $18r^3 - 24r^2 - 7r - 5$ 34. $4c^3 + 3c^2d + 17cd^2 + 42$

Page 40 Products of Polynomials

1. $9c^3 + 10c^2 + 46c + 5$ 2. $c^3 - 2c^2d + 6cd^2 - 5d^3$
3. $4x^3 + 14x^2y - 9xy^2 - 4y^3$ 4. $7 + 44r + 13r^2 + 6r^3$
5. $20r^3 - 33r^2s + 30rs^2 - 25s^3$ 6. $16s^3 + 66s^2 - 25s + 9$
7. $7 - 29c + 12c^2 - 36c^3$ 8. $7x^3 - 16x^2 - 14x - 3$
9. $9x^3 + 65x^2y + 11xy^2 - 21y^3$ 10. $12c^3 + 17c^2d - 25cd^2 + 5d^3$
11. $6a^2 + 5a^2b - 8ab^2 - 3b^3$ 12. $42 - 23r + 11r^2 + 6r^3$
13. $8r^3 + 71r^2s - 41rs^2 + 4s^3$ 14. $45c^3 + 73c^2 + 4c - 14$
15. $72c^3 - 34c^2d - 23cd^2 + 6d^3$ 16. $7x^3 - 29x^2 - 2x + 24$
17. $49x^3 + 42x^2y + 40xy^2 + 25y^3$ 18. $16r^3 + 44r^2 + 2r - 36$
19. $42m^3 - 31m^2n + 25mn^2 - 12n^3$
20. $72a^3 + 7a^2b + 34ab^2 + 8b^3$ 21. $9 + 24s - 6s^2 - 35s^3$
22. $5c^3 - 48c^2 + 30c - 27$ 23. $30c^3 - 11c^2d - 25cd^2 - 6d^3$
24. $12r^3 + 36r^2 - 19r + 7$ 25. $7x^3 + 10x^2 - 11x - 6$
26. $35x^3 - 81x^2y + 26xy^2 + 10y^3$ 27. $16a^3 + 68a^2 - 16a + 9$
28. $15s^3 + 4s^2 + 5s + 6$ 29. $45r^3 - 76r^2s + 41rs^2 - 8s^3$
30. $8 - 60a - 33a^2 + 8a^3$ 31. $28 - 17c + 5c^2 - 6c^3$
32. $40c^3 - 67c^2d - cd^2 + d^3$ 33. $63s^3 + 2s^2 + 34s + 5$
34. $36r^3 + 43r^2t + 3rt^2 - 4t^3$

Page 41 Products of Binomials

1. $x^3 + 6x^2 - x - 30$ 2. $x^3 - x^2 - 50x - 48$
3. $25x^3 - 65x^2 + 47x - 7$ 4. $15x^3 - 14x^2 - 47x + 30$
5. $4x^3 + 24x^2 + 41x + 21$ 6. $3x^3 + 20x^2 - 21x - 98$
7. $80x^3 + 196x^2y + 90xy^2 - 36y^3$
8. $5x^3 - 48x^2y + 100xy^2 + 48y^3$ 9. $7x^3 - 41x^2 - 195x - 27$
10. $18x^3 - 9x^2 - 17x + 10$ 11. $50x^3 - 5x^2y - 11xy^2 + 2$

126

12. $168x^3 + 82x^2 - 311x + 105$ **13.** $98x^3 - 189x^2 - 132x - 20$
14. $8x^3 - 68x^2 + 174x - 135$ **15.** $8x^3 + 61x^2 + 115x + 50$
16. $378x^3 - 501x^2 + 22x + 56$
17. $18x^3 + 153x^2y + 193xy^2 + 28y^3$
18. $135x^3 - 354x^2 + 85x + 14$ **19.** $24 + 44x - 278x^2 + 45x^3$
20. $360x^3 - 221x^2y - 533xy^2 - 56y^3$
21. $216x^3 - 429x^2 - 169x - 14$ **22.** $140 - 471x + 510x^2 - 175x^3$
23. $36x^3 + 153x^2 + 182x + 45$ **24.** $63x^3 + 212x^2 + 13x - 168$
25. $64x^3 + 80x^2 - 47x - 63$ **26.** $49x^3 + 315x^2 + 72x - 324$
27. $35x^3 - 186x^2 - 179x + 210$ **28.** $105 - 218x + 85x^2 - 8x^3$
29. $36x^3 + 209x^2y + 150xy^2 + 25y^3$ **30.** $64x^3 + 8x^2 - 30x - 9$
31. $49x^3 - 196x^2 - 540x - 288$ **32.** $6x^3 - 31x^2 + 46x - 16$
33. $18x^3 + 183x^2 + 194x + 45$ **34.** $60x^3 - 212x^2y + 5xy^2 + 7y^3$

Page 42 Products of Binomials

1. $x^3 - 41x^2 + 108x + 224$ **2.** $x^3 + 19x^2 + 21x + 5$
3. $x^3 + 3x^2 - 14x - 15$ **4.** $225x^3 - 215x^2 - 32x + 48$
5. $64x^3 - 216x^2y + 230xy^2 - 75y^3$ **6.** $5x^3 - 46x^2 + 128x - 96$
7. $5x^3 - 77x^2 + 267x + 189$ **8.** $20x^3 + 64x^2y + 11xy^2 - 60y^3$
9. $421x^3 + 413x^2 + 106x + 8$ **10.** $12 + 88x - 71x^2 - 56x^3$
11. $15x^3 - 62x^2 - 37x + 360$ **12.** $14 + 51x - 21x^2 - 4x^3$
13. $40x^3 + 147x^2 + 77x - 12$ **14.** $4x^3 + 71x^2 + 339x + 216$
15. $189x^3 - 186x^2y - 56xy^2 - 64y^3$
16. $504x^3 - 515x^2y - 192xy^2 + 27y^3$
17. $10x^3 - 71x^2 + 144x - 63$ **18.** $6x^3 + x^2 - 166x - 336$
19. $336 - 50x - 447x^2 + 56x^3$
20. $210x^3 + 97x^2y - 166xy^2 + 24y^3$
21. $28x^3 + 149x^2y - 573xy^2 + 216y^3$
22. $72 - 243x + 241x^2 - 60x^3$
23. $72x^3 - 471x^2y - 813xy^2 - 216y^3$
24. $35 - 158x + 67x^2 + 20x^3$ **25.** $60x^3 - 193x^2 + 183x - 54$
26. $140x^3 - 67x^2 - 438x + 189$ **27.** $45 - 277x + 428x^2 - 160x^3$
28. $36 - 188x + 75x^2 + 189x^3$ **29.** $12x^3 + 104x^2 + 147x + 49$
30. $56x^3 - 225x^2 - 38x + 168$ **31.** $16x^3 + 62x^2 + 27x - 45$
32. $6x^2 - 35x^2y + 125$ **33.** $21 + 148x - 359x^2 + 90x^3$
34. $144x^3 - 252x^2y + 128xy^2 - 15y^3$

Page 43 Polynomial Equations

1. $x = -2$ **2.** $x = -1$ **3.** $x = -2$ **4.** $x = 1/2$ **5.** $x = 3$
6. $x = 8$ **7.** $x = -15$ **8.** $x = -33$ **9.** $x = 5$ **10.** $x = 3$
11. $x = 22$ **12.** $x = 1$ **13.** $x = -4$ **14.** $x = -5$ **15.** $x = 2$
16. $x = 5/8$ **17.** $x = -15$

Page 44 Polynomial Equations

1. $x = -4$ **2.** $x = 34$ **3.** $x = 1$ **4.** $x = 5$ **5.** $x = 2$ **6.** $x = 3$
7. $x = -4/7$ **8.** $x = -2$ **9.** $x = 2$ **10.** $x = 4$ **11.** $x = 2$
12. $x = -11$ **13.** $x = 2/3$ **14.** $x = -5/3$ **15.** $x = -3$
16. $x = -2/3$ **17.** $x = -9$

Page 45 Polynomial Word Problems

1. Brother: 19 yr, Jenny: 24 yr **2.** $40 **3.** 60 **4.** 104
5. 16 and 56 **6.** 25 **7.** 17m × 29m **8.** Rob: 9 yrs,
Cleve: 57 yr

Page 46 Polynomial Word Problems

1. $500 **2.** 90 km/h **3.** 40 **4.** 5 cm × 15 cm
5. Charlotte: $100, Art: $121 **6.** 121 cm² **7.** 160 people
8. $a = 23$ cm, $b = 48$ cm

Page 47 Polynomial Word Problems

1. Brother: 6 yr; Tom: 8 yr **2.** 6 km/h **3.** 15 m **4.** $11
5. 55 ft **6.** 5 cm **7.** 243 m **8.** 5 cm

Page 48 Polynomial

1. $630 **2.** 5 yr **3.** 9 **4.** 44 in. **5.** 42 ft **6.** 36 ft
7. 22 in. **8.** 32.5 cm²

Page 49 Using Exponents

1. a **2.** b^3 **3.** b^5 **4.** cd^3 **5.** $6x^2y^5$ **6.** $-2m^4n^2$
7. $(a^5b^3)/4$ **8.** $-(x^8y)/3$ **9.** $-(1/2y^3)$ **10.** $1/4x^2y^2$
11. $-(x^4/3y^2)$ **12.** $a^2/2b^5$ **13.** a^4 **14.** $-3x^2$ **15.** $1/3a^4$
16. $y^5/4$ **17.** $2/3a^3$ **18.** $t^7/3r^6$ **19.** a^{4-r} **20.** x^{5-t}
21. x^{m-2} **22.** $2m^{8-r}$ **23.** $(b^{2r})/(a^{2r})$ **24.** 10^3 **25.** 2^6
26. 3^5 **27.** 7^3 **28.** 11^3 **29.** $(a^4b^2)/4$ **30.** $(9x^5y)/4$
31. $(4x^{2r-5}y^{2t-7})/3$ **32.** $(8a^{3m-6}b^{3t-2})/5$
33. $(7a^{s-r}b^{y-t})/11$ **34.** x^ry^{3r} **35.** $(a^{5m})/b^{3m}$
36. $(d^{4p})/c^{3p}$

Page 50 Using Exponents

1. x^3 **2.** b^5 **3.** n^4 **4.** m^3n **5.** $5a^5b^2$ **6.** $(12a^3b)/5$
7. $(a^8b)/5$ **8.** $-(x^7y^8)/4$ **9.** $1/(4x^2y^6)$ **10.** $1/(8x^3y^5)$
11. $-(x^3/3y^5)$ **12.** $m^3/(3n^7)$ **13.** $3a^3$ **14.** $8x^3$
15. $1/(2x^3)$ **16.** $(a^3b^2)/3$ **17.** $1/(3s^4)$ **18.** $(a^7b^9)/3$
19. x^{7-m} **20.** a^{10-n} **21.** $(x^{r-2})/3$ **22.** $(m^{12-x})/2$
23. x^ty^t **24.** 5^7 **25.** 7^5 **26.** 13^3 **27.** 3^2 **28.** 12^2
29. x^6y^4 **30.** $(2x^3)/(9y^2)$ **31.** $(a^{3m-3}b^{3n-2})/2$
32. $(a^{3r-7}b^{3s-6})/2$ **33.** $(x^{m-s}y^{n-t})/2$ **34.** $(a^{3x})/b^x$
35. $(m^{4r})/(n^{2r})$ **36.** p^sq^s

Page 51 Division of Polynomials

1. $r + s$ **2.** $c + d$ **3.** $1 + 3x$ **4.** $5x + 1$ **5.** $3a^2 - 2b^3$
6. $2r^2s + 3s^3$ **7.** $4a^2 + 5b^5$ **8.** $2a^6b^3 + 4a^4b$ **9.** $3a^3b^2c - 4a$
10. $5c^2d^6 - 8c^5de$ **11.** $-4r^5s^2t^2 + 6r^2s$ **12.** $-6x^6y + 4x^2y^6z$
13. $4a^7b^8 - 6a^3b^5$ **14.** $5a^2b^6 - 2a^3b^2$ **15.** $1 + 3x - 4x^2$
16. $5a^3 - 3a^2 + 1$ **17.** $1 - 2cd + 3c^2d^2$ **18.** $6a^3b^3 - 3ab + 1$
19. $-1 - 3ab + 4a^2b^2$ **20.** $-12x^5y^5 + 6x^2y^2 - 1$
21. $m^2n^4 + 2m^4n - 3m^6$ **22.** $5a^6b^3 - 4a^4b^2 + a^2b$
23. $4s^7t^2 - 2s^5t^5 - s^3t^7$ **24.** $ab^6 - 3a^3b^3 - 6a^7b$

Page 52 Division of Polynomials

1. $a + b$ **2.** $2x + 2y$ **3.** $1 + c$ **4.** $1 + 2r$ **5.** $4m - 3n$
6. $3x^2y - 2x^3y^2$ **7.** $3ab^2 + 2b^3$ **8.** $4 + 5ab^3$
9. $-2cd^3e + 3c^2d$ **10.** $2x^5y^2 - 3xyz$ **11.** $4b^4 - 6a^7b^2c^2$
12. $4p^4q^3r^4 - 4p^5$ **13.** $-7 - 10m^2n^2$ **14.** $-3a^4b - 4a^2b^6$
15. $3 + 7a^2 + 12a^4$ **16.** $9x^6 + 5x^3 + 8$ **17.** $5x^2y - 3x + 1$
18. $3a^4b^2 - 2a^2b + 1$ **19.** $-1 + 3x^2y^3 + 5x^4y^6$
20. $-1 - 6m^3n - 9m^8n^4$ **21.** $m^4 - 4m^2n^3 + 5m^6n^4$
22. $c^5d^4 - 3cd + 4d^3$ **23.** $2x^7 + 3x^3y^2 + 5y^4$
24. $3a^8 + 5a^4b^4 + 9b^8$

Page 53 Quotients of Polynomials

1. $x + 7$ **2.** $x + 5$ **3.** $x + 4$ **4.** $x + 5$ **5.** $2x + 3$ **6.** $3x + 2$
7. $4x - 2$ **8.** $5x - 3$ **9.** $2x + 7$ **10.** $3x - 2$ **11.** $3x - 8$
12. $5x - 2$ **13.** $2x - 5$ **14.** $7x + 3$ **15.** $x^2 - 6x + 5$
16. $x^2 + 3x + 2$ **17.** $x^2 - 5x + 2$ **18.** $x^2 + 2x - 3$
19. $x^2 - 9x + 18$ **20.** $x^2 - 3x + 10$ **21.** $x^2 - x - 30$
22. $x^2 + x - 12$ **23.** $x^2 + 4x + 3$ **24.** $x^2 + x - 20$
25. $x^2 - 3x - 18$ **26.** $x^2 - 39x - 70$ **27.** $x^2 + x + 1$
28. $9x^2 + 3x + 1$ **29.** $x^3 - 4x^2 + 16x - 64$
30. $8x^3 - 4x^2 + 2x - 1$ **31.** $x^4 + 2x^3 + 4x^2 + 8x + 16$
32. $81x^4 - 27x^3 + 9x^2 - 3x + 1$

Page 54 Quotients of Polynomials

1. $x - 5$ **2.** $x + 2$ **3.** $x + 7$ **4.** $x + 9$ **5.** $2x + 3$ **6.** $3x + 2$
7. $4x - 1$ **8.** $5x + 2$ **9.** $3x + 5$ **10.** $4x + 1$ **11.** $2x - 3$
12. $3x - 2$ **13.** $x - 5$ **14.** $2x + 1$ **15.** $x^2 - x - 6$
16. $x^2 - x - 20$ **17.** $x^2 - 2x + 3$ **18.** $x^2 + 9x + 20$
19. $x^2 - x - 6$ **20.** $x^2 - 2x - 8$ **21.** $2x^2 + 5x - 3$
22. $x^2 + 2x + 3$ **23.** $3x^2 - 5x + 2$ **24.** $3x^2 + 4x + 3$
25. $x^2 + 3x + 5$ **26.** $x^2 - 7x + 2$ **27.** $x^2 + 4x + 7$
28. $x^2 + 7x - 10$ **29.** $x^2 + 6x + 36$ **30.** $16x^2 - 4x + 1$
31. $27x^3 + 9x^2 + 3x + 1$ **32.** $x^3 + 4x^2 + 16x + 64$

Page 55   Quotients of Polynomials

1. $x + 3 + [5/(x - 1)]$ 2. $x + 7 + [-3/(x - 11)]$
3. $x - 7 + [1/(x - 3)]$ 4. $x + 9 + [8/(x - 12)]$
5. $x + 4 + [7/(x + 5)]$ 6. $x - 15 + [-15/(x + 5)]$
7. $x + 2 + [-5/(x - 9)]$ 8. $x + 20 + [-10/(x + 8)]$
9. $x - 6 + [-3/(x - 5)]$ 10. $x - 7 + [16/(x + 13)]$
11. $x - 9 - [12/(x + 12)]$ 12. $x - 3 + [20/(x + 5)]$
13. $x + 6 + [6/(x + 4)]$ 14. $x + 7 + [-10/(x + 10)]$
15. $x - 9 + [-7/(x + 7)]$ 16. $x + 5 + [10/(x - 17)]$
17. $2x + 1 + [-8/(x - 1)]$ 18. $2x + 11 + [12/(x - 7)]$
19. $2x + 5 + [5/(x + 3)]$ 20. $x - 4 + [4/(2x - 9)]$
21. $3x + 1 + [10/(x - 2)]$ 22. $2x - 9 + [-11/(2x + 1)]$
23. $2x + 5 + [4/(2x + 1)]$ 24. $3x - 7 + [31/(2x + 3)]$
25. $3x + 4 + [-3/(2x - 3)]$ 26. $5x + 8 + [-14/(x + 7)]$
27. $5x + 7 + [7/(3x - 5)]$ 28. $4x - 5 + [-17/(x - 8)]$
29. $4x - 9 + [13/(x + 7)]$ 30. $3x + 1 + [13/(3x + 5)]$
31. $x + 10 + [10/(2x - 11)]$ 32. $2x - 3 + [-7/(9x + 1)]$
33. $10x - 1 + [-20/(x + 5)]$ 34. $3x - 5 + [-8/(5x - 4)]$

Page 56   Quotients of Polynomials

1. $x - 9 + [22/(x - 11)]$ 2. $x + 3 + [-9/(x - 2)]$
3. $x + 21 + [-22/(x + 7)]$ 4. $x + 17 + [-37/(x + 11)]$
5. $x + 22 + [20/(x - 10)]$ 6. $x - 13 + [3/(x - 9)]$
7. $x + 17 + [9/(x + 3)]$ 8. $x + 15 + [20/(x + 3)]$
9. $x - 21 + [33/(x - 7)]$ 10. $x - 21 + [-18/(x - 18)]$
11. $x + 11 + [-38/(x + 8)]$ 12. $x - 13 + [19/(x + 8)]$
13. $x + 50 + [-25/(x + 2)]$ 14. $x - 30 + [-90/(x - 10)]$
15. $x - 23 + [-53/(x - 11)]$ 16. $x - 29 + [-17/(x + 2)]$
17. $3x + 2 + [-8/(4x - 1)]$ 18. $8x + 2 + [-24/(3x - 8)]$
19. $3x - 4 + [18/5x - 8)]$ 20. $2x - 4 + [-38/(7x + 1)]$
21. $2x - 14 + [-34/(4x - 1)]$ 22. $10x + 1 + [-6/(5x - 4)]$
23. $3x + 11 + [-50/(2x - 5)]$ 24. $8x + 10 + [-20/(9x - 2)]$
25. $4x + 3 + [-11/(4x - 3)]$ 26. $5x - 9 + [1/(5x + 9)]$
27. $5x + 2 + [-8/(5x - 2)]$ 28. $14x + 11$
29. $7x + 3 + [19/(3x + 2)]$ 30. $9x + 4 + [-18/(5x - 3)]$
31. $11x - 4 + [30/(3x - 5)]$ 32. $14x - 5 + [35/(5x + 6)]$
33. $5x - 20 + [-20/(4x - 10)]$ 34. $7x - 11 + [245/(3x + 10)]$

Page 57   Quotients of Polynomials

1. $x^2 + 3x - 5 + [3/(x - 2)]$ 2. $x^2 - 5x + 2 + [6/(x + 3)]$
3. $x^2 + 3x + 2 + [-5/(x - 5)]$ 4. $x^2 - 5x + 7 + [2/(x + 7)]$
5. $x^2 - 3x + 4 + [-1/(2x + 1)]$ 6. $x^2 - 5x + 1 + [-8/(3x - 2)]$
7. $x^2 + 7x + 3 + [4/(3x - 7)]$ 8. $x^2 + 5x + 7 + [-7/(x - 5)]$
9. $x^2 - 3x + 4 + [4/(x + 3)]$ 10. $2x^2 - 3x + 5 + [-8/(2x + 3)]$
11. $3x^2 - x + 2 + [-5/(3x + 1)]$ 12. $x^3 + 5x^2 + 3x + 2 + [5/(x - 5)]$
13. $x^3 - 4x^2 + 3 + [7/(x + 4)]$ 14. $2x^3 - 7x^2 + 5 + [-2/(2x + 3)]$
15. $x^3 + 3x^2 - 4x - 2 + [1/(4x - 1)]$ 16. $x^3 - 2x - 3 + [5/(2x + 1)]$
17. $x^3 - 3x + [-9/(3x - 2)]$

Page 58   Quotients of Polynomials

1. $x^2 + 4x + 11 + [10/(x - 1)]$ 2. $x^2 - 7x - 1 + [-6/(x + 4)]$
3. $x^2 - 6x + 3 + [5/(x - 3)]$ 4. $x^2 - 4x + 1 + [3/(x + 5)]$
5. $x^2 - 7x + 2 + [6/(2x + 3)]$ 6. $x^2 - 4x + 3$
7. $x^2 + 6x + 2 + [-12/(x - 6)]$ 8. $x^2 - 4x + 1 + [-7/(x + 4)]$
9. $2x^2 - x + 4 + [-3/(2x + 1)]$ 10. $3x^2 + x + 1 + [2/(3x - 1)]$
11. $x^3 + 4x^2 + 2x + 1 + [4/(x - 4)]$ 12. $x^3 - 6x^2 + 1 + [2/(x + 6)]$
13. $2x^3 - 5x^2 + 1 + [5/(2x + 5)]$
14. $3x^3 - 2x^2 - 3x + 1 + [6/(3x + 2)]$
15. $x^3 - 2x^2 - 3x + [5/(5x + 2)]$ 16. $x^3 - x + 1 + [-4/(2x + 3)]$
17. $x^3 - 2x + 3 + [-5/(3x - 1)]$ $x^3 - (2/3)x^2 - (20/9)x +$
$(13/9) + [(-3 - 2/3)/(3x - 1)]$

Page 59   Greatest Common Factors

1. $2 \cdot 5$ 2. $3 \cdot 5$ 3. $2^2 \cdot 3$ 4. $3 \cdot 7$ 5. $2 \cdot 3^2$ 6. 2^4
7. $2^3 \cdot 3$ 8. $2 \cdot 3 \cdot 5$ 9. $2^2 \cdot 3^2$ 10. $2^3 \cdot 5$ 11. 5^2
12. $3 \cdot 13$ 13. $3^2 \cdot 5$ 14. $3 \cdot 17$ 15. $2^2 \cdot 17$ 16. $5 \cdot 13$
17. $2 \cdot 7^2$ 18. 2^6 19. 5   20. 4   21. 4   22. 9   23. 1
24. 25   25. 12   26. 9   27. 30   28. 1   29. 16   30. 10
31. 13   32. 14

Page 60   Greatest Common Factors

1. $2^3 \cdot 3$ 2. $5 \cdot 7$ 3. $2 \cdot 11$ 4. 7^2 5. $7 \cdot 13$ 6. 3^3
7. $3 \cdot 11$ 8. $2^3 \cdot 3^2$ 9. $2^4 \cdot 3$ 10. $3^2 \cdot 7$ 11. $3 \cdot 5^2$
12. $2 \cdot 19$ 13. $2^4 \cdot 5$ 14. $2^2 \cdot 5^2$ 15. $2 \cdot 5 \cdot 11$ 16. 3^4
17. 5^3 18. $5 \cdot 17$ 19. 9   20. 4   21. 13   22. 16   23. 1
24. 7   25. 8   26. 3   27. 14   28. 1   29. 6   30. 29
31. 17   32. 28

Page 61   Greatest Common Factors

1. 3   2. 3   3. $2c$ 4. $36b$ 5. y 6. x 7. 1   8. $23ab$
9. $15xy$ 10. $30x$ 11. 1   12. 1   13. $3a^2b^3$ 14. $21z$
15. $16mn^2$ 16. $18a^2b^2$ 17. $8s$ 18. $16a^2b^3$ 19. $3(a + b)$
20. 1   21. $5x^7y^4$ 22. $11u^3z^2c$ 23. 1   24. $25rst$
25. $2(a + b)^2$ 26. $x + y$ 27. $16x^3y^2$ 28. 1   29. $11a^3b^2$
30. 1   31. $2m^3n^2$ 32. $2(r + s)$ 33. $7(a + b)$
34. $2(c - d)$

Page 62   Greatest Common Factors

1. 4   2. $3x$ 3. $5x$ 4. $4b$ 5. $5y^3$ 6. $16a^2$ 7. $4z$
8. $14r^2s^2t$ 9. $15xy$ 10. $28a^2b^3$ 11. $5b^2$ 12. s^3t^2 13. 3
14. $29mn^2$ 15. $15a^2b^5c^3$ 16. $7a^2b^3$ 17. 1   18. 1
19. $23p^2q^2r$ 20. $14a^2b^2c$ 21. $20m^2n^2r$ 22. $5mn^2$
23. $a + b$ 24. $25x^3y^2z^2$ 25. $8(r + s)^2$ 26. 1   27. $11mn^2$
28. $3(x + y)$ 29. $(y + z)$ 30. $12a^2z^2$ 31. $8x^2y^2z$ 32. $a + c$
33. mn^2 34. $5(m - n)$

Page 63   Factoring

1. $2x(x - 5)$ 2. $5x(1 - 4x)$ 3. $x^2(y - 3)$ 4. $b^2(a + 4)$
5. $z(x^2 + y^2z)$ 6. $c^2d^2(c^2 + d)$ 7. $8(x - 2y)$ 8. $5(3a + 5b)$
9. $4(a + 5b)$ 10. $6(m - 2n)$ 11. $3(x - 2y + 4)$
12. $4(a - 2b + 4c)$ 13. $5(1 + 3n + 9m)$ 14. $7(1 + 4a - 5b)$
15. $13a(a - 13)$ 16. $15a(1 + 15a^2)$ 17. $8x(1 - 7x^2)$
18. $3a^2(1 + 4a^2)$ 19. $7u^2(2 + 5u^2)$ 20. $23x^2(x^3 - 2)$
21. $u^2(17u^2 + u - 3)$ 22. $x^2(x^2 - 3x + 17)$ 23. $3x(x^2 + x + 2)$
24. $5a(a^3 - a + 5)$ 25. $x(x^2 + 3xy + 3y)$
26. $x^2(x^2 + 3xy^2 + 12y^3)$ 27. $4ab(a^3 - 4ab + b^3)$
28. $6ab(a^2b - 2ab^2 + 3)$ 29. $15x^2y^2(1 + 15xy + x^2y^2)$
30. $13ab(a^2b + 3a - 2b^3)$ 31. $3x(5x^2 + 8x + 12)$
32. $7c(c^2 - 4cd + 5d^3)$ 33. $ay(a^2y^2 + ay + 1)$
34. $mn(1 + 5mn - 12mn^2)$

Page 64   Factoring

1. $3x(x - 2)$ 2. $7(b + 2c)$ 3. $2(5a - 9b)$ 4. $6(x + 4y)$
5. $a^2b(a^2b - 1)$ 6. $x^2y^2(x + y)$ 7. $2(7x - 9y)$
8. $3(1 - 4a + 5c)$ 9. $3(a + 8b)$ 10. $13x(x^2 - 2)$
11. $2(x - 4y + 7)$ 12. $3(a + 4b + 5)$ 13. $7(1 - 3m + 5n)$
14. $12(2x^4 - y)$ 15. $4a^2(4a - 3)$ 16. $13x^2(x + 3)$
17. $12x^2(x + 12)$ 18. $8r^3(r - 3)$ 19. $a(a^2 + 2ab - b^4)$
20. $5ab(3a^2b - 6ab^2 + 1)$ 21. $5x(x^2 + x - 2)$
22. $m^2n(mn - n + 5m^2n^2)$ 23. $a^2(a^2 - 3ac + 9c^3)$
24. $5(1 + 4r - 5s)$ 25. $2ab(2 - ab + 5a^2b^2)$
26. $4rst(2t^2 - rs + 6r^2t^3)$ 27. $13xy(x^3y + 2xy + 1)$
28. $7a^2b^2(4a + 1 - 5b)$ 29. $ab(a^2bc + 3ab + 10c)$
30. $x^2y^2z^2(xz^3 - 5 + 12x^3)$ 31. $xy(x^2yz - 10z + 5x^3y^2)$
32. $3a^3b^2c(1 + 2a^3bc - 3ac)$ 33. $12xy(x^2 + 12xy + 5y^2)$
34. $22ab(a^2 - 2ab^2 + 3b^3)$

Page 65   Factoring

1. $(m - 5)(m + n)$ 2. $(r + 3)(r + s)$ 3. $(6 + b)(a + b)$
4. $(5 - m)(m - n)$ 5. $(1 + a - b)(a + b)$
6. $(3 + x + y)(x + y)$ 7. $(x + y)(x - y + 2z)$
8. $(a - b)(5a + 4b)$ 9. $(2r + s)(3r - 2s)$
10. $(a + b)(a - b)(-a + 3b)$ 11. $a(b + c)(2ab + ac + 1)$
12. $t^2(3r + 2s)(2rt + st + 1)$ 13. $6(2a + 1)$ 14. $2x(3x + 2y)$
15. $3a(5a + 2b)(-12a^2 + 3a - 5b + 3ab)$
16. $2m(3n - 2m)(n + m)(3 + 4m)$ 17. $5xy(3x + 2y)(4x - 9y)$

128

Page 66 Factoring

1. $(4 - q)(p + q)$ 2. $(8 + s)(r - s)$ 3. $(a + b)(12 + a)$
4. $(20 - x)(x + y)$ 5. $(m - n)(1 + m - n)$
6. $(r + s)(1 - r + s)$ 7. $(a + b)(a - b + 2c)$ 8. $(r + s)(3t + s)$
9. $2x(2x - y)$ 10. $(2a - b)^2(a + 2b)$
11. $x(a - b)(2ax + 3bx + 1)$ 12. $a^2(b + 2c)(3a^2b + a^2c + 1)$
13. $6(3x + 2)(x - 1)$ 14. $6n(m - 2n)$
15. $7x(3x - 5)(6x^2 - 7x + 10)$ 16. $3r(7r + 3s)(2r + 3s)$
17. $6ab(2a + 3b)(2a^2b - 10a + 15b)$

Page 67 Factoring

1. $(x + 9)(x - 9)$ 2. $(2x + 5)(2x - 5)$ 3. $(3x + 5)(3x - 5)$
4. $(x + 8)(x - 8)$ 5. $(2x + 9)(2x - 9)$ 6. $(5x + 3)(5x - 3)$
7. $(4 - 5x)(4 + 5x)$ 8. $(4x - 1)(4x + 1)$ 9. $(5 - x)(5 + x)$
10. $(3 - 7x)(3 + 7x)$ 11. $(10x - 1)(10x + 1)$
12. $(7 - x)(7 + x)$ 13. $(2a + b)(2a - b)$
14. $(2xy - 3)(2xy + 3)$ 15. $(3r - 2t)(3r + 2t)$
16. $(12a^2 - b)(12a^2 + b)$ 17. $(xy - 3z)(xy + 3z)$
18. $(3x + 4y)(3x - 4y)$ 19. $(20a + 3b)(20a - 3b)$
20. $(xyz - 2)(xyz + 2)$ 21. $(3x + 7y)(3x - 7y)$
22. $(x^3y^2 - 8z)(x^3y^2 + 8z)$ 23. $(20x - 7y)(20x + 7y)$
24. $(19ab - 3c)(19ab + 3c)$ 25. $(2r + 7t)(2r - 7t)$
26. $(15a^3 - 4b)(15a^3 + 4b)$ 27. $(16x^2 - 3y)(16x^2 + 3y)$
28. $(13x^2 - 4y)(13x^2 + 4y)$ 29. $(17x^3y - z)(17x^3y + z)$
30. $(15a^3 - 4b)(15a^3 + 4b)$ 31. $(a - b - c)(a - b + c)$
32. $(c - d - z)(c - d + z)$ 33. $(r - p - q)(r + p + q)$
34. $(z - x - y)(z + x + y)$

Page 68 Factoring

1. $(x + 1)(x - 1)$ 2. $(x + 2)(x - 2)$ 3. $(x + 4)(x - 4)$
4. $(2x - 1)(2x + 1)$ 5. $(x - 7)(x + 7)$ 6. $(x + 6)(x - 6)$
7. $(3x + 1)(3x - 1)$ 8. $(2x + 3)(2x - 3)$ 9. $(x + 5)(x - 5)$
10. $(x + 3)(x - 3)$ 11. $(3x + 4)(3x - 4)$ 12. $(3x - 2)(3x + 2)$
13. $(x + 9y)(x - 9y)$ 14. $(x - 8y)(x + 8y)$
15. $(2x + 5y)(2x - 5y)$ 16. $(3x - 5y)(3x + 5y)$
17. $(5x + 3y)(5x - 3y)$ 18. $(2x - 7y)(2x + 7y)$
19. $(6x - 7y)(6x + 7y)$ 20. $(4x + y)(4x - y)$
21. $(2x - 9y)(2x + 9y)$ 22. $(4x^2 - 5y)(4x^2 + 5y)$
23. $(4a^2b - 7)(4a^2b + 7)$ 24. $(3ab - 7)(3ab + 7)$
25. $(4ab - 3c^3d^2)(4ab + 3c^3d^2)$
26. $(4ab - 9c^2d^3)(4ab + 9c^2d^3)$ 27. $(5a - cd)(5a + cd)$
28. $(7a^3 - cd)(7a^3 + cd)$ 29. $(8mn + 3)(8mn - 3)$
30. $(9rs - 2)(9rs + 2)$ 31. $(a + b + c)(a + b - c)$
32. $(r + s + t)(r + s - t)$ 33. $(z - x + y)(z + x - y)$
34. $(m - n + r)(m + n - r)$

Page 69 Factoring

1. $(x + 1)^2$ 2. $(x + 3)^2$ 3. $(x + 5)^2$ 4. $(2x + 7)^2$ 5. $(3x - 1)^2$
6. $(2x - 3)^2$ 7. $(4x - 5)^2$ 8. $(x - 7)^2$ 9. $(6x + 1)^2$
10. $(4x - 1)^2$ 11. $(x - 9)^2$ 12. $(5x \times 7)^2$ 13. $(10x + 1)^2$
14. $(4x + 9)^2$ 15. $(3a - 7b)^2$ 16. $(3a + 4b)^2$ 17. $(8x - y)^2$
18. $(5x - 2y)^2$ 19. $(12r - s)^2$ 20. $(7m - 2n)^2$ 21. $(5x^2 - 4y)^2$
22. $(8a^2 - 5b)^2$ 23. $(6xy - 7)^2$ 24. $(9mn + 1)^2$
25. $(16r^2 + 1)^2$ 26. $(13s^2 - 2)^2$ 27. $(5p - 8q)^2$
28. $(18r + s^2)^2$ 29. $(7t - 4s)^2$ 30. $(30x^2 - 1)^2$
31. $(a + b + 1)^2$ 32. $(c - d + 1)^2$ 33. $(r - s - 1)^2$
34. $(m + n - 1)^2$

Page 70 Factoring

1. $(x + 2)^2$ 2. $(2x + 1)^2$ 3. $(5x + 1)^2$ 4. $(x + 4)^2$
5. $(2x - 5)^2$ 6. $(7x - 1)^2$ 7. $(10x - 7)^2$ 8. $(4x + 3)^2$
9. $(x + 6)^2$ 10. $(2x - 9)^2$ 11. $(10x - 3)^2$ 12. $(6x - 5)^2$
13. $(13x + 4)^2$ 14. $(7x + 3)^2$ 15. $(3a + 2b)^2$ 16. $(x - 8y)^2$
17. $(8r - 3s)^2$ 18. $(4a + 7b)^2$ 19. $(9c^2 + 2)^2$ 20. $(7r^2 - 5)^2$
21. $(10x^2y - 9)^2$ 22. $(3p^2 - 5)^2$ 23. $(3r^2 - 8t)^2$
24. $(5a^2 + 3b)^2$ 25. $(15t^5 + 1)^2$ 26. $(8x^4 - 7)^2$
27. $(5r^2 + 9s)^2$ 28. $(9m^3 - 4n)^2$ 29. $(20a^4 - 1)^2$
30. $(5x^2y + 6z)^2$ 31. $(p + q + 1)^2$ 32. $(x - y + 1)^2$
33. $(g - h - 1)^2$ 34. $(v + w - 1)^2$

Page 71 Factoring

1. $(x + 3)(x + 2)$ 2. $(x + 5)(x + 4)$ 3. $(x + 6)(x + 1)$
4. $(x + 3)(x + 7)$ 5. $(x + 8)(x + 7)$ 6. $(x + 2)(x + 1)$
7. $(x + 4)(x + 4)$ 8. $(x + 1)(x + 1)$ 9. $(x + 3)(x + 4)$
10. $(x + 6)(x + 7)$ 11. $(x + 4)(x + 1)$ 12. $(x + 5)(x + 9)$
13. $(x + 3)(x + 3)$ 14. $(x + 5)(x + 1)$ 15. $(x + 6)(x + 4)$
16. $(x + 2)(x + 2)$ 17. $(x + 7)(x + 1)$ 18. $(x + 6)(x + 6)$
19. $(x + 6)(x + 3)$ 20. $(x + 9)(x + 7)$ 21. $(x + 8)(x + 2)$
22. $(x + 9)(x + 3)$ 23. $(x - 4)(x - 2)$ 24. $(x - 5)(x - 6)$
25. $(x - 2)(x - 1)$ 26. $(x - 8)(x - 1)$ 27. $(x - 9)(x - 4)$
28. $(x - 7)(x - 8)$ 29. $(x - 4)(x - 4)$ 30. $(x - 6)(x - 2)$
31. $(x - 9)(x - 3)$ 32. $(x - 8)(x - 9)$ 33. $(x - 7)(x - 4)$
34. $(x - 3)(x - 3)$

Page 72 Factoring

1. $(x + 5)(x + 2)$ 2. $(x + 8)(x + 5)$ 3. $(x + 3)(x + 1)$
4. $(x + 4)(x + 2)$ 5. $(x + 5)(x + 5)$ 6. $(x + 9)(x + 1)$
7. $(x + 6)(x + 2)$ 8. $(x + 7)(x + 7)$ 9. $(x + 6)(x + 9)$
10. $(x + 7)(x + 4)$ 11. $(x + 8)(x + 8)$ 12. $(x + 3)(x + 5)$
13. $(x + 9)(x + 9)$ 14. $(x + 8)(x + 3)$ 15. $(x + 5)(x + 6)$
16. $(x + 7)(x + 2)$ 17. $(x + 9)(x + 2)$ 18. $(x + 7)(x + 5)$
19. $(x + 8)(x + 1)$ 20. $(x + 6)(x + 8)$ 21. $(x + 9)(x + 4)$
22. $(x + 8)(x + 9)$ 23. $(x - 8)(x - 4)$ 24. $(x - 5)(x - 3)$
25. $(x - 9)(x - 6)$ 26. $(x - 5)(x - 1)$ 27. $(x - 6)(x - 6)$
28. $(x - 2)(x - 2)$ 29. $(x - 7)(x - 2)$ 30. $(x - 8)(x - 5)$
31. $(x - 9)(x - 1)$ 32. $(x - 3)(x - 1)$ 33. $(x - 7)(x - 7)$
34. $(x - 6)(x - 4)$

Page 73 Factoring

1. $(x + 3)(x - 1)$ 2. $(x + 4)(x - 2)$ 3. $(x + 8)(x - 5)$
4. $(x + 9)(x - 6)$ 5. $(x - 6)(x + 8)$ 6. $(x - 4)(x + 7)$
7. $(x + 6)(x - 5)$ 8. $(x + 5)(x - 3)$ 9. $(x + 9)(x - 1)$
10. $(x - 4)(x + 9)$ 11. $(x - 3)(x + 8)$ 12. $(x + 9)(x - 2)$
13. $(x + 7)(x - 2)$ 14. $(x + 7)(x - 5)$ 15. $(x + 5)(x - 2)$
16. $(x + 9)(x - 8)$ 17. $(x + 8)(x - 1)$ 18. $(x + 6)(x - 2)$
19. $(x - 9)(x + 2)$ 20. $(x - 6)(x + 5)$ 21. $(x - 8)(x + 5)$
22. $(x - 8)(x + 6)$ 23. $(x - 5)(x + 2)$ 24. $(x - 3)(x + 1)$
25. $(x - 9)(x + 1)$ 26. $(x - 8)(x + 1)$ 27. $(x - 9)(x + 4)$
28. $(x - 9)(x + 6)$ 29. $(x - 6)(x + 2)$ 30. $(x - 3)(x + 2)$
31. $(x - 5)(x + 3)$ 32. $(x - 7)(x + 4)$ 33. $(x - 9)(x + 8)$
34. $(x - 7)(x + 2)$

Page 74 Factoring

1. $(x + 7)(x - 1)$ 2. $(x + 8)(x - 7)$ 3. $(x + 9)(x - 6)$
4. $(x + 5)(x - 4)$ 5. $(x + 2)(x - 1)$ 6. $(x + 3)(x - 2)$
7. $(x + 6)(x - 1)$ 8. $(x + 6)(x - 3)$ 9. $(x + 6)(x - 4)$
10. $(x + 9)(x - 5)$ 11. $(x + 5)(x - 1)$ 12. $(x + 7)(x - 3)$
13. $(x + 4)(x - 2)$ 14. $(x - 3)(x + 4)$ 15. $(x + 9)(x - 4)$
16. $(x + 8)(x - 2)$ 17. $(x + 14)(x - 7)$ 18. $(x + 7)(x - 6)$
19. $(x + 9)(x - 3)$ 20. $(x + 4)(x - 1)$ 21. $(x - 6)(x + 5)$
22. $(x - 9)(x + 3)$ 23. $(x - 9)(x + 8)$ 24. $(x - 8)(x + 1)$
25. $(x - 12)(x + 3)$ 26. $(x - 6)(x + 2)$ 27. $(x - 20)(x + 2)$
28. $(x - 14)(x + 4)$ 29. $(x - 13)(x + 5)$ 30. $(x - 7)(x + 4)$
31. $(x - 15)(x + 8)$ 32. $(x - 8)(x + 7)$ 33. $(x - 14)(x + 6)$
34. $(x - 20)(x + 6)$

Page 75 Factoring

1. $(2x + 3)(x + 2)$ 2. $(2x + 7)(x + 3)$ 3. $(2x + 1)(x + 1)$
4. $(2x + 5)(x + 4)$ 5. $(2x + 9)(x + 2)$ 6. $(2x + 9)(x + 6)$
7. $(2x + 1)(x + 7)$ 8. $(2x + 4)(x + 3)$ 9. $(3x + 1)(x + 3)$
10. $(3x + 5)(x + 4)$ 11. $(3x + 2)(x + 8)$ 12. $(4x + 3)(x + 2)$
13. $(4x + 3)(x + 6)$ 14. $(4x + 7)(x + 3)$ 15. $(2x + 3)(x + 6)$
16. $(2x + 9)(x + 4)$ 17. $(3x + 2)(x + 4)$ 18. $(4x + 5)(x + 1)$
19. $(2x + 7)(x + 7)$ 20. $(3x + 2)(x + 6)$ 21. $(4x + 3)(x + 4)$
22. $(2x + 5)(x + 3)$ 23. $(3x - 4)(x - 2)$ 24. $(4x - 7)(x - 7)$
25. $(3x - 5)(x - 7)$ 26. $(2x - 5)(x - 8)$ 27. $(3x - 7)(x - 2)$
28. $(2x - 7)(x - 1)$ 29. $(4x - 9)(x - 2)$ 30. $(3x - 7)(x - 5)$
31. $(2x - 9)(x - 7)$ 32. $(3x - 1)(x - 5)$ 33. $(4x - 7)(x - 5)$
34. $(3x - 7)(x - 9)$

Page 76 Factoring

1. $(3x + 4)$ $(x + 3)$ **2.** $(2x + 7)$ $(x + 2)$ **3.** $(4x + 5)$ $(x + 3)$
4. $(2x + 7)$ $(x + 4)$ **5.** $(3x + 7)$ $(x + 4)$ **6.** $(5x + 2)$ $(x + 3)$
7. $(6x + 5)$ $(x + 1)$ **8.** $(2x + 5)$ $(x + 2)$ **9.** $(3x + 2)$ $(x + 2)$
10. $(4x + 5)$ $(x + 2)$ **11.** $(5x + 3)$ $(x + 5)$ **12.** $(2x + 9)$ $(x + 1)$
13. $(3x + 7)$ $(x + 3)$ **14.** $(5x + 1)$ $(x + 5)$ **15.** $(5x + 7)$ $(x + 6)$
16. $(6x + 5)$ $(x + 3)$ **17.** $(4x + 1)$ $(x + 3)$ **18.** $(2x + 3)$ $(x + 3)$
19. $(2x + 9)$ $(x + 7)$ **20.** $(5x + 2)$ $(x + 8)$ **21.** $(6x + 5)$ $(x + 8)$
22. $(2x + 5)$ $(x + 4)$ **23.** $(3x - 4)$ $(x - 6)$ **24.** $(5x - 3)$ $(x - 7)$
25. $(4x - 5)$ $(x - 5)$ **26.** $(6x - 5)$ $(x - 7)$ **27.** $(2x - 7)$ $(x - 6)$
28. $(6x - 7)$ $(x - 4)$ **29.** $(5x - 4)$ $(x - 9)$ **30.** $(3x - 4)$ $(x - 5)$
31. $(4x - 1)$ $(x - 1)$ **32.** $(2x - 5)$ $(x - 1)$ **33.** $(5x - 2)$ $(x - 9)$
34. $(3x - 4)$ $(x - 9)$

Page 77 Factoring

1. $(3x - 1)$ $(x + 7)$ **2.** $(2x - 3)$ $(x - 1)$ **3.** $(4x + 1)$ $(x + 5)$
4. $(5x + 2)$ $(x - 6)$ **5.** $(2x - 1)$ $(x - 3)$ **6.** $(5x - 8)$ $(x + 8)$
7. $(4x - 7)$ $(x + 1)$ **8.** $(3x + 1)$ $(x + 1)$ **9.** $(2x + 9)$ $(x + 5)$
10. $(3x + 8)$ $(x - 7)$ **11.** $(4x + 3)$ $(x - 7)$ **12.** $(5x + 6)$ $(x - 9)$
13. $(6x - 5)$ $(x - 6)$ **14.** $(2x - 9)$ $(x + 3)$ **15.** $(3x + 5)$ $(x + 1)$
16. $(4x - 1)$ $(x + 2)$ **17.** $(4x + 9)$ $(x - 5)$ **18.** $(5x + 6)$ $(x + 5)$
19. $(2x + 7)$ $(x - 5)$ **20.** $(3x + 7)$ $(x - 6)$ **21.** $(5x + 7)$ $(x - 7)$
22. $(4x - 9)$ $(x - 1)$ **23.** $(3x - 1)$ $(x + 6)$ **24.** $(5x + 7)$ $(x + 7)$
25. $(6x - 1)$ $(x - 9)$ **26.** $(2x + 9)$ $(x - 8)$ **27.** $(3x + 7)$ $(x + 7)$
28. $(5x - 1)$ $(x + 8)$ **29.** $(4x + 7)$ $(x - 4)$ **30.** $(3x - 5)$ $(x - 6)$
31. $(2x + 3)$ $(x + 5)$ **32.** $(5x + 4)$ $(x - 3)$ **33.** $(4x + 3)$ $(x - 1)$
34. $(3x + 1)$ $(x + 9)$

Page 78 Factoring

1. $(2x + 5)$ $(x + 6)$ **2.** $(3x - 2)$ $(x - 1)$ **3.** $(4x + 3)$ $(x - 5)$
4. $(3x + 4)$ $(x + 8)$ **5.** $(5x - 2)$ $(x + 5)$ **6.** $(6x - 7)$ $(x - 5)$
7. $(2x - 1)$ $(x - 4)$ **8.** $(3x + 1)$ $(x - 4)$ **9.** $(4x - 1)$ $(x + 7)$
10. $(5x + 3)$ $(x - 8)$ **11.** $(6x + 1)$ $(x + 4)$ **12.** $(5x + 7)$ $(x + 3)$
13. $(5x + 7)$ $(x + 2)$ **14.** $(3x + 2)$ $(x + 1)$ **15.** $(5x + 3)$ $(x - 7)$
16. $(5x + 6)$ $(x - 8)$ **17.** $(6x - 7)$ $(x + 7)$ **18.** $(4x - 1)$ $(x - 4)$
19. $(2x + 1)$ $(x - 2)$ **20.** $(3x - 5)$ $(x + 2)$ **21.** $(5x + 7)$ $(x + 5)$
22. $(6x + 7)$ $(x - 9)$ **23.** $(4x + 3)$ $(x - 3)$ **24.** $(3x + 2)$ $(x - 3)$
25. $(6x + 1)$ $(x + 6)$ **26.** $(5x + 6)$ $(x - 6)$ **27.** $(7x - 1)$ $(x - 3)$
28. $(2x + 5)$ $(x - 7)$ **29.** $(5x + 4)$ $(x + 9)$ **30.** $(6x + 1)$ $(x - 7)$
31. $(5x + 4)$ $(x - 4)$ **32.** $(7x + 3)$ $(x + 4)$ **33.** $(2x + 5)$ $(x + 9)$
34. $(3x + 5)$ $(x - 8)$

Page 79 Factoring

1. $(2x + 5)$ $(2x - 9)$ **2.** $(3x - 7)$ $(4x + 1)$ **3.** $(4x + 7)$ $(3x - 2)$
4. $(5x - 7)$ $(3x - 1)$ **5.** $(5x + 2)$ $(5x + 1)$ **6.** $(7x - 1)$ $(5x + 6)$
7. $(6x - 1)$ $(2x - 7)$ **8.** $(3x - 7)$ $(7x + 1)$ **9.** $(5x - 6)$ $(7x + 3)$
10. $(7x - 9)$ $(2x + 3)$ **11.** $(4x + 5)$ $(7x - 5)$
12. $(6x + 1)$ $(4x + 5)$ **13.** $(6x + 7)$ $(2x - 7)$
14. $(2x - 5)$ $(2x - 7)$ **15.** $(7x - 4)$ $(5x - 1)$
16. $(3x + 7)$ $(5x + 6)$ **17.** $(5x + 6)$ $(2x + 3)$
18. $(6x + 5)$ $(6x - 7)$ **19.** $(7x + 2)$ $(10x + 3)$
20. $(12x - 5)$ $(3x + 1)$ **21.** $(7x - 2)$ $(2x - 1)$
22. $(3x + 4)$ $(5x + 3)$ **23.** $(7x + 4)$ $(2x - 9)$
24. $(4x - 5)$ $(2x + 5)$ **25.** $(3x - 1)$ $(3x + 7)$
26. $(7x + 1)$ $(7x - 3)$ **27.** $(5x + 2)$ $(12x + 1)$
28. $(13x - 3)$ $(2x - 1)$ **29.** $(4x - 3)$ $(5x + 9)$
30. $(5x + 2)$ $(3x + 9)$ **31.** $(6x - 5)$ $(3x - 2)$
32. $(7x - 3)$ $(2x + 3)$ **33.** $(4x + 3)$ $(3x - 7)$
34. $(7x + 1)$ $(2x - 3)$

Page 80 Factoring

1. $(3x + 1)$ $(2x - 9)$ **2.** $(5x - 1)$ $(3x - 7)$ **3.** $(7x - 2)$ $(3x + 1)$
4. $(3x + 1)$ $(5x + 1)$ **5.** $(5x + 2)$ $(5x + 9)$ **6.** $(5x + 2)$ $(5x - 8)$
7. $(3x + 2)$ $(2x - 5)$ **8.** $(5x - 9)$ $(2x + 3)$ **9.** $(6x - 5)$ $(4x + 3)$
10. $(6x + 5)$ $(7x - 5)$ **11.** $(7x + 6)$ $(3x - 1)$
12. $(2x + 9)$ $(2x + 1)$ **13.** $(6x + 7)$ $(2x + 1)$
14. $(5x - 9)$ $(7x + 1)$ **15.** $(7x - 4)$ $(4x - 3)$

16. $(4x + 3)$ $(5x - 6)$ **17.** $(5x + 7)$ $(5x - 9)$
18. $(7x - 1)$ $(7x + 4)$ **19.** $(7x - 3)$ $(3x + 4)$
20. $(5x - 4)$ $(5x - 3)$ **21.** $(4x + 3)$ $(4x + 5)$
22. $(3x + 1)$ $(2x + 3)$ **23.** $(5x - 4)$ $(2x - 7)$
24. $(5x + 2)$ $(7x - 4)$ **25.** $(4x - 3)$ $(5x - 2)$
26. $(7x + 2)$ $(2x - 7)$ **27.** $(2x + 1)$ $(2x - 3)$
28. $(7x + 2)$ $(4x + 1)$ **29.** $(4x - 9)$ $(3x + 7)$
30. $(7x + 2)$ $(7x - 8)$ **31.** $(6x + 1)$ $(3x + 2)$
32. $(4x + 9)$ $(6x - 7)$ **33.** $(3x + 7)$ $(10x + 1)$
34. $(10x + 3)$ $(5x - 6)$

Page 81 Factoring

1. $x(3 - y)$ **2.** $x(2 + y)$ **3.** $4(x + y)$ **4.** $x(3 + y)$ **5.** $b(1 + c)$
6. $n(x - y)$ **7.** $3(2x + 7)$ **8.** $27(y - 3)$ **9.** $a^2b(3m - n)$
10. $mn^2(3x - 2)$ **11.** $3x^3y^2(5x + 6y)$ **12.** $5a^2b(3a + 2b)$
13. $6x^2y^4(7x + 3y^2)$ **14.** $9mn^5(3m - 7n^2)$ **15.** $5a(a - 5)$
16. $10b(x - 3y)$ **17.** $10x^2y(3y - 2)$ **18.** $15a^3b^2(8n - 3m)$
19. $6ab(2x^2 + x - 5)$ **20.** $12m^2n(3x^2 + 7x - 2)$
21. $(r - 5)$ $(r + 2)$ **22.** $(m + 8)$ $(m - 3)$ **23.** $(2p - 3q)$ $(p + q)$
24. $(3a + 1)$ $(a - 2)$ **25.** $(m - 2n)$ $(m + 2n)$
26. $(3x - 2y)$ $(3x + 2y)$ **27.** $(7x - 3)$ $(7x + 3)$
28. $(6r - 7t)$ $(6r + 7t)$ **29.** $(m - 2n)^2$ **30.** $(3x + 2y)^2$
31. $(a - 3b)$ $(a + 2b)$ **32.** $(x - 4y)$ $(x + 3y)$
33. $(3b - a)$ $(b + 2a)$ **34.** $(4y - x)$ $(y + 5x)$

Page 82 Factoring

1. $5(m - n)$ **2.** $y(3 + y)$ **3.** $x(10 + y)$ **4.** $5(a + b)$
5. $a(b + c)$ **6.** $m(x - y)$ **7.** $4(2x + 7)$ **8.** $15(y - 3)$
9. $a^2b(2m + n)$ **10.** $mn^2(3x + 2)$ **11.** $3x^3y^2(2x - 5y)$
12. $5a^2b(2a - 5b)$ **13.** $6x^2y^4(3x - 2y^2)$
14. $9mn^5(2m + 3n^2)$ **15.** $7a(5 - a)$ **16.** $9b(3y - x)$
17. $7xy^2(2 - 3y)$ **18.** $8ab(5m - 6n)$ **19.** $12a^2b(3x^2 - x + 9)$
20. $9mn^2(2x^2 - 9x + 3)$ **21.** $(r - 3)$ $(r + 2)$
22. $(m + 8)$ $(m - 5)$ **23.** $(3p - q)$ $(2p - 3q)$
24. $(3a + 1)$ $(a - 5)$ **25.** $(4a + 9b)$ $(4a - 9b)$
26. $(5a - 13y)$ $(5a + 13y)$ **27.** $(a - 5b)^2$ **28.** $(5x - 2y)^2$
29. $(x - 7y)$ $(x + 4y)$ **30.** $(x - 7y)$ $(x + 2y)$
31. $(7x - y)$ $(x + 2y)$ **32.** $(5x + y)$ $(3x + 2y)$
33. $(5 - 9x)$ $(5 + 9x)$ **34.** $(13x - 12y)$ $(13x + 12y)$

Page 83 Factoring

1. $3(5x + 2)$ $(x + 2)$ **2.** $10(3 + cd)$ $(2 - 7cd)$
3. $5(6a - 5b)$ $(6a + 5b)$ **4.** $7(8x + 1)$ $(8x + 1)$
5. $6a(a + 2)$ $(a + 4)$ **6.** $9x(x + 9)$ $(x + 4)$ **7.** $7x(2x - 3)^2$
8. $3y(4x - 3)$ $(4x + 3)$ **9.** $xy(5x + 8)$ $(x - 5)$
10. $pq(2pq - 3)$ $(pq + 8)$ **11.** $ab(3 - 7ab)$ $(3 + 7ab)$
12. $rs(12r^2s^2 - 13rs + 11)$ **13.** $x^2y^2(5x - 2)$ $(2x - 5)$
14. $a^2b^3(9 - 2ab)$ $(9 - 2ab)$ **15.** $x^3y(x + 7)$ $(x + 1)$
16. $ac(6a + 5)$ $(4a + 1)$ **17.** $3b(4a + 1)^2$
18. $5mn(5mn - 2)$ $(5mn + 2)$ **19.** $5c^2d(2c - 3)$ $(7c + 6)$
20. $11a^3b(1 + 3ab)$ $(1 - 5ab)$ **21.** $72xy^2(x - 7y)$ $(x - y)$
22. $20a^2b(3a - 7b)$ $(a - b)$ **23.** $9a^3b^2(3 + 4ab - 9b^2)$
24. $3mn^4(7m^4 - 13m^2 - 15)$ **25.** $5cd^3(4c - 5)$ $(7c + 2)$
26. $12ab^2(a - 9)$ $(a + 2)$ **27.** $-3x^3(5x - 3)$ $(5x + 3)$
28. $-7c^7(10c - 3)^2$ **29.** $-5x^2(x + 8)$ $(x - 6)$
30. $8b^2(10b + 1)$ $(6b - 5)$ **31.** $7x^3y^2(3xy - 7)^2$
32. $-12m^3n^3(2 - 7mn)$ $(2 + 7mn)$ **33.** $25ab(a^4 + b^4)$
34. $35cd(3 + 4cd)$ $(1 - 4cd)$

Page 84 Factoring

1. $4(2x + 1)$ $(x + 5)$ **2.** $9(4a^4 + 10a^2b^2 + 11b^4)$
3. $7a^3(2a + 7b - 3ab^2)$ **4.** $5(6a - 5)^2$
5. $9x(2x - 3)$ $(2x + 3)$ **6.** $3y(y + 7)$ $(y + 4)$ **7.** $3a(3a - 5)^2$
8. $5d(4d^2 + 7)$ $(2d^2 - 3)$ **9.** $ab(a + 6)$ $(a + 2)$
10. $pq(8p - q)$ $(8p + q)$ **11.** $pq(5p + 7)$ $(2p - 3)$
12. $st(3s + 2)$ $(s - 5)$ **13.** $r^3s^2(19s - 3 + 10t)$
14. $m^2n(25m^2 + 16n^2)$ **15.** $xy^4(7x - 1)$ $(7x + 1)$

16. $cd^3(c - 8)$ $(c + 2)$ **17.** $-7xy(2x - 3)$ $(x + 9)$
18. $rst(4rs - 5)$ $(4rs + 5)$ **19.** $3m^2n(n - 9)$ $(n + 6)$
20. $-4p^2q(7 + q)$ $(q + 6)$ **21.** $8ab^3(4a + 3)^2$
22. $7z^3(14z^2 + 35z + 25)$ **23.** $3m^2n^2(6m - n)$ $(2m - 9)$
24. $11v^2w^2(7vw + 3)^2$ **25.** $15rst(5rst - 6)$ $(5rst + 6)$
26. $12za(4za + 1)$ $(za - 8)$ **27.** $5pq^4(7p - 3)$ $(5p + 1)$
28. $-8mn(10m - 3)$ $(2m - 7)$ **29.** $-2r^2t^3(r - 3)$ $(r - 2)$
30. $5r^3t^2(r - 8)$ $(r + 8)$ **31.** $3a^4b(3b + 4)$ $(b + 1)$
32. $7m^3n(9n - 2)^2$ **33.** $7xy^4(3x + 1)^2$
34. $5aw^2(a + 9)$ $(a - 7)$

Page 85 Factoring

1. $(x + c)$ $(x - a)$ **2.** $(c - e)$ $(c + d)$ **3.** $(a + c)$ $(2a + b)$
4. $(x - z)$ $(3x + y)$ **5.** $(3x + z)$ $(2x + y)$
6. $(2a + d)$ $(5a + b)$ **7.** $(x + y - z)$ $(x + y + z)$
8. $(a + b + 3c)$ $(a + b - 3c)$ **9.** $(m + n - 4p)$ $(m + n + 4p)$
10. $(r + s - 6t)$ $(r + s + 6t)$ **11.** $(s - m + n)$ $(s + m - n)$
12. $(a - b + c)$ $(a + b - c)$ **13.** $(3a + 1)$ $(a + 1)$ $(a + b)$
14. $(x + 3)$ $(x + 2)$ $(x + y)$ **15.** $(x + y + 2)^2$
16. $(a + b + 3)^2$ **17.** $(r + s + 4)^2$ **18.** $(m + n + 5)^2$
19. $(2x + 5)$ $(x + 1)$ $(3x + y)$ **20.** $(5a - 2)$ $(a - 3)$ $(4a + b)$
21. $(2a - 3)^2$ $(2a + 3b)$ **22.** $3(x - 1)$ $(x - 4)$ $(3x + 2y)$
23. $(2x + 3y)$ $(x - 5)$ $(3x - 1)$
24. $(3x + 3y - 2)$ $(5x + 5y + 1)$
25. $(4a + 4b + 3)$ $(2a + 2b + 3)$
26. $(4c + 4d + 1)$ $(7c + 7d - 2)$

Page 86 Factoring

1. $(c - d)$ $(a + b)$ **2.** $(t + u)$ $(r + s)$ **3.** $(a - c)$ $(2a + 3b)$
4. $(2x - z)$ $(3x + y)$ **5.** $(2m - 3n)$ $(3m + 2)$
6. $(2x - 5y)$ $(5x + 3)$ **7.** $(x + y - 2z)$ $(x + y + 2z)$
8. $(a + b - 4c)$ $(a + b + 4c)$ **9.** $(r + s - 8t)$ $(r + s + 8t)$
10. $(c + d - 9)$ $(c + d + 9)$ **11.** $(x - y - z)$ $(x + y + z)$
12. $(4a - b - c)$ $(4a + b + c)$ **13.** $(a + b + 1)^2$
14. $(c + d + 3)^2$ **15.** $(4 + r + s)^2$
16. $(5 + m + n)^2$ **17.** $(2x + y)$ $(x + 3y)$ $(3x + 1)$
18. $(3x + 4y)$ $(x + y)$ $(2x + 1)$ **19.** $(2x + 3)$ $(x + 2)$ $(5x + y)$
20. $(3x + 2y)$ $(x - 5y)$ $(4x + 3)$
21. $(5m + 2n)$ $(m - 3n)$ $(2m - 5)$
22. $3(c + d)$ $(c - 4d)$ $(2c + 7)$
23. $(7r + 5)$ $(r - 3)$ $(2r + t)$
24. $(7x + 7y - 2)$ $(5x + 5y + 1)$
25. $(3x + 3y - 5)$ $(2x + 2y + 1)$

Page 87 Factoring

1. $5a(2x + 3)^2$ **2.** $(p + t)$ $(p + q)$ **3.** $5x(x + 2)$ $(x - c)$
4. $9y(6x + 1)$ $(x + 1)$ **5.** $(x^2 + 16)$ $(x + 4)$ $(x - 4)$
6. $8x^2(x + 6)$ $(x + 5)$ **7.** $13x^2(x - 5)$ $(x + 4)$
8. $6a^2(5x - 2)$ $(3x + 1)$ **9.** $8m(4x + 3)$ $(3x + 5)$
10. $(x + 3y + 1)$ $(x + 3y - 1)$ **11.** $3a(a - 4)$ $(a + 4)$
12. $(4 + x^2)$ $(2 + x)$ $(2 - x)$ **13.** $(a - 2b - 2)$ $(a - 2b + 2)$
14. $6a(a - 3)$ $(a + b)$ **15.** $9y^2(3x + 1)$ $(2x - 3)$
16. $7x(3x - 1)^2$ **17.** $(r - 5)$ $(r - t)$
18. $8p(3p - 7)$ $(p - q)$ **19.** $3a(2m - 5)$ $(2m + n)$
20. $7x^2(2x + 5)$ $(2x - 5)$ **21.** $5x(x - 6y)$ $(x + 3y)$
22. $4t(6x + 5)$ $(2x - 3)$ **23.** $(4a^2 + 9b^2)$ $(2a + 3b)$ $(2a - 3b)$
24. $5x^3(x + 7)$ $(x + 3)$ **25.** $12a(3x - 5)$ $(2x + 1)$
26. $7z(y + t)$ $(2x + 3)$ **27.** $4x^2y^2(3x - y)$ $(7x + 2y)$
28. $6ab(5a + b)$ $(2a - 3b)$ **29.** $2az(a + 5)$ $(a + 3z)$
30. $(25 + 4a^2)$ $(5 - 2a)$ $(5 + 2a)$ **31.** $(a + b + 2)$ $(a + b + 1)$
32. $(x + y - 7)$ $(x + y + 2)$ **33.** $(a + b - 5)$ $(a + b + 2)$
34. $(x + y + 7)$ $(x + y + 4)$

Page 88 Factoring

1. $(x^2 + 25y^2)$ $(x + 5y)$ $(x - 5y)$ **2.** $(x + 4y - 5)$ $(x + 4y + 5)$
3. $7r(r - 5)$ $(r + 3)$ **4.** $7a^2(a + 7)$ $(a + 3)$
5. $2a(2x + y)$ $(2x + 3)$ **6.** $3m(2p + 7)$ $(p - q)$
7. $4t^3(3a + 1)$ $(5a - 2)$ **8.** $5x(x - y)$ $(3x + 2)$ **9.** $3x(3x + 5)^2$

10. $3a(4a + 1)$ $(2a + 7)$ **11.** $5z(x + 3)$ $(2x + y)$
12. $13r(r + 5)$ $(r - 5)$ **13.** $8n(5m - 3)$ $(3m + 1)$
14. $(16 + 9r^2)$ $(4 - 3r)$ $(4 + 3r)$ **15.** $(x - 5y - 4)$ $(x - 5y + 4)$
16. $(c + 7)$ $(c + v)$ **17.** $3r(3a + 4)$ $(2a + 7)$
18. $(49 + x^2)$ $(7 + x)$ $(7 - x)$
19. $(4x^2 + 25y^2)$ $(2x - 5y)$ $(2x + 5y)$ **20.** $9z^2(3 - 2z)$ $(5 + z)$
21. $(a + b)$ $(a - 2t)$ **22.** $4a^4(a + 7)$ $(a + 2)$
23. $7x(5a - 4)$ $(5a + 4)$ **24.** $3b(b + c)$ $(6a + 1)$
25. $6c(4c + 3)$ $(2c + 5)$ **26.** $12r(4r - 3)^2$
27. $3r(y - z)$ $(2x + 3)$ **28.** $3a^3(4a + 1)$ $(3a - 2)$
29. $5m^2(x - 5)$ $(x + 2)$ **30.** $r^2(7r + 2)$ $(3r - 5)$
31. $(4a + b + 3)$ $(4a + b + 2)$ **32.** $(2a - b + 5)$ $(2a - b + 3)$
33. $(3a + b + 3)$ $(3a + b - 1)$ **34.** $(5a + b + 4)$ $(5a + b + 1)$

Page 89 Polynomial Equations

1. $x = 7$ or -5 **2.** $x = -4$ or -15 **3.** $x = 2/3$ or $-19/2$
4. $x = 17/5$ or $7/2$ **5.** $x = 5/6$ or $-3/4$ **6.** $x = 1/7$ or $-5/2$
7. $x = -6$ or 5 **8.** $x = -11$ or 10 **9.** $x = -29/2$ or 5
10. $x = -32/3$ or 5 **11.** $x = -7/8$ or $-4/5$ **12.** $x = -4/7$ or $8/3$
13. $x = -2/11$ or $-7/2$ **14.** $x = -1/13$ or $-4/3$
15. $x = 15$ or -13 **16.** $x = 27$ or -20 **17.** $x = -9/7$ or $11/9$
18. $x = 4/5$ or $3/10$ **19.** $x = -13/3$ or $7/2$
20. $x = -10/7$ or $5/4$ **21.** $x = 11/2$ or $5/2$ **22.** $x = 7/3$ or 3
23. $x = 1/5$ or $-1/3$ **24.** $x = -2/13$ or $5/7$ **25.** $x = -14$ or 3
26. $x = -12$ or 2 **27.** $x = 7/5$ or $5/2$ **28.** $x = -5/8$ or $-1/2$
29. $x = -1/2$ or $-15/2$ **30.** $x = -3/4$ or $-5/3$
31. $x = -14$ or $-1/14$ **32.** $x = -1/13$ or -13
33. $x = 4/7$ or $-8/9$ **34.** $x = 9/7$ or $-3/5$

Page 90 Polynomial Equations

1. $x = 15$ or -7 **2.** $x = 14$ or -8 **3.** $x = -7/3$ or 5
4. $x = -9/2$ or 6 **5.** $x = \pm2$ **6.** $x = \pm1/2$ **7.** $x = -7/5$ or $-13/7$
8. $x = -9/8$ or $-11/5$ **9.** $x = -17/2$ or 9 **10.** $x = -10/3$ or 5
11. $x = -3/7$ or $4/11$ **12.** $x = 5/12$ or $-2/9$ **13.** $x = -2/3$ or -2
14. $x = -3$ or $-5/2$ **15.** $x = 4/5$ or $1/2$ **16.** $x = 2/3$ or $1/2$
17. $x = -11/7$ or 12 **18.** $x = 9/8$ or 11 **19.** $x = 7$ or $-49/6$
20. $x = -10/3$ or $7/2$ **21.** $x = 7/11$ or $-5/4$
22. $x = -4/9$ or $3/7$ **23.** $x = 1/16$ or $-8/3$
24. $x = 2/15$ or $-4/5$ **25.** $x = -5/7$ or $1/2$ **26.** $x = 1/5$ or $-1/2$
27. $x = 7/5$ or $9/2$ **28.** $x = 8/7$ or $7/3$ **29.** $x = 16$ or -20
30. $x = -25$ or 21 **31.** $x = 15/2$ or $-2/7$ **32.** $x = -14/5$ or $2/3$
33. $x = 1/4$ or -2 **34.** $x = -2$ or $2/3$

Page 91 Polynomial Word Problems

1. 6, -7 **2.** 40 cm $\times$ 51 cm   **3.** 21, 7 **4.** 4 m
5. 11 m $\times$ 11 m   **6.** 25 s   **7.** 7 m $\times$ 8 m   **8.** 7 cm
9. 13 and 14 and 15 or -9 and -10 and -11

Page 92 Polynomial Word Problems

1. 11, -10 **2.** 20 cm $\times$ 5 cm   **3.** 20 and 12 **4.** 3 cm
5. 58 cm $\times$ 39 cm   **6.** 30 s   **7.** 15 m $\times$ 25 m   **8.** 6 cm
9. 19 and 20 and 21 or -17 and -16 and -15

Page 93 Polynomial Word Problems

1. 9 **2.** 16 m $\times$ 24 m   **3.** 17 and 6 **4.** 6 m   **5.** 5 cm
6. 20 s   **7.** 20 m $\times$ 30 m or 15 m $\times$ 40 m   **8.** 8 m
9. 8 and 10 and 12 or -2 and 0 and 2

Page 94 Polynomial Word Problems

1. 13 and 14 **2.** 10 cm $\times$ 14 cm   **3.** 17 and 18 **4.** 4 m
5. 20 cm $\times$ 45 cm   **6.** 20 s   **7.** 20 m $\times$ 80 m or 40 m $\times$ 40 m
8. 5 m   **9.** 17 and 19 and 21 or -21 and -19 and -17

Page 95 Fractions

1. $(t + 2)/(t - 7)$ **2.** $(b + 1)/(b - 1)$ **3.** m/n **4.** c/d
5. $(3 + y)/(4 + y)$ **6.** $(2 + x)/(3 + x)$ **7.** a/b **8.** m/n
9. $3/4$ **10.** $9/5$ **11.** $(3m - n)/(2m + n)$
12. $(3x - 2)/(3x + 2)$ **13.** $(5x + 2)/(2x - 5y)$
14. $(3a + 2b)/(2a - 5b)$ **15.** $(7x + 3y^2)/(3x - 2y)$

131

16. $(3m - 7n^2)/(2m + 3n^2)$ **17.** -5/7   **18.** -10/9
19. $-10x/7y$ **20.** $-(15a^2b)/8$
21. $(2x^2 + x - 5)/[2a(3x^2 - x + 9)]$
22. $[4m(3x^2 + 7x - 2)]/[3n(2x^2 - 9x + 3)]$
23. $(r - 5)/(r - 3)$ **24.** $(m - 3)/(m - 5)$ **25.** $(p + q)/(3p - q)$
26. $(a - 2)/(a - 5)$

Page 96   Fractions

1. $(b - 5)/(b + 3)$ **2.** $(t + 2)/(t + 3)$ **3.** x/y **4.** a/b
5. $(y - r)/(y + r)$ **6.** $(2 + 7m)/(4 + 7m)$ **7.** x/y **8.** t/v
9. 4/5   **10.** 6/5   **11.** $(2z - 5)/(2z + 3)$ **12.** $(5x + 3)/(5x - 3)$
13. $[2(2b - 3)]/[3(2b + 3)]$ **14.** $[3(2a + 3b)]/[4(2a - 3b)]$
15. $[2x(5x^2 + 2y^2)]/[3y(5x - 3y)]$
16. $(3r + 2s)/[2(2r + 3s)]$ **17.** 9/8   **18.** $3a/4b$ **19.** $4a/5$
20. $2a/3b$ **21.** $[2(3x^2 + 2x + 9)]/[3(5x^2 - x + 7)]$
22. $[3(5r^2 + 3r + 12)]/[5(6r^2 + 2r + 7)]$ **23.** $(x + 2)/(x + 3)$
24. $(m + 2)/(m - 5)$ **25.** $(2x + 3y)/(2x + 5y)$
26. $(3r - 5)/(2r - 1)$

Page 97   Fractions

1. $3a^2b^2$ **2.** $3c^2/b^2$ **3.** $8n^3/m^3$ **4.** $2z^3/3y^2$
5. $6y^3/(7x^2z^2)$ **6.** $(3a^2x^2y^2)/15b^2$ **7.** $7m^2/6n^2r^2$
8. $(49a^2r)/30b^3$ **9.** $[2(x - 2)]/(x + 2)$
10. $(a + 2b)/[3(a + 3b)]$ **11.** 2/5   **12.** 2/5   **13.** -2/3
14. -2/3   **15.** $-(r + 3s)/(2r + s)$ **16.** $-(2b + c)/(b - c)$
17. $(x + y)/3$ **18.** $[(2r + s)(r + s)]/(2r - s)$
19. $[3(b - a)]/4$ **20.** $[(2x + 3)(1 - 2x)]/(2x + 5)$
21. $15/[4x(x - y)]$ **22.** $28a^2/[3(a + b)]$
23. $15r^2s/[2(2s - 5)]$ **24.** $[5ab^2(ab + 1)]/21$
25. $[-3x^3y(x + y)]/[2(3x + y)]$ **26.** $28ab/(4b^2 - a^2)$

Page 98   Fractions

1. $4x^3y^2$ **2.** $c/3d^2$ **3.** $4r^3t^3/5$ **4.** $3a^5/2b^2$
5. $2ac^2/3d$ **6.** $25mr^2/6nt^2$ **7.** $15x^2/8yz^2$
8. $(21ab^2c^2)/20$ **9.** $(b - 3)/[2(b + 3)]$ **10.** $[3(r + s)]/(2r + s)$
11. $(3x + 1)/[5(2x + 3)]$ **12.** $(3r + 1)/[4(3r - 1)]$
13. $[6(a - b)]/(2b - 3a)$ **14.** $-(r + s)/(r + 2y)$
15. $-(2x + 3y)/(x + 3y)$ **16.** -2/3   **17.** $[5(a + b)]/6$
18. $-[3(x + y)]/2$ **19.** $-1/[2(2r + 1)]$ **20.** $5/[3(4x + 3y)]$
21. $15a^2/[2(a - 2b)]$ **22.** $1/[3(3a - 4)]$
23. $5r^2/[3s^2(4r + 5s)]$ **24.** $[3a(10a - 9b)]/2b$
25. $-5(t + 3s)/[4(7t + 5s)(3s + 2t)]$ **26.** $[5(8m - 1)]/3$

Page 99   Fractions

1. $3/[(x + 3)(x - 5)]$ **2.** $[5(a - 3)]/(a - 2)$ **3.** $(x - 3)/(2x + 1)$
4. $(5a - 3)/(a + 3)$ **5.** $x(x + 1)$ **6.** $x(x - 5)$
7. $[(r - 7)(r + 2)]/r$ **8.** $1/[q^2(p + 2q)]$ **9.** $1/[(2x - 7y)(x + y)]$
10. $1/(4a^2 + 8a + 3)$ **11.** $(r + 3s)(r + s)$ **12.** $r + 5s$
13. $[(x + 5)(2x - 1)]/[(2x + 3)(x + 2)]$
14. $[(2a - 1)(2a - 7)]/[(a - 7)(2a - 3)]$ **15.** $(m - 2n)/(m + n)$
16. $[(2r + 3s)(r + s)]/[(2r - 3s)(r - s)]$
17. $[-3(x - 4)]/[(x - 5)(x + 1)]$
18. $[-5(y - 4x)]/[(x + y)(y - 2x)]$
19. $[-2(a + 3)]/[(3a + 4)(2a + 1)]$
20. $[-(10 + 13a)]/[2(2a + 1)]$ **21.** $[2(r + 2t)]/r^2$
22. $(2x + 3y)/3xy$ **23.** $(3m + n)/4$
24. $[3(2x + y)]/[16x(x - 5y)]$ **25.** $-3/[(2a + b)(a + b)]$
26. $-4/[(a + 2)(4a + 3)]$

Page 100   Fractions

1. $5/[(x - 7)(x + 2)]$ **2.** $[4(2a - b)]/[3(a - b)(a - b)]$
3. $2(4x + 1)/(x - 3)$ **4.** $[10(2x + 1)]/(5x - 3)$ **5.** $x(x + 3)$
6. $1/[a(a + 4b)]$ **7.** $x(x + 3)$ **8.** $m/(m + 3n)$
9. $(2a + 1)(2a + 3)$ **10.** $1/[(x - 1)(x + 4)]$
11. $1/[2(3x + 2)(3x + 1)]$ **12.** $3(5 - a)$
13. $[(x + 5)(x - 1)]/[(x - 3)(2x - 1)]$ **14.** $(2a + 3)/(a + 2)$
15. $(r + 1)/(2r - 1)$ **16.** $[(2a + 1)(2a - 1)]/[(4a + 1)(2a - 3)]$
17. $-4/(2a - b)$ **18.** $-(2x - y)(x + y)]/[5(x - 3y)]$
19. $3(r + s)/[(r - s)(2s - r)]$
20. $-[(3y + 2x)(x + 2y)(x + 3y)]/[5(y + 3x)(y - 2x)]$

21. $1/2x$ **22.** $[2(y + 2)]/(y - 3)$ **23.** $(x + 3)/[2(x - 4)]$
24. $(y - 5)/[2y^2(2y + 3)]$ **25.** $-3/[2(x - 2y)$
26. $[-4(b + 3a)(a + b)]/[5(b - 3a)]$

Page 101   Fractions

1. $y^3(y + 6)$ **2.** $(2x + 5)/y$ **3.** x/y^3 **4.** x^5/y^3 **5.** y/x **6.** x
7. $(x + y)(3x - y)$ **8.** $(x - y)(2x + 3y)$ **9.** $3/4x$ **10.** 5
11. $x^2/9$ **12.** $x^2/7$ **13.** $(x + 5)/(x + 11)$
14. $[(x + 3)(x - 12)]/[(x + 7)(x + 7)]$
15. $[(x - 10)(x - 10)(x + 4)]/[(x - 9)(x + 2)(x + 2)]$
16. $(x + 7)/(x + 6)$ **17.** 1   **18.** $(x - 1)/(x + 1)$
19. $(10x - 1)/(x + 5)$ **20.** 1/4   **21.** $(2x + 5)/(x - 7)$ **22.** 1
23. $[14(x + 3)]/(x - 2)$ **24.** $[24(3x + 4)]/(x - 1)$
25. $(x + 9)/(2x - 5)$ **26.** $(2x - 1)/3x - 1)$

Page 102   Fractions

1. $(y - 5)/y$ **2.** $y^4(3y - 2)$ **3.** $2x^4/y^6$ **4.** $x^2/3y^7$ **5.** $1/xy^2$
6. x/y **7.** $[(x - y)(2x + y)]/2$ **8.** $(2x + 5y)(5x + 2y)$
9. $7/10x$ **10.** $11x/20$ **11.** $[x^2(2x + 1)]/[2(x - 1)]$ **12.** $7x/5$
13. $(x + 5)/(x - 1)$ **14.** $(x - 3)/(2x - 1)$
15. $[(x - 4)(2x + 1)]/(x + 3)^2$ **16.** $(x - 3)/(x + 4)$
17. $(x + 4)/(3x + 2)$ **18.** $(x + 3)/(2x - 7)$ **19.** $(x + 9)/(x - 7)$
20. $x + 5)/(4x + 1)$ **21.** $[(5x + 3)(x - 2)]/(3x + 4)^2$
22. $(3x - 1)(4x + 3)]/(4x - 3)^2$ **23.** $4(x + 5)/(3x - 7)$
24. $5(5x + 3)/(4x - 1)$ **25.** $(x + 5)/(2x + 3)$
26. $(x - 5)/(x - 9)$

Page 103   Fractions

1. $(10ax^2)/by^2$ **2.** $8a/49x$ **3.** 8/63   **4.** $-5/[2(2x + 5)]$
5. $3b/[2a(a + b)(2b + 1)]$ **6.** -4/3   **7.** $xy^2/[2(x - y)]$
8. $5n^2/(n - 1)$ **9.** $[(x - 1)(x + 1)]/54x^3y$ **10.** $4/x$
11. $-[xy(x + 2y)]/[2(1 - 2x)(x + y)]$
12. $-(x - 4y)^2/[5x + y)(x + 3y)(y - x)]$ **13.** $(a + 5b)/(3a + b)$

Page 104   Fractions

1. $2xy$ **2.** $2s^2/3br^2$ **3.** $(r + s)^2/[12(t + u)^2]$ **4.** $2/[x(2x + 3)]$
5. $[2(x - y)^2]/3x^2$ **6.** 1   **7.** $4b/[5a(2a + b)]$ **8.** $r + 2$
9. $5y^2/[2(2x + 3)]$ **10.** $-[2(2x - 5)]/[3(5x - 2)]$
11. $-[3(x + 3y)]/[5(x + 6y)]$ **12.** $-(b + a)/(3a + b)$
13. $(m - 3n)/(3m + n)$

Page 105   Least Common Multiple

1. $12abc$ **2.** $9xyz$ **3.** $15mnt$ **4.** $20bcd$ **5.** $24r^2s^2$
6. $60x^2y^2$ **7.** $75a^2b^3$ **8.** $210m^2n^3$ **9.** $(x - y)(x + y)^2$
10. $(r - 2s)^2(r + 3s)$ **11.** $(2x + 1)^2(2x - 1)^2$
12. $(a + 3b)^2(a + 2b)^2$ **13.** $(x + 3)(x - 4)(x + 4)$
14. $(2a + 3)(2a - 1)(3a + 2)$ **15.** $(x + 5)(x - 1)(x + 3)$
16. $(3a + 2)(3a - 1)(2a + 1)$ **17.** $(x + y)(x - y)(x + 2y)$
18. $(a + b)(a - b)(2a + b)$ **19.** $(2a - 3b)(2a + 3b)(2a + 3b)$
20. $(2a + 1)(a + 5)(a - 5)$ **21.** $(a + 3)(a - 5)(a - 2)$
22. $(x - 3y)(x + y)(x - 2y)$ **23.** $(2a + 1)(a + 3)(2a - 1)$
24. $(2a + b)(2a - b)(3a + b)$ **25.** $(m + 3n)(m - 3n)(m - 2n)$
26. $(5x - y)(5x + y)(3x - y)$ **27.** $(x + y)(x - y)(2x + y)$
28. $(x + 5)(x - 4)(x + 6)$ **29.** $(3x + 2)(2x + 3)(3x - 5)$
30. $(2x + 1)(2x + 3)(3x - 1)$ **31.** $(2r + s)(2r - s)(2r + 5s)$
32. $(5x + 3y)(5x - 3y)(5x + 2y)$

Page 106   Least Common Multiple

1. $12mnt$ **2.** $25xyz$ **3.** $20rst$ **4.** $14abc$ **5.** $60r^2s^3$
6. $60m^3n^2$ **7.** $36a^3b^3$ **8.** $105x^2y^3$ **9.** $(x - 5)(x - 1)^2$
10. $(3x + 2)(2x - 1)^2$ **11.** $(x + 2)^2(x + 3)$ **12.** $(x - 7)(x - 3)^2$
13. $(x - 5)(x + 2)(x + 3)$ **14.** $(2x + 1)(2x + 3)(2x - 5)$
15. $(2x + 1)(x + 3)(x + 4)$ **16.** $(3x - 1)(x + 2)(x + 3)$
17. $(p + q)(p - q)(p + 2q)$ **18.** $(r + 2s)(r - 2s)(r + 3s)$
19. $(m + 3n)(m - 3n)(m + 2n)$
20. $(2x + 3y)(2x - 3y)(2x + y)$ **21.** $(x + 2y)(x - 3y)(x - 4y)$
22. $(3a + 1)(2a - 1)(a - 2)$ **23.** $2(2r + 3s)(2r - s)(2r - 3s)$
24. $2(2m + n)(2m + 3n)(m - 5)$ **25.** $(x - 2y)(x + 2y)(3x - y)$
26. $(3a - 2b)(a + 3b)(3a + 2b)$

132

27. $(2x - 5y)(x + 3y)(2x + 5y)$
28. $(4m - n)(4m + n)(n + 2m)$
29. $(5x + 3y)(5x - 2y)(2x - y)$ **30.** $(2r + 3s)(r - 4s)(3r + 2s)$
31. $(r - s)(r + s)(r + 3s)(r - 5s)$
32. $(2x + 3)(2x - 3)(2x + 1)(3x - 1)$

Page 107 Equivalent Fractions

1. $8a$ **2.** $9c$ **3.** $30abc$ **4.** $21mx^2y$ **5.** $9x(2x + 1)$
6. $3r(r - 3t)$ **7.** $4t(t - 1)$ **8.** $8a(3 + 2a)$ **9.** $(x + 3)(x - 5)$
10. $(2x + 1)(x - 2)$ **11.** $(2a - 5)(a + 3)$
12. $(4a + 2b)(2a + 3b)$ **13.** $(3m + n)(m + 2)$
14. $(a + 2m)(a + 3m)$ **15.** $(5r + t)(r + 3t)$ **16.** $(2r + t)(r + t)$
17. $(3x + 2y)(x - y)$ **18.** $(4x + y)(5x - 2y)$
19. $(3a - 5b)(2a + 3b)$ **20.** $(2x + 3y)(x + 2y)$
21. $(3 + 2t)(3 - t)$ **22.** $(7x - y)(2x - 5y)$
23. $-(2m + 5n)(n + 2m)$ **24.** $-(6x + 1)(3 + x)$
25. $(5x - 3y)(x - y)(x^2 + y^2)$ **26.** $(2b + c)(b + c)(b^2 + c^2)$

Page 108 Equivalent Fractions

1. $12x$ **2.** $21b$ **3.** $16abc$ **4.** $28dxy^2$ **5.** $3m(3m + n)$
6. $5h(h + 3t)$ **7.** $5x(x - 3y)$ **8.** $7c(5a - 3b)$
9. $(x + 7)(3x + 2)$ **10.** $(2a + 9)(2a - 5)$
11. $(3m - 5)(3m + 2)$ **12.** $(c + d)(3c - 4)$
13. $(2r + 3t)(5r - t)$ **14.** $(3x + y)(x - 4y)$ **15.** $(3r - 1)(2r - 3)$
16. $(4a - b)(2a - 9b)$ **17.** $(7a - 3b)(a - 2b)$
18. $(a + 3b)(3a + 5b)$ **19.** $(x + 2y)(5x + 4y)$
20. $(6r + 5t)(3r - 7t)$ **21.** $(3t - 7)(3t - 4)$
22. $-(a + b)(3a + 5b)$ **23.** $-(r + 2t)(r + 5t)$
24. $(3x - 7)(3x - 1)$ **25.** $(3m + 1)(m - 2)(m^2 + 4)$
26. $(2a + 3)(a + 3)(a^2 + 9)$

Page 109 Addition of Fractions

1. $(9x + 5)/12$ **2.** $(20x + 7)/15$ **3.** $(3 + 5a)/54$
4. $(3 + 4a)/32$ **5.** $(45x + 28y)/648$ **6.** $(21x + 10y)/252$
7. $(10a + 3)/75$ **8.** $(20a + 3)/64$ **9.** $(15x + 14y^2)/100$
10. $(8x + 9y^2)/60$ **11.** $(8y^2 + 3x)/20xy$
12. $(66y^2 + 7x)/18xy$ **13.** $(4x^2 + 5z^2)/6xz$
14. $(24x^2 + 15zt)/40xz$ **15.** $(3a^2 + 2b^2)/9ab$
16. $(3a^2 + 2b^2)/8ab$ **17.** $(10x^2 + 9y)/48x$
18. $(27x^2 + 10y)/78x$ **19.** $(14x^2 + 10)/196x^2$
20. $(27x + 35)/360x^3$ **21.** $(3y^2 + 20/72xy^2$
22. $(35y^2 + 12)/70x^2y^2$ **23.** $(15a + 4b)/20a^2b^3$
24. $(3 + 2b^2)/6a^2b^3$ **25.** $(21x + 12y)/28x^2y^2$
26. $(3 + 2xy)/4x^2y^2$

Page 110 Addition of Fractions

1. $(24x + 2)/9$ **2.** $(28x + 11)/32$ **3.** $(77 + 16b)/196$
4. $(56 + 27b)/192$ **5.** $(2y + 2x)/21$ **6.** $(14y + 15x)/280$
7. $(15x + 9)/80$ **8.** $(13x + 13)/38$ **9.** $(12x^2 + 5y)/75$
10. $(3x^3 + 5y^2)/55$ **11.** $(14b^2 + 7a)/12ab$
12. $(3b^2 + 7a)/9ab$ **13.** $(15y^2 + 10x^2)/12xy$
14. $(10y^2 + 9x^2)/6xy$ **15.** $(12y^2 + 15x)/5xy$
16. $(18y^2 + 9x^2)/13xy$ **17.** $(55a^2 + 22b)/90a$
18. $(65ax + 52b)/170x$ **19.** $(45a + 55)/78a^3$
20. $(12a + 3)/23a^3$ **21.** $(7b^3 + 16)/14a^2b^3$
22. $18b^3 + 14)/21a^3b^3$ **23.** $(80 + 36y)/75x^2y^2$
24. $(28x + 15y)/64x^2y^3$ **25.** $(60y + 28)/87x^2y^3$
26. $(392y + 225)/756x^2y^3$

Page 111 Subtraction of Fractions

1. $29x/60$ **2.** $11x/30$ **3.** $(55x - 16y)/180$
4. $(98a - 15y)/175$ **5.** $(5xy - 3x^2)/105$ **6.** $(4ab - 3bc)/72$
7. $(21z - 12z^2)70$ **8.** $(16x - 9x^2)/60$ **9.** $(3u^2 - 4u)/66$
10. $(5x^2 - 12x)/160$ **11.** $(5ac - 3b)/15c^2$
12. $(3m^2 - 2n^2)/12mn$ **13.** $(8b^2 - 15a^2)/36ab$
14. $(28cy - 9dx)/60xy$ **15.** $(8y^3 - 21x^2)/36xy^2$
16. $(20rt - 21s)/75t^2$ **17.** $(4z^2 - 25t)/30tz^2$ **18.** $19/26x$
19. $(30 - 35x)/168x^2$ **20.** $(7 - 2a)/4a^2$
21. $(2y^3 - x^3)/60x^2y^2$ **22.** $(5y^3 - 3x^3)/35x^2y^2$ **23.** $1/(x + 1)$

Page 112 Subtraction of Fractions

1. $-5a/48$ **2.** $-(31a)/84$ **3.** $(65b - 68c)/120$
4. $(96m - 65n)/150$ **5.** $(3x - 6y)/28$ **6.** $(35mn - 2n^2)/70$
7. $(4rt - 3t^2)/72$ **8.** $(35a - 36b^2)/60$ **9.** $-3m/35$
10. $(4z^2 - 15z)/108$ **11.** $(3p - 2q)/30t$ **12.** $(5r - t)/15s$
13. $(45z^2 - 24a^2)/70az$ **14.** $(9az - 22a)/48z^2$
15. $(9rt - 14xs)/78xt$ **16.** $(49xn - 30my)/84mn$
17. $(12z - 8)/57z^2$ **18.** $(46y - 15)/34xy$
19. $(65 - 36x)/75x^3$ **20.** $(38b^2 - 21a^2)/66a^2b^2$
21. $(35b^2x - 36a^2y)/75a^2b^2$ **22.** $(15b^2c - 28a^2c)/80a^2b^2$
23. $-2/[r^2(r + 2)]$ **24.** $(-2 - r)/[r(r - 3)]$
25. $(-2a^2 + 7a)/[(a - 2)(a + 1)]$
26. $(-2b^2 - 4)/[3b(b - 2)]$

Page 113 Addition and Subtraction of Fractions

1. $7/6a$ **2.** $7/12a$ **3.** $11/2a$ **4.** $25/3a^2$
5. $(bc + ac - ab)/abc$ **6.** $(2b^2c^2 + 2a^2c^2 - 2a^2b^2)/a^2b^2c^2$
7. $(b^2c + a^2c - ab)/abc$ **8.** $(b^3c^2 + a^3c^2 - a^2b^2)/a^2b^2c^2$
9. $(4xy + 4z - xyz)/2y^2$ **10.** $(3xy + 3z - xyz)/y^3$
11. $(20xy - 9x)/12y^2$ **12.** $(40xy - 15x)/12y^3$
13. $(4xz + z^2 - 24x)/6z^2$ **14.** $(6xz + z^2 - 60x)/10z^2$
15. 0 **16.** $-z^2/(z^2 - 1)$ **17.** $(x^2 - x + 2)/[x(x - 1)]$
18. $(2x^2 + 2x + 2)/[x(x - 2)]$ **19.** $(y + x - 1)/xy$
20. $(2b + 2a - 2)/ab$ **21.** 0 **22.** $3y/4x$
23. $(2x^2 + y^2)/3xy$ **24.** $(5x^2 + y^2)/7xy$
25. $(8x^2 - 45z^2)/12xz$ **26.** $(-30x^2 - 147z^2)/70xz$

Page 114 Addition and Subtraction of Fractions

1. $(20 - 3y)/15xy$ **2.** $(20 - 3y)/30xy$ **3.** $25/3x$
4. $33/5x^2$ **5.** $(5y^2z^2 + 5x^2z^2 - 5x^2y^2)/2x^2y^2z^2$
6. $(12y^2z^2 + 9x^2z^2 - 2x^2y^2)/6x^2y^2z^2$
7. $(4x^2z + 9y^2z - xy)/6xyz$
8. $(12x^4z^2 + 30y^4z^2 - 10x^2y^2)/15x^2y^2z^2$
9. $(10ab + 5z - 3abz)/4b^2$
10. $(40a^2b + 6c - 10a^2bc)/15b^3$
11. $(220ab - 99a)/84b^2$ **12.** $209a/85b^2$
13. $(24ab + 3b^2 - 748a)/34b^2$
14. $30a^2b + 5b^2 - 484a^2)/44b^2$ **15.** $(3x^2 - 3x)/(4x^2 - 9)$
16. $(7x^2 - 4x)/(9x^2 - 4)$
17. $(5x^2 - 25x + 10)/[x(5x - 2)]$
18. $(12x^2 - 12x + 4)/[x(3x - 1)]$
19. $(7y + 7x - 15)/(xy - x - y + 1)$
20. $(22y + 22x - 67)/4xy - 6x - 6y + 9)$
21. $(7a^2 + 3b^2)/3ab$
22. $(20a^4 + 21b^4 - 2a^2 - 3b^2)/15a^2b^2$
23. $(5a^2 - 5b^2)/4ab$ **24.** $(55a + 63b^6 - 12a^2)/77ab^3$
25. $(14x^2y + 55y^3 - 140x)/35xy^2$
26. $(16x^2 - 9xy^2 - 144y^2)/12x^2y$

Page 115 Addition and Subtraction of Fractions

1. $2a/[(a - b)(a + b)]$ **2.** $-2b/[(a + b)(a - b)]$
3. $(a^2 + b^2)/[(a + b)(a - b)]$ **4.** $-2ab/[(a + b)(a - b)]$
5. $(a^2 - ab - b^2)/(a + b)$ **6.** $(-x^2 - x - 1)/(x - 1)^2$
7. $(-x^2 - 1)/[x(x + 1)^2]$ **8.** $(2x + 1)/(x + 1)^2$
9. $(-x^3 + x^2 + 2)/(x - 1)^3$ **10.** $(x^2 + 1)/(x - 1)^4$
11. $(-2x + 1)/[x^2(x - 1)^2]$ **12.** $(x^2 + 1)/x^3$
13. $(5x + 2)/6x^2$ **14.** $(5x - 3)/6x^2$
15. $(-x^2 - 1)/[x(x + 1)(x - 1)]$
16. $(6x^2 + 2)/[(x + 1)(x - 1)]$
17. $(3x + 5)/[(x + 1)^2(x + 2)]$ **18.** $-1/[x(x - 3)(x + 1)]$
19. $5/[(x - 2)(x + 3)^2]$
20. $(2x + 3)/[(x + 1)(x - 5)(x + 2)]$
21. $(-2x + 3)/[(x - 1)^2(x - 2)^2]$
22. $(x^2 + 5x + 11)/[(x - 2)(x + 3)^2]$ **23.** $1/(x + 3)$
24. $(3x - 3)/[(3x + 2)(3x - 2)]$ **25.** $1/(2x - 5)$
26. $(3x + 3)/[(3x + 4)(3x - 4)]$

Page 112 Subtraction of Fractions

24. $(2 - x^2)/(x^2 - 1)$ **25.** $(-x^2 + 3x)/(x^2 - 1)$
26. $(-x^2 - 1)/[2x(x - 1)]$

Page 116 Addition and Subtraction of Fractions

1. $4x/[(2x - y)(2x + y)]$ 2. $-2y/[(2x + y)(2x - y)]$
3. $(x^2 - xy + 2y^2)/[(x + 2y)(x - 2y)]$
4. $(x^2 - 3xy - 2y^2)/[(x + 2y)(x - 2y)]$
5. $(3x^2 - 6xy^2 + 9y^3)/(4x^2 - 9y^2)$
6. $(-4a^2 + 2a + 9)/(2a - 3)^2$
7. $(-18x^2 - 12x - 8)/[3x(3x + 2)^2]$ 8. $(13x - 2)/(4x - 1)^2$
9. $(-x^2 + 5x + 5)/(x - 5)^3$
10. $(9x^3 + 42x^2 + 49x + 3)/(3x + 7)^4$
11. $(-a^3 + 44a^2 - 132a + 99)/[a^3(2a - 3)^2]$
12. $(4a^2 + 21a + 25)/a^3$ 13. $(4x - 10)/15x^3$
14. $(20 + 7x + 7x^2)/35x^2$
15. $(-x^3 + 3x^2 + x + 3)/[x^2(x + 3)(x - 3)]$
16. $(20x^2 + 4)/[(2x + 3)(5x - 1)]$
17. $(4x + 7)/[(x - 2)^2(x + 3)]$ 18. $-5/[x(x + 5)(x - 2)]$
19. $7/[(x + 8)^2(x + 1)]$
20. $(2x - 1)/[(x - 3)(x - 9)(x + 2)]$
21. $(-10x + 5)/[(x + 2)^2(x - 3)^2]$
22. $(-x^2 - 12x + 1)/[(x - 1)^2(x + 5)]$
23. $(x - 3)/[(x - 4)(x - 7)]$ 24. $5x/[(5x - 1)(5x + 1)]$
25. $(6x + 9)/[(6x + 1)(6x - 1)]$
26. $(8x + 6)/[(8x + 7)(8x - 7)]$

Page 117 Addition and Subtraction of Fractions

1. $(x^2 - 9)/[(x - 9)(x + 4)(x - 1)]$
2. $(2x^2 - 9x + 15)/[(x - 5)(x + 1)(x - 3)]$
3. $(x^2 + 4x - 1)/[(x + 1)(x - 1)]$
4. $(-10x + 40)/[3(x - 4)(x - 7)(x - 9)]$
5. $2/[(x + 8)(x - 6)]$ 6. $-1/(x + 4)$
7. $(-x^2 - 104x - 4)/[(x + 7)(x + 2)(x - 8)(x - 2)]$
8. $1/[(x - 8)(x - 6)]$ 9. $14/[(x - 2)(x + 5)]$
10. $(-66x + 22)/[(3x - 1)(2x - 1)(6x - 1)]$
11. $2/[(2x - 1)(2x + 9)]$
12. $-1/[(4x - 3)(3x - 2)]$ 13. $-5/[(9x - 4)(4x - 3)]$

Page 118 Addition and Subtraction of Fractions

1. $(x^2 - 2x - 4)/[(x - 4)(x - 2)(x - 3)]$ 2. $x/(x - 1)$
3. $(-x^2 + 5x + 2)/[(x - 1)(x + 1)]$ 4. $42/[(x - 8)(x + 6)]$
5. $7/[(x - 2)(x - 9)]$ 6. $-6/[(x - 2)(x - 5)]$
7. $2/[(x + 3)(x + 7)]$ 8. $(34x - 25)/[(3x - 2)(2x - 1)(4x - 3)]$
9. $(-37x + 80)/[(2x - 3)(x - 2)(x - 5)]$
10. $(-4x^2 + 14x - 19)/[(3x + 2)(2x - 5)(x - 7)]$
11. $(-19x^2 - 13x - 1)/[(7x - 1)(4x + 5)(x + 3)]$
12. $(19x^2 - 8x - 20)/[(4x - 5)(3x - 5)(3x - 5)]$
13. $(3x^2 - 7x + 98)/[(5x - 4)(2x + 7)(x - 3)]$

Page 119 Mixed Expressions

1. $(2x + 1)/x$ 2. $(3x^2 - 1)/x^2$ 3. $(x^2 + 2)/x$ 4. $(2x^2 - 3)/x$
5. $(2x^2 - 2x - 2)/(x - 1)$ 6. $(2x^2 + 2x + 1)/(x + 1)$
7. $(3x^2 - 4x)/(x - 1)$ 8. $(2x^2 + 3x + 2)/(x + 1)$ 9. $2x/(x + 2)$
10. $x^3/(x - 2)$ 11. $(3x + 3y)/2$ 12. $(7x - 10y)/3$
13. $(x^2 - 2x + 1)/[(x - 2)^2]$ 14. $(-2x^2 - 3x + 3)/(x + 1)^2$
15. $(a^2 + 4ab - b^2)/[(a - b)(a + b)]$
16. $(4a^2 + 27b^2)/[(2a + 3b)(2a - 3b)]$
17. $(a^2b - ab^2 + b + a)/ab$ 18. $(2a^2b + 2ab^2 + b - a)/2ab$
19. $(y^2 + xy - x + y)/xy$ 20. $(-x^2 - xy + 2x + 2y)/xy$
21. $(a^2b - ax - ab^2 - bx)/ab$ 22. $(a^2 + abx + b^2 - ax)/ab$
23. $(2x^2 + 7xy + 2y^2)/2xy$ 24. $(6x^2 - 5xy - 9y^2)/3xy$
25. $(2a^4 - 3a^2b^2 + 2b^4)/2a^2b^2$ 26. $(2a^4 - a^2b^2 + 2b^4)/a^2b^2$

Page 120 Mixed Expressions

1. $(-5x^2 - 1)/x^2$ 2. $(-8x^2 + 1)/2x^2$ 3. $(4x^2 - 3)/x$
4. $(15x^2 + 2)/3x$ 5. $x^2/(x + 1)$ 6. $(2x^2 + x - 4)/(x - 1)$
7. $(-2x - 3)/(x + 1)$ 8. $(-6x - 4)/(2x + 1)$ 9. $(-1 - x^2)/(x + 1)$
10. $(6x^2 + 5x - 1)/(2x + 1)$ 11. $(x^2 + 4x + 4)/(x^2 + 4)$
12. $(2x^2 - 3x - 8)/(x^2 - 4)$ 13. $(a^2 + b^2 - a + b - 2ab)/ab$
14. $(a^2 + 2a - 2b^2 + 3b - 6ab)/2ab$ 15. $(-a^2 + 2a + 3)/a^2$
16. $(4ab + 10a + 4b)/[a(5a + 2b)]$
17. $(a^2 + ab - ab^3 + ab^2 - a^2b^2 - b^3)/ab^2$
18. $(-2a^2 + 2a^2b - 2ab^2 + ab - b^2)/2ab$
19. $(3x^2y - 3xy - 3y^2 + xy)/3xy$ 20. $(8x^2 + xy - 18y^2)/12xy$
21. $(-a^2 + ab + 4b^2 + 2a)/2ab$ 22. $(9a^2 + 14ab - 6b - 2b^2)/6ab$
23. $(a^2 + b^2 + 2ab - 1)/ab$ 24. $(-2a + b)/a$
25. $(-9a^3 + a^2 - ab - 12b)/3a^2$
26. $(4a^2 - 2ab - 40a^2b - 5a - 5b)/10ab$

Page 121 Complex Fractions

1. $1/4$ 2. $4/3$ 3. $5/7$ 4. 1 5. $2/3b$
6. $(x^2 + 5)/(x^3 + 3x^2)$ 7. $(x^2 + 2x + 1)/(x^2 - 2x + 1)$
8. $(x^3 + 4x)/(x^3 - 2)$ 9. $(2a^2 + ab + b^2)/(2a^2 - ab + b^2)$
10. $(2x - 1)/(-2x^2 + 5x + 3)$ 11. $(x^2 + 2xy - y^2)/(x^2 + y^2)$
12. $(3x + 8)/(3x + 5)$ 13. $(x^2 - x - 4)/(x^4 - 5x^2 - 2x)$
14. $-(x^5 + x^3 - 10x^2 - 6x)/(2x + 9)$

Page 122 Complex Fractions

1. $2/5$ 2. $2/3x$ 3. $3/40$ 4. $49/26$ 5. $3/8y$
6. $(2x^2 - 4)/(x^3 - 2x^2)$ 7. $(6x^2 - 5x - 21)/(6x^2 + 5x - 21)$
8. $(5x^3 + 20x^2 - x)/(5x^2 + x + 22)$ 9. 1
10. $(a^2 + 4a - 6)/(-2a^3 + 3a^2 + 10a + 15)$
11. $(4a^2 - 5ab + 3b^2)/(4a^2 + ab - 3b^2)$
12. $(20x^2 - x - 123)/(20x^2 - 10x - 100)$
13. $(8x^3 + 2x - 2)/(8x^4 + x)$
14. $(12x^3 - 10x^2 + 10x - 7)/(12x^3 - 14x^2 - 10x + 7)$